VITAL SIGNS

VITAL SIGNS
Psychological Responses
to Ecological Crisis

Edited by
Mary-Jayne Rust and Nick Totton

KARNAC

First published in 2012 by
Karnac Books Ltd
118 Finchley Road
London NW3 5HT

"What if it were true …?" by Jerome Bernstein was originally delivered as a lecture at the CG Jung Institute, San Francisco on Earth Day, April 17, 2010.

"Gaia living with AIDS: Towards reconnecting humanity with ecosystem autopoiesis using metaphors of the immune system" by Peter Chatalos first appeared in *Psychotherapy and Politics International*, 4(3): 213–222 (2006).

"The politics of transformation in the global crisis" by Mick Collins, William Hughes and Andrew Samuels first appeared in an earlier version in *Psychotherapy and Politics International*, 8(2): 162–176 (2010).

"Dangerous margins: Recovering the stem cells of the psyche" by Chris Robertson first appeared in an earlier version in *Psychotherapy and Politics International*, 9(2): 87–96 (2011).

British Library Cataloguing in Publication Data

A C.I.P. for this book is available from the British Library

ISBN-13: 978-1-78049-048-9

Typeset by Vikatan Publishing Solutions (P) Ltd., Chennai, India

Printed in Great Britain

www.karnacbooks.com

CONTENTS

PART IV: WHAT TO DO—POSSIBLE FUTURES

PART V: WHAT TO DO—INFLUENCING ATTITUDES

PART VI: WHAT TO DO—CLINICAL PRACTICE

ABOUT THE EDITORS AND CONTRIBUTORS

Astri Aasen is an experienced kindergarten teacher with a degree in early childhood education and further education in pre-school children's play in natural environments from Telemark University College. At present employed at Meaksmoen kindergarten, Notodden municipality, Norway.

Jerome S. Bernstein, M.A.P.C., NCPsyA, trained as a Clinical Psychologist and is currently a Jungian Analyst in private practice in Santa Fe, NM. He was the founding President of the Jung Institute of Greater Washington, D.C., and Past President of the Jung Institute of New Mexico, where he is a member of the teaching faculty. He is the author of *Living in the Borderland, Power and Politics*, and Co-Editor of *C. G. Jung and the Sioux Traditions*, as well as numerous articles on international conflict, shadow dynamics, and various clinical topics. He has had a forty-year relationship with Navajo and Hopi Indian cultures and for the past sixteen years has been working with a Navajo medicine man in a collaborative clinical model.

Inger Birkeland holds a PhD in human geography from University of Oslo and is associate professor at Telemark University College in Norway, where she teaches geography. She has research experience on the role of place for human development and sustainable community development. Amongst her books is *Making Place, Making Self: Travel, Subjectivity and Sexual Difference* (Ashgate, 2005). Research expertise in nature-society relations, social and cultural valuation of place, landscape and nature, culture and development, place-based learning and place pedagogies.

Susan Bodnar, PhD, is in clinical practice in New York City. She teaches and supervises at Teachers College at Columbia University and at The Mitchell Relational Center. She also serves as an associate editor for Psychoanalytic Dialogues and serves on the editorial board of Contemporary Psychoanalysis.

G. A. Bradshaw, PhD, is the founder and executive director of the Kerulos Center (www.kerulos.org) and author of *Elephants on the Edge: What Animals Teach Us About Humanity* (Yale University Press: 2009) and *Being Sanctuary: A Guide to Compassionate Living with Animal Kin* (2011). Her discovery of Post-Traumatic Stress Disorder (PTSD) in free living elephants established the field of trans-species science and psychology.

Peter A. Chatalos, MSc, is a London-based consultant, holistic therapist, group facilitator and human ecologist on the governing board of the Commonwealth Human Ecology Council. He is engaged in developing integrated, sustainable, and collaborative approaches to human ecological challenges. He has been involved in environmental, humanitarian and inter-faith projects, ranging from urban food growing to international development programmes.

Mick Collins is a lecturer in the School of Allied Health Professions, Faculty of Medicine and Health Sciences, University of East Anglia, Norwich, UK. He has published widely on the subject of spirituality and the transpersonal dimension of human occupation. Mick is currently working towards a PhD by publication; focusing on the interface between doing and being in the transformative journey through spiritual emergencies.

Tom Crompton has worked in the environment movement for fifteen years. For the first ten, he worked on environment policy. But he became increasingly frustrated at the lack of political commitment to adequately address environmental challenges. For the last five years he has worked with social scientists, exploring the importance of cultural values in underpinning public expressions of social and environmental concern.

He is author of *Weathercocks and Signposts: The Environment Movement at a Crossroads* and (with Tim Kasser) *Meeting Environmental Challenges: The Role of Human Identity*—both available at www.wwf.org.uk/change. His most recent report, *Common Cause: The Case for Working with Our Cultural Values*, has led to extensive debate across the third sector in the UK, and its recommendations are now being incorporated into the strategies of many UK-based NGOs.

Joseph Dodds, CPsychol, MPhil, MA, BSc, University of New York in Prague, lectures in various courses in psychoanalysis and psychology at several universities and is a psychotherapist in private practice. Dodds' research interests include the dialogue between psychoanalysis and neuroscience, and the application of psychological and psychoanalytic insight into the domains of society, art and nature. Currently his main focus is on climate change and his chapter in *Vital Signs* is based on his recent book *Psychoanalysis and Ecology at the Edge of Chaos: Complexity theory, Deleuze I Guattari, and psychoanalysis for a climate in crisis* (Dodds, 2011).

Kelvin Hall has been an integrative psychotherapist for twenty-five years; also a professional storyteller, supervisor and trainer. He has tutored numerous courses on storytelling and on therapeutic practice, and accompanied many groups of young people on wilderness trips, including the Sinai Desert and the Crimea. He has carried out several long-distance horseback journeys in Britain. A keen rider, his pursuit of the true art of horsemanship led him to investigate inter-species communication and the human bond with nature. He tutors the course on the Ecological Self at the Bath Centre for Psychotherapy and Counselling (of which he has been a trustee) and now includes equine–assisted therapy in his practice. He is the author of *Beyond the Forest: the Story of Parsifal and the Grail* (Hawthorn Press, 2000), and many articles on story, therapy and nature. He is firmly rooted in Gloucestershire and is married with three children and two grandchildren.

William Hughes is a Fellow of the Royal College of Psychiatrists and a Jungian Analyst in Private Practice; he is Honorary Senior Lecturer at the University of East Anglia and Founding Member of the European Society for Trauma and Dissociation. He trains and supervises for The Guild of Analytical Psychology and Spirituality.

Martin Jordan is a chartered counselling psychologist, UKCP registered psychotherapist and counsellor. He is also a senior lecturer in counselling and psychotherapy at the University of Brighton. He is on the editorial board of both the US and European ecopsychology journals.

Margaret Kerr works as an integrative psychotherapist. Central to her practice is understanding the human psyche as part of a wider world— ecological, historical, and socio-political. She works with David Key to facilitate the Natural Change Project and to develop writing and research in Ecopsychology. Before becoming a psychotherapist, Margaret worked as a medical doctor. She holds a BA (Hons) in Psychology, an MSc in Psychological Research Methods, and a postgraduate diploma in Transpersonal Psychology. She has lived all her life in Scotland and loves exploring the mountains and the sea.

David Key is an internationally qualified outdoor leader with over fifteen years experience working with groups in wild places to facilitate change. He is a fellow of the Centre for Human Ecology and co-led the postgraduate Ecopsychology module at the University of Strathclyde in Scotland for seven years. He now facilitates the Natural Change Project with Margaret Kerr and teaches Ecopsychology at Schumacher College in Devon with Mary-Jayne Rust, while training as a psychotherapist. Dave lives in Cornwall with his partner and daughter.

Paul Maiteny is an ecologist, anthropologist, and transpersonal psychotherapist in private practice. He has worked in ecological education and research for thirty years, held research fellowships at Oxford and Open Universities, and tutored Education for Sustainability at London South Bank University since 1996. He is a staff member of the Centre for Counselling and Psychotherapy Education, London. He has written and spoken widely on psycho-spiritual and cultural dimensions of ecology, sustainability, learning, and behaviour. He integrates scientific and mytho-religious ways of knowing in seeking to understand the evolving role of the human, person and species, as intrinsic to the ecosystem. Contact: Paul@PsychEcology.Net.

Hilary Prentice is an Integrative Psychotherapist, who has been lucky enough to live and work on Dartmoor in Devon for the last eleven years. She co-founded one of the first working groups of Transition Town Totnes (TTT), the "Heart and Soul" Group, in 2006, and was a member of the TTT Core Group. In earlier years, she was very active in the early UK ecopsychology movement, and has organized, taught ecopsychology, spoken at numerous events, facilitated numerous workshops, and had many articles published. She has degrees in Social Anthropology and in Medical Sociology as well as in Psychotherapy, and has been involved in the women's movement and the peace movement. Loves gardening, singing in choirs, birdsong, and a life journey of integrating political, ecological, psychological and spiritual insights and practice, both in healing and towards transformation, personal and planetary.

Rosemary Randall is a psychoanalytic psychotherapist and co-founder of the charity Cambridge Carbon Footprint. Her work focuses on practical ways of bringing a deep psychological perspective to work on climate change, whether this is in the community, in business or in policy. She developed the group-based Carbon Conversations project (www.carbonconversations.org) that brings a psychological perspective to individual work on carbon reduction. She writes and lectures widely on psychological aspects of climate change, carbon reduction, and climate change communication. Her blog can be found at www. rorandall.org.

Chris Robertson has been a psychotherapist and trainer since 1978. He is the co-author of *Emotions and Needs* (OUP) and a co-founder of Re•Vision (www.re-vision.org.uk). He has been the convener of several conferences on the themes of his chapter including *Sacred Margins* (2009) and the co-creator of the workshop *Borderlands and the Wisdom of Uncertainty*, which in 1989 became the subject of a BBC documentary. He works in London, works on the ecopsychology training at Re•Vision and also offers "Emergent Space" workshops in Sweden and the Netherlands.

Mary-Jayne Rust is an art therapist and Jungian analyst. Alongside her private practice she writes, lectures and facilitates workshops in the field of ecopsychology. In the 1980s she worked at the Women's Therapy Centre with women with eating problems; this led to a wider interest in the roots of consumerism, the connections between body and psyche, land, and soul. Two journeys to Ladakh in the early 1990s alerted her to the seriousness of the environmental crisis, and gave her a brief glimpse of an almost intact traditional culture. On return she joined the PCSR ecopsychology group. This group of ten therapists met monthly for five years, discussing theory and exploring the practice of ecopsychology. She grew up beside the sea and is wild about swimming. Now she lives and works beside ancient woodland in North London.

With a background in environmental and human rights work, **Viola Sampson** is a craniosacral therapist with a continuing commitment to social and environmental change. Alongside a diverse craniosacral practice, including humans, horses and trees, she is part of the grassroots climate change movement, the Activist Trauma Support Network, and is a campaigns communications specialist for a global environmental organization. Those who have influenced her work include a childhood apple tree, Tasmanian rainforest, limestone, horse and many human teachers, living and dead, to whom she extends deep gratitude.

Andrew Samuels is Professor of Analytical Psychology at the University of Essex and holds visiting chairs at London, Roehampton and New York Universities. He is a Training Analyst for the Society of Analytical Psychology, and in clinical practice in London. He works internationally as a political consultant. Andrew is co-founder of Psychotherapists and Counsellors for Social Responsibility, and Chair of the United Kingdom Council for Psychotherapy. His books have been translated into nineteen languages and include *The Plural Psyche*, *The Political Psyche*, and *Politics on the Couch*. www.andrewsamuels.com.

Nick Totton is a therapist and trainer with nearly thirty years experience. Originally a Reichian body therapist, his approach has become broad based and open to the spontaneous and unexpected. Nick has an MA in Psychoanalytic Studies, and has worked with Process-Oriented Psychology and trained as a craniosacral therapist. He has a twenty-five-year-old daughter. He has written several books, including *Body Psychotherapy: An Introduction*; *Psychotherapy and Politics*; *Press When Illuminated: New and Selected Poems*; and most recently, *Wild Therapy*, published by PCCS Books. See www.erthworks.co.uk. He lives in Calderdale with his partner and grows vegetables.

Sandra White works as an ecopsychologist and ceremony maker. She has a background in cultural change within government and business, particularly in the fields of race equality and humanizing the workplace. All her work is rooted in Jungian analytical psychology. A founding member of Transition Hertford, her published articles and chapters include "Exile from earth" in GreenSpirit Journal, "Denial, stories and visions" in Greenpeace Business, and "White lilies: Sacrifice, transformation and renewal in our civilised age" in *Thoughts on Sustainability, Vol 2*, published by Ashridge Business School.

INTRODUCTION

The actual outlook is very dark, and any serious thought should start out from that fact.

—George Orwell

We do not and cannot know whether we are here to serve as deathbed attendants for our world or as midwives to a new chapter of life on earth.

—Joanna Macy

Psychological practitioners reflect the society we live in—including its divisions. At our best, we also reflect *on* it, identifying its problems and offering possible ways forward; and, indeed, reflect on our relationship with it. All of these processes can be seen at work in this anthology, which is intended to illustrate the range and diversity of responses from the psychological world—counselling, psychotherapy, Jungian analysis, psychoanalysis, and to a lesser extent psychology—to the multiple ecological crises with which our society is faced. The main focus in what follows is on work done in the UK; but also included are a few chapters from authors in the United States and in Europe which we feel offer important insights. Some of the chapters are quite scholarly in style, and some very much not; the majority are somewhere in the middle.

"Vital signs" are, of course, the basic physiological measures of functioning which health practitioners use to assess the gravity of a patient's predicament. This anthology focuses not so much on our physical predicament, with so many of the earth's systems severely stressed and beginning to fail—there are plenty of other places to read about this (e.g., Lovelock, 2010). Instead we focus on our psychological predicament, as news of the situation slowly penetrates our defences and we struggle as individuals and as a society to find an adequate response. By "vital signs" we also mean signs that such a response is beginning to take shape: signs of hope, signs of healing.

Just as Western society in general has taken decades to begin seriously to confront the interlocking crises that in retrospect have been apparent at least since the 1950s, so with psychological practitioners. Perhaps the first initiative in the UK was in the mid-1980s, when Paul Fink and others established a British section of the Interhelp Network (Senders, 1994), inspired by Joanna Macy's "Despair and Empowerment" work (Macy, 1983); the primary focus at that point was on the nuclear bomb, but environmental issues were always part of the mix. Other individuals, such as Paul Maiteny, Graham Game, and Jenny Grut, were also beginning to make links between ecology and psychology around this time. Later, in 1995, and inspired partly by developments in the USA (Roszak, 1992; Roszak et al., 1995), Hilary Prentice and Tania Dolley formed an ecopsychology group as part of the newly founded organization Psychotherapists and Counsellors for Social Responsibility (PCSR); Mary-Jayne Rust became a member of this group. A couple of years later Hilary and Tania started the UK Ecopsychology Network, whose current descendant is the Ecopsychology UK Online Network (www.ecopsychologyuk. ning.com), with over 600 participants. Nick Totton consciously connected with ecopsychology in around 2003, influenced by his partner Hélène Fletcher; Nick and Hélène, together with Mary-Jayne and Hilary, organized an ecopsychology gathering at Laurieston Hall, near Dumfries, in 2004. These are just snapshots of a gradually accelerating process of development and connection.

But environmental issues have been slow to enter the therapy mainstream, as they have been slow to enter the cultural mainstream. As we write, it seems likely that a cross-modality alliance of UK therapists and therapy organizations will be formed, aiming to bring together the different groups and individuals within the field who are trying to address the situation. PCSR is still playing an important role here. There have been a number of conferences and other events on ecopsychological themes in the last few years. As a result of all this activity, Oliver Rathbone of Karnac Books invited us to produce this anthology, and offered to fast-track its publication.

Oliver gave us pretty much a free hand, and we considered several different possible anthologies: for instance, a European one, one focused on clinical applications, or one drawing on work worldwide which particularly excited us. All of these seemed either too complicated to assemble, or offering either too much or too little material. Because so much writing in this field has emerged from the USA, we settled on the idea of an anthology of UK authors, though not rigidly so, and aiming to show the range and variety of work being done rather than to select only work with which we ourselves feel closely aligned. Many of our authors have not yet been published, or hardly so, though all have been active in ecopsychology. We feel that ecopsychology in Britain has a distinctive voice and unique contributions to make.

In doing so, we hope to facilitate debate and dialogue within the field, in the hope that this will lead eventually to more developed theory and practice. Things are still at quite an early stage in the construction of ecopsychology as a discipline, and the articulation of relationships of compatibility or incompatibility between various approaches. It will take time for the field to reach maturity, to agree on terminology (or agree to use different terminologies), and to develop organizational forms. This is a familiar process for any new way of looking at things.

At the same time as recognizing this slow maturation, we are of course equally aware of the extraordinary urgency of the external situation which it is one of the missions of ecopsychologists to address. While there would in theory still be an important role for ecopsychology if we were not facing environmental meltdown—exploring the complex relationships between human and other-than-human, and the therapeutic value of bringing the two together—in practice ecopsychology has been completely shaped by a sense of catastrophic loss, of the irreversible destruction of complexity and the impending threat to the systems that sustain life on this planet.

From this point of view, ecopsychology is part of a much larger movement seeking to develop awareness of climate change together with all the other developing ecological crises (pollution, over-consumption of resources, destruction of habitats, etc.). What distinguishes ecopsychology from many of the other players in this larger movement, however—apart from the psychological focus itself—is a very widespread perception of human beings as just one element in the global ecosystem; and an agreement, both ethical and practical, that humanity cannot save itself by throwing other species out of the sledge. The ecosystem stands or falls as a whole, human, other-than-human, and more-than-human; and a failure to recognize this is itself a symptom of our culture's dissociation from its place in the larger whole, which is one of the causal factors leading to our current situation.

Among people who have been working in this area for some time, there is a growing question: what if we fail? What if our society does not manage a transition to a carbon-free economy—and all of the other transformations of culture and practice which are required alongside this? In all probability time is getting extremely short; considerable damage to global ecosystems is already certain, and runaway "tipping point" effects are predicted by many scientists. Although awareness of this crisis is far greater than it was a decade ago, there is still little sign of a serious shift in public attitudes. Indeed in the UK, and elsewhere, ecological concerns have been eclipsed by the recent economic crisis with seemingly little recognition that of course ecological, social, and economic crisis are completely interwoven. While the future can never be predicted with certainty, there is not much concrete basis for optimism. What then?

It may well be that the future role of ecopsychology will be to help people manage the pain and despair that will accompany "the end of the world", and to preserve some sort of hope. Not that the world will literally end—so far as we can see now; but our current human world, the world we grew up in, will cease to be viable: millions or billions of us and trillions more other-than-humans will die, the mass extinction of species that is already underway will accelerate, and a large proportion of the planet will become uninhabitable by humans. In all probability, however, something will survive; and the small fraction of humanity which is likely to be part of that "something" will need all the help it can get in staying sane, and in carrying forward the seeds of a sane culture, founded in ecological consciousness. Ecopsychology as it now exists may well be the beginnings of a theory and practice for such a future.

We are not yet at that point, though—despite the suffering of those in other parts of the world who are the victims of our affluent lifestyles—and ecopsychology is certainly not yet at the point of being able to take on this task. This anthology offers a number of samplings of where ecopsychology has got to so far, and where it seems to be heading. We hope that they will be of interest and of use: to those already involved with the field, in developing and refining their thinking; to those becoming aware, in finding out more about what is going on and where they might join in; and to anyone concerned about human relationships with the ecosystems of which we are part, in discovering ways of looking at those relationships and what makes them problematic.

We have divided the book into six parts, which as usual in these cases have a slightly arbitrary nature: many of the chapters could reasonably be placed in more than one part, and many contain material from more than one part. In particular, almost every chapter considers at least to some extent what can be done given the seriousness of our situation. However, it feels more helpful than not to create some subdivisions, and these are the ones which we have chosen.

The first part, "Contexts", contains four chapters which focus on various aspects of where we are now: the ecological crisis and its psychological effects and causes. In the opening chapter, Viola Sampson offers an embodied, rather than an intellectual exploration of climate change, seeking to ground our rational responses in the emotional soil, to situate our local realities in the cosmic field, and to connect with love for the physical world as the only effective basis for action. Susan Bodnar provides a different sort of grounding for our theories, reporting the detailed responses to climate change of some New York inhabitants in a piece of what we might call psychoanalytic micro-anthropology. Peter Chatalos, in probably the oldest piece included here, develops the metaphor of AIDS as a planetary immune response to our "cultural autism". Paul Maiteny, in a chapter that usefully cuts across the grain of most other contributions, considers what is *special* about the role of human beings on this planet, and how that specialness might be used creatively rather than destructively.

Picking up on Viola's chapter, the next part focuses on "The other-than-human and more-than-human", phrases which are increasingly being used to describe other species and phenomena on the planet in terms which place them on at least an equal footing with human beings. Margaret Kerr and David Key write about relationship with place, and how spending time alone in wild places can open us to the unconscious and to transpersonal experiences. In very different styles, Kelvin Hall and G. A. Bradshaw both point out the assumptions of superiority built into our relationships with other species, how destructive this is for our way of being in the world, and how much there is to gain from rebuilding these relationships on a basis of equality. Finally in this part Inger Birkeland and Astri Aasen describe very beautifully the creative relationship which a group of children in Norway have developed with a small and local more-than-human place—as children instinctively will do given the opportunity. The strong message of all four chapters, as of several others in the book, is that humans need to look beyond their own species concerns to find ways forward in this crisis.

In contrast, the part entitled "The View from Postmodernism" offers ways of looking at ecology which express themselves more intellectually than emotionally, and which critique what they see as simplistic and romantic accounts of "nature" (a word which we have, for good reasons, avoided using in this introduction). Using several varieties of critical theory, notably the work of Deleuze and Guattari, Martin Jordan and Joseph Dodds each explore the possibility of an ecopsychology which rigorously questions its own assumptions and privileged concepts. This approach is very different in both flavour and content from more familiar ones, but we suggest that it adds a vitally self-questioning element to the field.

The three final parts all explore different aspects of the question: what can we do? The first, "What to do: Possible futures", includes four overviews of how our culture might be entering into a profound change of heart—versions of what Joanna Macy calls "The Great Turning". Mary-Jayne Rust focuses on the need to rediscover an intimacy with the other-than-human and more-than human, and on the wounds that the loss of that intimacy has created. Mick Collins and his co-authors use Stan Grof's concept of "spiritual emergence" as a central image of such a change: according to Grof and others, many individual emotional crises—what have traditionally been called "breakdowns"—are also "break-*throughs*", opportunities for creative transformation, and this chapter suggests that the same may be true on a planetary scale. Hilary Prentice contributes some history of the relationship between ecological and psychological currents in the UK, and an account of one recent flowering of this history in the formation of a "Heart and Soul Group" as part of the first UK Transition Town in Totnes, together with her reflections on "ecos and psyche". And Jerome

Bernstein's warm and approachable chapter summarizes his concept of Borderland consciousness, "shaped from forces outside of the ego, to open itself up more to the fact that all living systems are inter-related and inter-dependent"—parallel, though in a different language, to the spiritual emergence described by Collins et al.

"What to do: Influencing attitudes" offers four psychologically informed approaches to changing people's behaviour around environmental issues. Tom Crompton draws on his extensive experience as an environmental campaigner, as well as on research findings, to argue that "the more individuals endorse intrinsic goals and self-transcendence values, the more they also express positive attitudes and behaviours towards other-than-human nature"—and that therefore campaigning simply to change what people *do* will on its own be of limited value. Sandra White offers an approach to understanding what blocks people from acting with environmental awareness, focusing on denial, and on the meaning of sacrifice. The last two papers in this part each discuss specific practical initiatives. Rosemary Randall describes the "Carbon Conversations" project in Cambridge, working with small groups to facilitate change to a lower-consumption lifestyle. And in a second contribution David Key and Margaret Kerr tell the story of their "Natural Change Project", set up by WWF Scotland, which tries to put ecopsychology into practice by working in wilderness areas with small groups of invited individuals who are seen as being of influence in a variety of fields, none of them previously environmentally active.

Most, though not all, of our contributors are psychotherapists, counsellors or analysts; so it is interesting that little has been said in the chapters discussed so far about therapy itself. This is the theme of the book's final part, "What to do: Clinical practice". Nick Totton's chapter explores how ecological thinking and feeling might really change the practice of psychotherapy, rather than just being used as a "bolt-on". And in a beautifully written piece, Chris Robertson moves back and forth between clinical vignette and general ecological themes to suggest how each can illuminate the other, and how, for his client, "the very nature of his complaints, his failings" can "become the ingredients of his sense of connection with the more-than human and a consequent sense of being held".

What themes stand out from the enormous richness and range of contributions? Perhaps not surprisingly given its source, the writing collected here emphasizes the depth of psychological change required before we can make the practical changes which the situation requires. As we said earlier, there is a tension between the urgency of the situation, and the scale of the emotional shift which it demands. We might wish that a lot of things had happened much sooner; but they didn't, and therefore no doubt couldn't. It is important now, in the psychological realm as in the technological, to keep working steadily at the rate which is possible rather than losing our skilfulness to panic reflex.

Beyond that, there is very little, other than the seriousness of the situation, on which all of the authors agree. The most obvious theme is actually difference: every author expresses a different perspective from most of the others, each brings their own diagnosis and/or remedy to some aspect of the situation. It is not even obvious that everyone is engaged in the same task or part of the same discipline. A reader might be left asking whether a recognisable field of "ecopsychology" actually exists. But this seems to us a sign of health—a vital sign!—rather than a shortcoming. On the psychological plane just as on the practical plane we are seeing an efflorescence of creative ideas and partial solutions, and at this point no one can tell which of them, or what combination of them, will be most useful. (We can be fairly sure, though, that the recurrent theme in this book of dissolving boundaries between humans and other species, between the individual and the world, between "inside" and "outside", will be important in what develops.)

As Viola Sampson says in her chapter, referencing some frequent motifs of environmentalism, perhaps we are just shuffling deckchairs on the Titanic, keeping ourselves intellectually busy in the face of something too big to comprehend, let alone affect. To some degree this is certainly so. But a fundamental principle of activism is that no one can change the world alone; the task is always too big, and we just have to do as much as we can, in the way that we can. As we have tried to argue above, it seems to us that one aspect of the current task, and one which has value on several levels, is to consider the psychological aspects of ecological crisis; and that the chapters herein collected make a major contribution to that task.

PART I

CONTEXTS

CHAPTER ONE

The darkening quarter: an embodied exploration of a changing global climate

Viola Sampson

Home

I live on a hilltop who tips me out into the fresher winds and broader horizons to the north of the city. This hill shoulders old villages swallowed many years ago in London's urban gobble. Its paths through ancient woodlands, of oak and hornbeam, jay and blue tit, will soon be softened by fallen leaves—the dank wind in my nostrils tells me it is autumn now.

Autumn. I share my days with yellow plums squashed underfoot near the bus stop, and rain-swollen blackberries cloaked in mildew. Ripe, green figs hang far out of reach in my neighbour's tree. Heavy with fragrant sweetness, they empty ooze onto the roof of the shed, hanging slack before sliding to the ground and completing a year-long gesture of fruition and nourishment. Each year a flock of starlings descend in noisy feasting and leave in one quick swoosh. I am waiting for them. To me, they mark the season in this increasingly uncertain time, when the chemistry of the climate is stirred by humanity's hand.

What of this home? This house on a hill in London. This city, a historical centre from where the great British set out to colonize lands, creatures, and cultures. A city perched at the base of a small, green island. This island, laid out on the northern face of this blue-green planet swooping through the heavens, and spinning on a midline pointing to the distant North Star. This face of the planet now tilted towards the winter skies in the outer reaches of the sun's rays.

Our industrial growth society is rushing headlong into a darkening age, clamouring to keep the lights on and the accelerator pressed down: a moth mistaking the hot streetlight for the moon. This is a time when the wildness of life on earth as we know it, is dependent on industrial civilization for survival. In its linear hero's quest for progress and growth, industrial civilization has acted as if we could cut loose from the web of life and ignore the cyclical nature of earthly systems. Climate change is one of many pressing symptoms of this disorientation.

This is a time of emergency: new models of enquiry and knowing are emerging and informing our decisions and priorities, systems theories of feedback and balance are generating new stories of earthly intelligence, and there are other vital signs of our evolving consciousness.

As an ecopsychologist, I am interested to explore what earth, as an intelligent system, may be calling into our awareness through climate change. This question reverberates through my days, through my work and my ponderings.

As a craniosacral therapist, I am interested in how the airy, intellectual exchange of facts and figures, that feature in climate change discussions, can be brought back down to earth and explored through embodiment. I search for a collaboration between our high-flying eagle intellect and the earth-bound snake of our gut feelings and passions (Peters, 1987).

As a climate activist, I find myself asking people to become interested in air. We speak in tonnes of CO_2, using the language of science to give us gravitas. But how can such a measurement describe this apparently weightless and invisible sea pervading every cell of our bodies? How can it portray these hurricanes in our nostrils we co-created with the green grasses and all life on earth? We are immersed in a common field, sharing breath with this living planet—with soil microbes and elephants, forests and seaweed. Air? We are now called into conscious relationship with the earth's changing atmosphere—a word rooted in the ancient Sanskrit, *atman*, meaning soul (Abram, 2010a) and *atma*, intelligence, mind, and heart. Through the evolution of languages from both Latin and Greek, air is linked to the words psyche, spirit, and soul (Abram, 1996). Perhaps these words speak more deeply than metrics to the challenges we are facing, and can inspire the task in our hands.

Alongside the cycling currents of ocean and air, the great carbon and water cycles are central to global climate stability. As they move through us, the air and the global landscape, these cycles show us to be small in relation to the life-sustaining capacity of this planet. Perhaps as we build our homes higher and cut deeper into wild spaces, we struggle with our smallness and dependence on these vast cycles beyond our control. Yet they are highly sensitive and, as the climate shows signs of disruption, we are realizing our awesome destructive power over them.

Over the past five years in the UK, we have lived through the hottest summer since records began (two centuries ago), the driest spring and one of the coldest winters. In this part of the world, the seasons are where we can have a bodily understanding of a changing climate (Knebusch, 2008, pp. 242–262). Through attending to the seasons, I have deepened into my embodied understanding of the cycles our planet maps through the heavens, in relationship to the source of life energy—the sun.

Equinox: balance

It is Equinox. The days have been receding to equal night, as the sun dips lower in its ancient circle dance. The relationship between earth and sun is the basis of myths and stories that fed the imagination of older cultures, but no longer fills us with awe.

For us the changing seasons simply mean comments on the unwelcome chill rain, and our changing wardrobe. But the beech tree in the nearby woodland still bends to this dance; the flourishing of spring and fullness of summer is already giving way to winter's crackle of empty branches, and the metallic grey of her bark is cold against my cheek.

The transition between night and day is also overlooked. Humanity's collective brilliance lights the night sky with orange streetlights, and the hum of cars holds at bay the deep stillness suspending the stars. In the daytime, we like to forget the night's skinny fox, police cars, and creeping wind, as we busy ourselves with our daily lives.

This Equinox, the Harvest Moon is waning, and I feel grateful for this soft beacon shining with the same light now gracing the far side of the earth. Night—the great shadow of this planet body—draws us into the intimacy of the earth's celestial relationships (Abram, 2010) with whom our own bodies stretch and swell, ebb and flow.

School physics taught me that the force binding these celestial bodies together in their dance of intergalactic yearning, is the same force gifting us with weight, embedding us in the airy, watery surface of earth. Without gravity and their earthly ground, we learned, astronauts float clumsily, their muscles degenerating and their toothpaste squirling upwards. Gravity pulls us and the earth together at a speed of 9.81 metres per second. Yet we, continuously landing on planet earth, feel a quiet meeting of foot and ground, hoof and turf, rump and chair, head and pillow; a resting place.

We now understand gravity pulls the earth to orbit the sun, and the moon to orbit earth. But tales of chariots and night sea journeys depict something of humanity's earlier relationships with the burning sun and the gentle moon.

It was only around five hundred years ago that the astronomer Copernicus calculated that the earth orbits the sun, and a Spanish ship sailed across uncharted seas to complete the first circumnavigation of the globe. While the whales and birds, oceans and winds have long known the planet to be round, this was a radical change in human consciousness: within just one generation, the earth was no longer flat, nor the solid, heavy, fixed centre of the universe it once had been. The cosmos, once the realm of gods and dark mysteries, had succumbed to human reason in a mathematical aesthetic.

To understand the heliocentric theory, the human mind must be projected into the heavens, to look down at the earth, while the sun must be chosen as a central, commanding stillpoint. Objective reasoning overrules a subjective, embodied sense of a solid, still earth and moving sun. This worldview is now so close to our perception that we barely notice how it shapes our relationship with the wider than human world.

Copernicus's heliocentric theory sparked the scientific revolution. Objective reasoning generates an experience of fundamental separation between the experiencing human self (subject) and the objective facts that make up the world. For modern scientific reasoning, the factual world must be purely objective, that is, it must not contain subjectivity and therefore inherent meaning or conscious intelligence (Tarnas, 2006, pp. 1–26).

In this way of thinking, no pattern or meaning exists except as constructed by the human mind. The world is passive, inanimate, inarticulate, and non-participatory. This worldview underpins the dominant culture today, where consciousness and intelligence are *created* by the circuitry of the brain, rather than *received* by it as a fundamental, pervasive force of the universe. There is no continuity of subjectivity from the interior world of the human to the surrounding (and permeating) world. Responsive, creative intelligence, as well as consciousness, spirit or soul, are believed to be qualities only of the human world. Any recognition of human-attributed qualities in the encompassing world is dismissed as projection and anthropomorphic.

As the world is objectified and disenchanted, forests can be considered resources and natural limits ignored. Humanity's uniqueness in subjectivity becomes magnified, giving us a greater sense of freedom and power over the rest of the world. In today's society, quantity (an objective measurement) supersedes quality—a function of subjectivity, essential to an embodied, relational understanding of the world. As objectivity is over-privileged, the value of subjective experience can be easily dismissed and, with that, our empowerment to act on our experience of ecological crisis.

The story of how the waters of Copernicus's theory broke over civilization intrigues me. While many writers have charted defining moments in history, before and since the scientific revolution, that contributed to the emergence of today's dominant ecopsychological disposition, this story describes one step in a dramatic change in humanity's experience of place within the cosmic order. It gave us the powerful, reasoning intellect suited to solving many puzzles and technological challenges, but it also gave us an illusion of freedom from the marshy web of life and death, it undermined the value of our embodied, relational experience, and disenchanted the cosmos.

Within a tale that has breathed through much of western civilization, I see the heliocentric theory as one bite of the fruit from the Tree of Knowledge that changed our self-consciousness. When, in the Garden of Eden, Eve bites the fruit, the state of wholeness and unity falls into apparent opposites—good and evil, man and woman, life and death, subject and object, sickness and health, mind and body.

These dualisms are alive in our culture today, and I ponder this black and white thinking, as the Equinox days and nights occupy this greying of autumn into winter. This transitional time of cool dusk and gloaming holds light and dark in balance.

* * *

I began adult life as a scientist, studying molecular biology and genetic engineering, feasting on the fruits of objective enquiry and scientific reason, deeply fascinated by the invisible magic of living processes. I later applied my knowledge to environmental campaigning and grassroots activism. But it was seven years ago, at this time of year, when I found a practice uniting objective and subjective ways of knowing, as I embarked on a training in craniosacral therapy.

I was drawn to the training by a force I could not argue with. I wanted to learn a new *language*—the language of the body, form, and health. I learned, through experiencing, how life moves in deep breaths through the body, and the body's fluids are drawn in the undertow of tides. Deeper still, I found a wind glittering like the Aurora Australis sweeping through the body in a long, slow waft. I learned that this was an *intelligence* that pervaded the human body, and that of other living beings, constantly seeking health and wholeness. I learned how the muscle and sinew of each joint makes intelligent decisions more quickly than my intellect can grasp. And I learned how to sit, still, with the body's moment-to-moment coming into form.

Core to my craniosacral skills, I learned to listen from a state of balanced awareness—balancing my internal sensations with awareness of my external world, including the client's body (Sumner & Haines, 2010, pp. 19–22). This kind of listening, through a spacious, relational touch, is deeply synaesthetic; images, textures, smells, feeling tones, and even sound, all inform the practitioner of the process of health in the client's system. It is based on equanimity and presence. Craniosacral therapy is a perceptual practice that requires a balanced attention to objective awareness and subjective experience; to oneness and separation; to relationship.

A perceptual practice like this can nurture our sense of self that is of the world. As we deepen into our senses, the separation between us as an experiencing subject and the perceived as an object, diminishes (Sewall, 1999). The perceiver is interdependent with the perceived, different aspects of the same living field. Craniosacral practitioners recognize that deep listening is healing for the deeply heard, and we recognize that healing has reciprocity; both client and practitioner emerge changed from the shared therapeutic journey.

Samhain: darkness

Darkness causes us to sense differently. It banishes our vision and invites us to drop deep into our sensing bodies, listening for the edge of the coffee table that surprises us as we bruise our shin.

The earth's shadow looms over our hour of waking, darkness seeping into the daytime. But with a quick flick of a switch, electric light blasts the shadows, crudely announcing humans' power over darkness. In this city, it feels as though the pace of life is increasing and there is little time for twilight, liminal space, or not knowing.

One of the greatest difficulties with facing climate change seems to be *not knowing*. The emphasis on models, facts, targets and parts per million, feels to me like a desperate way to regain some sense of control, as if, in quantifying, we can reduce this enormous issue enough to fit inside boxes in our minds and bend to human reason. We demand ever more accurate predictions, but no model can compute all the variables, and scientists' understanding of vital intricacies in the global cycles—such as the oceans and Arctic tundra—is still in its infancy. Is it too late? Are we just in time to avert the worst with an array of glittering technologies and green jobs? Are we shuffling deckchairs on the Titanic? Should we just party while Rome burns? Maybe. We don't know. We cannot know.

Climate change faces us with darkness, a great uncertainty, and a fear of losing the electric excitement of our fossil-fuelled lifestyle. In the discomfort of not knowing, it can feel easier to pretend nothing is wrong, but also easier to pretend we know catastrophic climate change is inevitable and we humans, like a cancer, have no part to play in the earth's healing. Can we stay present to the stretch of possibility that either could be true—and perhaps somewhere in between, or even completely different? We cannot predict how an intelligent system, as we now know this planet to be, might respond, or what interventions it might make—for better or worse.

The objective, scientific analysis of earth's climatic systems has been vital in alerting us to climate change. However, perhaps a different kind of knowing might emerge, that can provide a path to navigate the climate crisis. Objective knowing is a cool unfettered thinking that permeates a singular truth from all angles. Subjective knowing is based in our embodied experience. It recognizes that we can see just one part of the truth, one side of the argument and one side of a rock. The rock keeps a side hidden from us. If we walk around it, the rock will reveal more of itself to us, but still conceals the other side in an unending dance of disclosure and privacy. Staying with the discomfort of not knowing can open us out to mystery, and allow us to rest in an experience much larger than ourselves.

* * *

There is an interiority that grows at this time of year. I spend more time under shelter—indoors or in my raincoat. My jumpers get thicker, my feet become booted and I feel less expansive and sociable. As the nights grow longer and the winter weather sets in, my world is made smaller. I hurry as I pull my coat tighter around me, and gaze only downwards as I shelter my face from the cold rain. When I arrive home, the lounge holds me closer within the pool of lamplight, as the rain on the window-panes melts the street outside, scattering the orange sparks of streetlight and softening the sound of the late rush hour traffic.

Winter weather pulls me to the immediacy of my skin and needs for warmth and food. We are vulnerable. Websites, iPhone apps, and TV channels are dedicated to predicting the weather twenty-four hours a day. But as the climate changes and weather patterns become more unpredictable and extreme, our vulnerability becomes keener. Weather wrecks our plans, and even our homes and communities. Weather can't be controlled. Weather is wild. Climate change shows us our human-sized powerlessness and vulnerability, and faces us with death—not least, the extinction of so many species as well as our own.

In this part of the world, many hundred years ago, a spirituality emerged from our relationship with the land, honouring the cycle of the seasons. As I begin to connect with my own indigeny, this has taken on meaning in my own experiences. In the great wheel of the year, with its cyclical motifs of life and death, this time is marked by a festival called Samhain; summer's end. It is better known as Halloween; the time of glowing, ghoulish pumpkins, death, witches, ghosts, and other night characters.

A week before Samhain, a full moon has risen low, golden and heavy, into a soft blue sky. It is called the Blood Moon, reflecting the sun's light, now growing scarce as we enter the night-time, lunar half of this earth-sun year. Moon teaches of cycles, as the thin, bright crescent grows into soft fullness before returning to silent darkness; a potency from which the sliver of light emerges once more. Through these phases, given the feminine depictions of maid, mother and crone, she teaches us of the visible and invisible, potential and whole. Her light depends on her relationship with the radiant, bodiless sun, but this is easy to forget as the quality of light is so much her own. The body of moon offers this light to guide us as we navigate the night's dreaming world of collective unconscious: moths in search of nectar. As we lie back to see her face, looking back at the earth with a gaze of an ancient partnership, she offers a planetary perspective in which to anchor our sense of self.

This Samhain, we sit and watch the night settle. Twilight: the shadows creep outwards, diffusing into the room, softening distinctions, reconciling furniture and air, form and flow, and mediating the transition from sunlight to moonlight. Darkness is often considered an absence. But this evening, we find a fullness and pervasiveness. It has depth and softness, felt by my eyes.

Death is often thought of as merely absence of life, but it too has a pervasiveness, an expanding-into and outwards. So while it is an absence for those of us who are left in the living, it is also an everywhereness. We think of death, like our own shadow on the pavement, as two-dimensional; an ending. But we forget that shadows have depth and volume, and that death is a profound journey in itself, for the one dying and those living. We are buried in the earth's darkness by those who love us.

Sleep, held in the darkness, lets us turn inwards and so slip outwards into the realm of dreams, the collective unconscious. Is this a taste of death's expansiveness? Perhaps it is this society's terror of death and darkness that keeps us running blindly towards extinction, taking with us so many of the beings with whom we share this earth, air, and water.

In the garden, we see death and decay is part of life, and all growth is also a death. In the compost bin, the uneaten pear loses form, relinquishing the warmth the tree had drawn from the sun, so that the mulch becomes hot with rot. The pear's potential expands outwards; a delicious opportunity missed and a pang of sadness. Samhain is both the end and the beginning of the festival cycle, reminding us that all death is a birth, all beginning also an ending.

At this dark planet time, there is so much death and grief. Where do we mourn our fellow beings torn from our world by floods, droughts, and habitat destruction? When grief, disempowerment, social conditioning, or trauma closes our hearts and minds to the devastation of earthly life, we become deadened, unable to respond in a healthy or creative way. We need to find ways to sustain our sensitivity and deepen our resilience.

Several years ago, I was sitting on the top deck of a crowded London bus, reading one of the free newspapers handed out in rush hour. I came across a small news article, buried deep in the later pages, about the sea butterfly; a minute mollusc named for the way it flies through the depths of the oceans. The article told me how, due to rising CO_2 levels increasing ocean acidity, these small creatures are becoming unable to bind the calcium to make their snail-like shells. The sea butterfly is a food source, directly or indirectly, for most of ocean life.

I began to cry at the significance of this news. My tears fell even thicker, because even if someone had noticed and enquired about my distress, I felt they would be baffled. I have seen no mention of the sea butterfly in mainstream news since, but a part of me still dives into oceans of grief as I bear witness to this enormous tale of one of the world's smallest creatures, unable to bear the brunt of our lifestyle choices.

I feel bearing witness, grieving, and facing squarely the pain of our collective responsibility, is one of the most important ecopsychological tasks of our time. Honouring our pain can give us an opportunity to grow, shaped by our relationship with our world, just as a tree growing on the edge of a cliff is shaped by the sea winds, and our muscle and bone is wrought from our interactions with our encompassing world. Grief is the process by which we enter a new relationship, wise from the knowledge that shattered our earlier certainties. Living as interconnected, feeling, responsive, and sentient beings, we can move away from trying to "save the planet", towards actions that are an expression of the earth to save itself—our Self.

Myths within many cultures tell how each night, the sun sinks into the sea, and the world is plunged into darkness, before the sun is reborn from the ocean womb at dawn. In some ancient stories, the sun is carried by boat through the underworld to the next sunrise. Night sea journeys describe a descent and an immersion in the unconscious. They are an archetypal motif commonly associated with grief or depression; the necessary dark prelude to rebirth. When we let our own brightness dissolve in the ocean of grief, we honour the daily cycle of death and rebirth enacted by the sun and earth, and slowly realign with a cosmic order from which we have become estranged.

And so I begin to see that this darkening quarter of the year is a journey of fullness, an expanding into the darkness. It is an opportunity to stay present to the darkness within and without, and not shrink from the cold or the world's grief. It is an opportunity to inhabit the greater darkness of the earth, allowing its shadow to imbibe me, and draw me inwards and downwards—into my roots.

Solstice: spark

In an age-old collaboration of rock and flame, the sun gives us light, while the earth gives us darkness. The sun gives us fire, the earth gives us fuel. In rust-red oil and blackness of coal, the earth buried many, many thousands of years of sunlight. In just a few hundred years, humanity has unleashed this energy, transforming the world and ourselves.

With the heliocentric theory, humans fixed the sun, one of a sea of stars in motion, at the centrepoint of our world—mirroring society's fixation on linear progress and growth that is always onwards, upwards, towards the light, and away from darkness, earth, and decay. We also displaced our earth-bound embodied reality, bowing to the commanding power of the sun and the mathematical model that gave it such fixity. Now, our relationship with our hero sun is changing. The heavenly source of life has become a death threat. But it is we who took on the power of a sun god, and our hubris, hanging around the planet in a smog of CO_2, that is trapping the sun's warmth and destabilising the finely balanced interchange of wet and dry, hot and cold, movement and stillness, we call climate.

In the longest night, as the planet turns its northern face into the darkest depths of the solar system, I notice a brightness—not the rich brightness of the sun at summer solstice, but the brightness of a cold, full moon and snow.

This is winter solstice, a festival taken over by the Christian church as Christmas. It speaks of returning light and the promise of life in the prayer-form of winter buds at the tips of their twigs, quietly awaiting their springtime swelling. This year, we go out into the longest night to light a candle in the snow; the spark of life is held deep in the dark and frozen earth.

As industrial civilization strains ever higher and brighter, some are going down, deeper, and wider, facing the shadows and opening to a different way of knowing. From here perhaps a spark of ecocentric consciousness can take hold, where humanity is a living expression of this alive planet's intelligence, and where the earth's gestures of humanness flower alongside those of python, mosquito, and rose.

In this time of bright darkness, holding a paradox of two apparently contradictory truths can let us expand beyond the dualistic mode of thinking so common in our culture. Paradox invites conscious awareness to be intrigued by a primordial, non-dualistic state. Within paradox is a potent creative tension. If we are able to hold the tension of two opposites, like the string on a bow powering an arrow, something new can arise. Opposites can become polarities of a newly figured whole.

Returning to that great scientific myth that initiated humanity's latest exploration of the cosmos, we can find a new dimension to the story. We know from Galileo's patient observations, it is mechanically true that the earth orbits the sun. We could assign the sun as the still centrepoint in an ever-moving universe, but it is also true that from where I am an earthly, embodied centre of the universe, the sun rises and sets, around the earth—around me. Holding those two truths together can allow a deep homecoming—here we are the very centre of the universe and yet also placed within the larger cycles of the cosmos.

In holding these two truths, I find the creative potential of paradox and a stillness. In this fast culture, stillness is considered a lack; an absence of movement. But my craniosacral practice has taught me that stillness can be a place of great potency from where new form can arise. It can have a fullness and dynamism, sometimes so rich it rings like a clear bell.

As we come to rest on the earth circling the sun, itself moving through the heavens filled with stars in motion, it is possible to sense stillness in this universe that is not the external, commanding stillpoint of a sun. It can be tasted most easily sitting on a meditation cushion, or on a mossy log deep within the forest, or at midday in the hot, red desert. This stillness is at the very ground of our being, a dynamic stillness, rich with an intelligence that breathes through us. Here, we can experience ourselves as a continuous expression of a pervasive field of universal intelligence. The stillness at our core contains the dark potential of deepest outer space, the ringing roar of the big bang, fuelling our moment-to-moment coming into form.

Returning home

An experience of our global self has emerged with computer technology and the internet: a human-centric world-wide web of communication—a human consciousness. Instead of intelligent, participatory relationship with our encompassing earth, we are immersed in communications reflecting humanity back to ourselves, like a hall of mirrors, and insensitive to the warning signs of ecological collapse.

Climate change is calling us into relationship with a different sense of global self—with whole-earth systems, an ecocentric world-wide web of pattern and balance—a planetary consciousness. To understand climate change, we come to understand ourselves as part of a sensitive global system in which we are no more or less important than the rest of life on earth. It is perhaps an opportunity to find our place in the cosmic order, both participant and recipient of the universal intelligence that flows through us.

Activism arises out of love. Perhaps it is no irony that the floating blue-green jewel of planet earth became an enduring symbol of the environmental movement when man exploring the dark side of the moon fell in love with the earth. In the thick of the scientific adventure several hundred years after the heliocentric theory emerged, perhaps these famous astronauts visualized the global identity we had been straining to perceive, and floating within the gravitational pull between the moon and the earth—a mutual attraction that lovers align their poems with—they were steeped in this expression of universal love from where the environmental movement was born.

Humanity's love for life on earth is a rich mix of longing, hatred, projection and idealization, fear of dependence, fear of merging, fear of separation, these and all those feelings that sweep through us in any intimate relationship. These feelings are expressed in tar sands mines visible from space, the agricultural wastelands, the charred scars of rainforest destruction and the fenced-out conservation parks. The love we yearn for cannot be sold to us in perfume bottles, from the larger-than-life screens of cinemas or between the sheets of chocolate bar wrappers. Perhaps this love is an age-old longing of the subject and object to become one—an expression of climactic union only possible following the experience of separateness.

Can we complete the intellectual leap of the scientific revolution with a dive into embodiment—ultimately enworldment? Can we reconcile this flight of human consciousness with an opening inwards—and thus outwards—to the depths and expanse of the collective unconscious, the intelligence of the universe?

Rich with the fruits of objective knowing, coming home to our sensing bodies, we might find ourselves at home in this earth who enfolds us, at home within this precious living planet floating deep in the darkness and brilliance of that unfathomable potential we call space. As a foetus, floating in the hotpot darkness of our mother's womb, our fingers differentiate as our hands form around our enormous, beating heart. Right now, those sensing hands hold a book and perhaps that bony, questioning gesture is, in turn, echoed by wing, hoof, flipper and fin, for at this time of crisis and opportunity, we hold nothing less than the fate of all life on this spinning, round earth in our hands.

CHAPTER TWO

"It's snowing less": narratives of a transformed relationship between humans and their environments

Susan Bodnar

For the past several years, I have been researching the transformed relationship between human and their ecosystems, assuming that the human relationship to the physical environment was another object relationship (Bodnar, 2008). I also stated that the same societal forces that adversely affect the environment also have a negative impact on people. This chapter brings forth more field data collected in the northeastern urban community of New York City. The people interviewed bring forth in their narratives how they have been affected by the same social practices that have altered the human relationship to the ecosystem.

Psychologists have approached the interface of psychology and environmental issues from a variety of theoretical positions (see Du Nann Winter & Koger, 2004 for an overview). Krupnik and Jolly (2002) present field studies from the Arctic. These indigenous observations demonstrate how physical environmental changes segue into transformations in cognition and meaning. Weather can't be predicted, the fishing is different, and the ice is shifting. Others, like Kahn (1999) have researched the ways in which human development is linked to relationships to the natural world. His studies in an under-resourced black community in Texas, in a small village in the Brazilian Amazon, in Prince William Sound (children affected by the Exxon Valdez disaster), and children in Lisbon Portugal demonstrate that there is an intense human need to affiliate to life ("biophilia": Wilson, 1984). Further Albrecht (2005; Albrecht et al., 2007) describes "solastalgia", a type of psychic distress brought on by environmental change.

While a group of anthropologists once understood ecological systems as determinants of social behavior (Rappaport, 1984/1948), human geographers with a psychoanalytic bent began thinking about the bi-directional influence of landscape and the human mind in the early seventies (see Bodnar, 2008, pp. 491–493). These geographers believe that relationships and the physical environment create interacting systemic valences that both limit and expand the capacity of mind, thought and behaviour. They are a part of each other. The land with its potential for generativity has always factored in the human story.

The philosopher Alva Noë (2009) also recognizes that the physical environment factors importantly in the construction of the mind. In a somewhat neuro-scientific elaboration of Durkheim, he argues that the mind is designed to directly communicate not only with the relational but also with the physical environment. Our minds exist in dynamic relationship to all forms of life. In Noë's view human behaviour expresses the environmental world that influences us. He wrote:

> It is a prejudice that constrains us like a straitjacket when we are trying to understand what we are and how we work. We spend all our lives embodied, environmentally situated, with others. We are not merely recipients of external influences, but are creatures built to receive influences that we ourselves enact; we are dynamically coupled with the world, not separate from it.
>
> (Noë, 2009, p. 181)

The demarcation, however, between what is natural and what is civilized does change. Further, an individual's capacity to draw that line for him or herself has also transformed. Certainly throughout the twentieth and now twenty-first centuries, the locus of control has shifted away from a locally and autonomously derived relationship to nature to one that is more institutionally (or hegemonically) determined. The loss of intimacy between people and their landscapes, a shift in the object relatedness, enables people to objectify and degrade those landscapes.

As a relational psychoanalyst (Mitchell, 1988) I assume that humans and their ecosystems exist in a multiply determined relationship. Nature has never been entirely unspoiled and pure, and it can be harshly dangerous. Civilization protects humans from nature's capricious threats, expresses the best of human gifts and also enslaves the human spirit. Archeologists, physical anthropologists, and even evolutionary biologists understand that humans were never free of their environments, nor were environments ever independent of their humans. Civilization is a panoply of mutually evolving and interdependent life forms, and the mind is an internalized aggregate of the systemic energy between these life forms (Bateson, 1980).

The meanings that people attribute to their relationship to the physical environment derive from inherently local, small group processes in geographic contexts (Durkheim, 1925/1961; Geertz, 1973, 1983). Even at the level of brain organization early infant interaction with interpersonal environments directly influences the neurological underpinnings of self or consciousness (Schore, 1999; see also Bronfenbrenner, 1979; Bruner, 1985; Lewin, 1976; Vygotsky, 1978, 1986). While large-scale concepts like families, peers, or educational institutions may frame a society's moral values and ethical choices for the observing scientist, an individual operates more like a *bricoleur*, internalizing and utilizing bits and pieces of information processed in small group interaction while also balancing needs, limits, priorities, and possibilities. Thus like all relationships, the way in which an individual relates to their physical environment is at once highly personal and culturally determined.

Heidegger (1977) foreshadowed the role that technology would play in that degradation. He specifically discussed how the technology that humans invent might soon re-invent the humans. As people transform the earth to meet the society's needs, they also alter their own consciousness. He warned that if people only know natural resources in terms of their usefulness for human consumption, they would only be capable of experiencing nature as a commodity and land as an instrument of human consumption. If technology becomes the dominant perceptual paradigm for a relationship to an eco-system—whether it be urban, rural, or wild—then peoples' actions will further organize the environment according to the principles of that technology.

Studies from the field

These following case studies are excerpts from interviews with people conducted in New York City in 2009 and 2010. Their narratives demonstrate how the same consumerist processes that are causing careless damage to the earth's ecosystems have also become a part of their personalities. An interesting pattern has also emerged. The complexity with which people think about their relationship to the ecosystem is similar to their type of relational experience with the physical landscape. In some cases, like those who conceptualize their ecosystem more like scenery, the environment functions as something of a self-object. In other cases, the environment is more like a symbolic transference object. Finally, people who have had complex experiences in the environment tend to also have very textured and nuanced thoughts about the environment and climate change. All reveal that they struggle to make sense of themselves in an increasingly technological world framed by the threat of climate change.

The earth as scenery

KL, a twenty-six-year-old single female, graduated from an Ivy League college two years ago and today works as a buyer for a large department store. While now living on Manhattan's Upper East Side, she grew up in a middle-class neighbourhood in North Central USA. Her parents both worked, she has a young brother. Both were always excellent students and athletes.

Despite access to abundant cultural resources, she spends her time "hanging out, we hang out, just get together, bars, mostly hang out in bars."

When asked about whether she enjoys the movies, theatre, dance art, she looked puzzled. "I don't know how to answer this really because it isn't something I think about, really. I know that stuff is out there and I would probably go if everyone was doing it but mostly it's just about having fun."

She explained the blend of her socializing behaviour and her sexuality, "It's just about fun. You go home with someone and I hardly think about it unless it's really weird the next morning and that rarely happens because anyone who takes it too seriously would be stupid."

Yet the notion of fun continued to seem hard to define. "Fun is fun," she explained. KJ liked to drink and flirt and considered herself very good at it and enjoyed feeling on the edge. "If I have sex with someone," she reiterated, "it has been a very good night, because then I can say that I had sex and that it was fun."

At her New York City apartment she owns a laptop, iPhone, CD and DVD player, a flat-screen television, a car and "every kitchen appliance you could ask for but I never cook."

Again she reminded, "It's all about having fun, feeling good and having style and enjoying yourself."

It became clear that her social groups largely defined what fun and having a good time meant for KJ. She had little sense of personal agency, and communicated awkwardly. When asked her about her future, however, she paused and momentarily seemed sad.

> Feels hard to think about that because I do things that don't allow me to think about it so much. I'm in a thing here with my best, best friends and sometimes I know it feels like I'm missing something but by then I'm onto the next thing. I kind of wonder what it would be like to get married and what will happen to our group when we do get married. Sometimes I am aware that maybe this isn't the best thing but it is what I know."

KL described her relationship to nature:

> We had an amazing view of the mountains where we lived, and I really miss it. I probably lived in one of the most beautiful places in the world that people would travel to come and see but for me it was mostly scenery. I would say I spent more time at the mall than doing anything outdoors, and by then we were already partying and there didn't seem to be a point. Now, I like the beach and we usually get a summer share at the beach but sometimes we just sleep all day and party at night and the beach is just beautiful to look at and soothing and it makes me feel good, but we don't focus on it so much. I guess we assume the beauty of it but I don't really think that we do much with it—the focus is more social because we just count on the beach being there.

KL said:

> I guess the creepy thing about global warming is finding out that the earth might not be there. In some ways this idea is in the back of

my mind but I don't focus on it really—even though in some way I think I'm very worried. But then I realize I have everything I could ever need or want. I guess I just assume some scientists will come along at some point and just fix it—but that does seem naive. But I think that's how I handle it. When I notice less snow and warmer winters, sometimes it just feels easier like, "Oh My God this is so much better". It sucks for skiing though. I guess if someone told me what to do I would do it, but I'm not so sure how much I would or could change. My life seems very settled right now. I kind of just go along with things.

Consider another interviewee, JT a thirty-two-year-old Hispanic male who grew up in a working-class neighbourhood in the Bronx. Recently married with no children, JT and his wife live in Brooklyn. He spends most of his time working as a concierge at a large Manhattan building and "hanging out watching TV, shopping and doing errands" and, he added proudly, "relaxing by my new pool. And sometimes a Mets game."

He no longer spends time in bars or hooking up, but he did when he was "younger." He enjoyed having a few drinks, getting some sex, "even though most of the people who were your best friends disappeared as soon as the alcohol dried up."

JT changed when he met a woman who was determined to marry him, and succeeded by taking charge of their life together.

"I went along with it" he said "because she wanted it, and I knew the way I was living wasn't a good thing, and now she organizes things and I work and just go along … it's a good life, and I like the safety and security of it."

JT described his relationship to the environment:

> When I grew up in the Bronx the whole world was right there, didn't have to worry, could walk anytime anywhere to all of our games, friends, leagues, summer day camp. Everything being right there, it was a great upbringing. It was all defined by the neighborhood. I've never been much of a camper. I don't have a relationship to the natural environment—I love going outdoors and seeing nature but not obsessed with it. I took a trip with my wife to the Shenandoah Valley and loved it. You can drive for miles and see the valley and it is beautiful. I think nature is great, and I like to look at it, but I admit that at times I don't care. It is there and that's it.

There should be areas set aside where it is untouched but I can't say it means something to me.

I don't know that much about climate change and global warming, but something is going on, that is for sure. I've read about polar ice caps and I understand that ice sheets are getting smaller and smaller. Something is going on and I don't like it—some animals could be extinct because of an infringement upon natural habitat—like mountain gorillas looking for food in a smaller and smaller area. When I was a little kid it used to snow a lot in the winter. Nowadays you have one heavy snowstorm and maybe a couple of things in between. The winters have changed a lot and I'm glad. I'm glad it doesn't snow that much. It's a hassle, only fun when you are a kid.

He added contemplatively:

Things are different, though. It doesn't warm up when it used to and it seems to be getting hotter when it shouldn't. It is a warmer winter and it's hot in the summer for long stretches and I am sure in other parts of the world it is even worse. There are droughts and famines and parched land and no rain. We are lucky here—we have a little bit of everything and don't have to think. I'm for alternative fuel sources and not something that will take twenty years. We need something now—and it is the government's fault. I fear more for children today that are growing up—thirty years from now growing up it will be a rough place between the environment, fuel, terrorism, unless things get lucky for them and even then, who knows. The environment—there is nothing I can do about it.

The earth is my symbol

Another group of people exhibited a more symbolic or transferential connection to their ecosystem. They experienced the earth as meaning-laden platform upon which to work out conflicts. They tended to think in broad political statements without challenging their consumerist choices.

CB is a twenty-nine-year-old performance artist and writer. She grew up with her parents in a lower-middle-class neighbourhood in Connecticut. They divorced when she was young but she had close contact with both of them. She came to New York about nineteen years ago to attend a top university that had a strong arts concentration. She spends her time involved with her creative work, goes to films, listens to bands, and sometimes camps or swims at nearby recreation areas. She was never part of the current social trends of her generation but she knows what happens around her.

She said:

> I find that people who do all that hooking up and intense partying have a hard time relating. It is a disconnection from self and society, and from human nature. Society has just become so empty and isolating and people are looking to fill the void. There is so much technology, so much searching, so much pressure and alcohol is numbing, and so is the sex. Me? I would rather feel pain than drink and sleep with someone I don't have some deep emotion for.

She owned the standard pieces of technology—a cell phone, MP3 player, laptop, stereo, TV, DVD, microwave, coffee maker—but no car. She thinks it is all too much, adding:

> People pile up enormous amounts of junk that they don't need and it's a huge waste—because we live in a media-saturated culture where we think we need these things. Capitalist society brainwashes people to buy, buy, buy, and spend. There is a huge amount of peer pressure and expectations, there is an image of what society expects and I think it is true. Society does expect it of them. But a brave person rejects it. I'm not always brave enough to reject it all but that is what I would aspire to be.

CB camped and took many trips to National Parks. She vacationed in Yellowstone and the Grand Tetons, hiked, swam and has lived in Nicaragua, drove cross country, backpacked through Europe, the White Mountains and the Berkshires. She even lived across the street from a farm, "always going across the street and spending time with animals. But the farmer didn't like it so it was frustrating. I was across the street from a deepening awareness of animals and the role that they played in the world, but it was something I could watch or visit, not something I knew, or could live."

Even though she now lives and works in New York City, she considers herself an environmentalist on a spectrum that is relatively left leaning. CB views the earth as a victim. She stated:

> Nature is being horribly abused by humanity, humans act like god feeling that they can destroy life, feeling have the right to dominate all life on this planet. Humanity is a duality and dichotomy—we are one of the most violent life forms who consider nature violent and uncivilized. We act distant from animals when really we are all part of the animal species and we are just one member.

CB understands that there is a systemic unity between life forms but she hasn't lived it. She has a deep intellectual recognition of nature's value, but she conceives of nature and civilization as two systems rather than one integrated entity. Her decisions about the environment reflect this uneasy tension. In her mind, nature is almost always good, and humans are bad. In her life she easily disconnects from her own aggression toward the earth.

CB recognizes the ongoing threat of climate change, but also seems ambivalent about her own personal choices. She explained, "There is less snow. I miss big snow storms, and the water being solid so you knew you could skate … but I am in NYC and I'm not sure what I can do about the snow, or the glaciers, other than donate money because right now, basically I'm fine."

DB is a forty-seven-year-old technology expert and accountant living in Brooklyn where he was born and raised. He is remarried with a small son, and has a son and daughter with his first wife. He spends his time reading and hanging out with his kids and is a big Mets fan. He stated, "I am not an outdoor nature person, but I like going into nature, hitting golf balls. We probably spend way too much time in front of the TV and the computer—but that's the nature of our lives."

He also works on causes—usually generating and participating in e-mail campaigns for Sierra Club, NRDC, and the Atlantic Yards projects.

A married man with kids, he feels very disconnected from current social trends. He has heard how out of control and wild it gets from his grown children, and has witnessed a young neighbour passed out in the hallway from too much drinking. He explained:

> I've participated in a bunch of different things when I was younger but none of those behaviors are a core component to my life. And they never were. I am, however, a big technology person—flat screen TV, 2 computers, VCR, DVR, stereo plus turntable, PDA, phones, a Prius, air conditioners, microwave, blender, Cuisinart—everything you could imagine for a kitchen. I'm domesticated and my house is set up for comfort.

He described his life as,

> limited and contained. I ran the environment committee at my synagogue but I haven't had much to do with the environment other than nice vacations and the work I do on e-mail campaigns. I was an early adopter of technology and to a certain extent I work around what I can do at home and on the computer.

Twenty-five years ago, DB was a member of many student activist organizations including the anti-nuclear power movement. He enacted his commitment to environmentalism by purchasing a Prius, volunteering as the recycling coordinator in his building and becoming involved with websites that promote petition signing and letter campaigns on issues like solar and wind power advocacy.

Similarly, DB observes the natural world more than experiencing it. He appreciates, admires and occasionally ventures into the separate entity known as nature. He elaborated, "It's not as important to appreciate nature by being in it. We go on hikes and love the beauty of the landscapes but we don't commune with nature. I mean, I'm allergic to bees. I enjoy green and fresh air but I don't necessarily like to be in nature."

He then added, "People tend to treat nature the way we see each other. The way we conceive of nature right now doesn't say much about our humanity."

These people feel committed to environmentalism. They have been in and explored nature. They have taken excursions. They appreciate the natural world but still feel separate from it even though at some level they intellectually recognize that people and animals, earth and civilization are interdependent units. The environment is something of a symbol through which they work out their observed conflicts between good and bad. They haven't internalized a conception of self, however, that is embedded in nature so they can't really imagine living with it differently.

The earth is part of me

The people who conceive nature as a component of the self have changed the way they live. The people in this group use far fewer appliances, focus less on digital media, and participate in more cultural events. They have also had deeper and more complex relationships to the ecosystems.

FT, a twenty-two-year-old male who majored in English at a NYC university, considers himself a blogger/writer with a day job, working in research at a New York City law firm. His environmentalism grew out of his newly learned Buddhism. He supports and has worked tirelessly for the movement to ban the use of plastic bags. He considers himself less mainstream and more of "a rarified group of kids who grew up in middle class liberal homes who attended private colleges and expect to express social values through what we do, trying to act on our social awareness and still pay the rent."

The changes he has made in his life since college hint at his multi-faceted decision-making process. Though a writer he works in a law firm to make sure that all of his ideas confront different perspectives. He explained that his life means "seeing all sides, taking into account perspectives different from my own."

He has evolved his "individual-centric college lifestyle" into "more organic living." It annoys him to talk about how his generational peers behave, even post-college. "It is always the same thing: we went to a party, got drunk, threw up and we hooked up. Of course, I've done it, and I'm coming to terms with it, but it never defined me. Now, I'm cooking organic meals at home, walking and using public transporta-tion, and practicing consumer activism—not buying from companies that have bad communal and environmental practices."

When I asked him to explain his thoughts about his life transitions he said:

> In our society there is an overall pattern of really reflexive promis-cuity, especially in fraternities and sororities and I think the media represents this as quasi hedonistic and a cutting loose from pressure thing but … I can see it from a Buddhist perspective. Being young

like this is a willful denial of mortality. Death is around the corner and this type of stuff just fends it off. We are afraid of the death of our world, we know it is happening and climate change is the beginning of the end. We know this. For me and my friends blacking out is a bad thing, but for a lot of other people my age it is the only thing."

He elaborated further:

Our world is melting down and we are getting fucked up. Think about our lives and all this colossal meltdown stuff we face—it is like watching holocaust movies all day long. I'm trying to move away from the helpless mentality into something more active even if the reduction of my personal carbon imprint won't matter, or change policy—it feels like positive change and that makes my life easier and more hopeful.

FT grew up in a rural environment. Farms, forests, and wide open fields were his childhood playground. His father worked in banking and his mother taught at the university. While his childhood was standard enough—divorced parents, good education, lots of friends and sports—camping and backpacking trips with his family stood out. In addition to his own free play outdoors, he spent weeks at a time, interacting with and working with the landscape on camping and backpacking trips. He recollected:

It wasn't exactly as if we were going on a trip, it was more like going more deeply into our lives. And the best part is that it is something my parents and even their new partners could do together ... and I really felt that there was something deeper in everyone that we could be in touch with when we were dealing with the contingencies of the wilderness, and in that sense there is a deeper part of me that is very much an extension of that wilderness.

Another slightly older adult male echoed similar sentiments. WB works in the financial industry and is married to a medical resident. Raised in the suburban northeast, WB, 32, attended boarding school before graduating from an Ivy League college and law school. According to WB, he could have easily been caught up in the "materialistic, bingeing culture" of his generation. The child of divorce, his emotionally reclusive father and his more open but preoccupied mother raised him in a cooperative and comported atmosphere. He didn't get caught up in excessive drinking, sexuality, and product consumptions.

He explained the behavior of his peers, especially when younger, through the metaphors of avatars—online, usually fanciful, representations of a person's identity used on the internet. He said:

> People cast themselves as different versions of themselves reflecting some lack of comfort with who they are. They have some fascination with what is going on in this other self, and find privacy by hiding behind an avatar. I think a great deal of what is going on in society is that in some ways people have real life avatars—this whole hooking up/drinking/Facebook thing—but there is some other real self behind all that they just don't like or feel comfortable with. Or maybe they don't feel real with.

He believed that everything about him would have predicted that he might have become the same type of typical goal-seeking, false-self person. Instead, he had an intense immersion in the outdoors that changed him. There he encountered an internal authenticity that felt different. Genuine interests began to motivate him rather than outcomes. A competitive streak that automatically shut others out transformed into openness when he understood himself as one person who was part of a larger field.

WB largely credits his reflective thinking to his experience at The Mountain School, a co-ed school in New Hampshire that provides high school juniors the opportunity to live and work on an organic farm.

He described this program. "There we lived and worked on an organic farm. Our day was spent taking calculus and feeding the pigs. Running this farm, and having to kill what meat we ate, made things that were normally distant far more close up. I didn't see how things worked; I was part of how they worked."

He continued:

> The Mountain School was absolutely the most important experience of my life and it sent me in a totally new direction … what happened there was definitional. I would call it an awakening, an epiphany, a self consciousness linked to nature, the environment, community, spirituality and appreciating the inter-relationship between these things. It was like a spatial example of connections

between the religious spiritual experience and the law of humans and land. We read Thoreau, Emerson, and I understood the man, god, nature triangle. If you understood one point you would understand the other three perfectly.

A three-day solo was the crucial high point of WB's experience. He recounted it:

> I only took one box of blueberries, because I was also fasting. That was part of it, to be as one with myself as I could be. The alone in the woods experience was really beyond anything I can say, it was so real. I slept and sat and thought and could pay attention to every little detail. It got to the point that even though I could obviously distinguish day from night, it was as though day and night were one entity. The thoughts I had came at me fast and yet slow and there was time for every one of them. The thing that was so exhilarating was recognizing, being, feeling a part of it. I was connected to this vast landscape, and also linked to the smallest little molecule of a spot of dew on a leaf. I was another manifestation of it. We, the environment and I, weren't separate in the way we usually think. It was all about the God, man and nature triangle—I focused and dove into it and started to appreciate all the intricacies.

He and his wife continue to spend a good deal of time out in nature. He mused, "it is where I go to know my truth, or a home plate. When there is nothing between you and the earth somehow you can find your vision turned toward more important things than the dividing lines between them."

Collaborative and interactive experiences in nature unite FT and WB. They don't regard the earth as separate. They recognize themselves to be an intimate part of it. Their decisions, therefore, tend to take in the bigger picture and accommodate to the interconnection physical and emotional landscapes.

Conclusion: people become the earth they know

This limited and small-scale psychoanalytic field investigation, however, suggests that early interactions with the physical landscape forms the kind of relationship people have to their ecosystem and who they become. The more consumerist practices shape those interactions, the more those interactions will shape human contact with the planet. The earth is a part of us. The earth influences us; we influence it. If the human impact on the environment significantly changes our ecosystem, how will the transformed landscape influence us? What happens if the people we become aren't able to adopt the changes necessary to preserve and save our planet?

Anyone enslaved by a bad relationship, substance abuse, or the need to check multiple times if the stove has been shut off, warrants psychological support. Why shouldn't our work now consider peoples' interactions with their ecosystem as part of our purview? According to the psychoanalyst Andrew Samuels, "We need an educational program that faces people with their decisions and choices rather than letting them be made for them by experts who will offer protection from the moral implication of what is being done" (Samuels, 1993a, p. 104).

In his book, *Averting Global Extinction: Our Irrational Society as Therapy Patient*, Louis Berger (2009) has written convincingly that therapeutic work might very well entail two people working together on the problem of their mutual patient: a hungry society that violates boundaries in order to perpetuate itself rather than the individuals and groups who constitute it.

I think WB said it best:

> I think it is possible that we may have already passed the point of correcting the problem, However, I do think we should put our best minds to work on this issue and dedicate significant resources to it. Either that or we are in for very dramatic changes over my lifetime, our lifetime.
>
> The changes will be and have to be very intense and bigger than we are prepared for, it will become a psychological problem as much as it will be economic, geological and biological and otherwise. The battle will be partly in our heads.

Perhaps the tenor of psychological work may shift away from creating the ideal of the bigger, better, healthier me and toward teaching people how to live within the limits and boundaries of their landscapes and how to make use of rather than being used by their technologies.

James Gustave Speth wrote in a recent edition of *Harvard Business Review*:

> Soon developed countries will begin the move to a postgrowth world where working life, the natural environment, communities and the public sector will no longer be sacrificed for the sake of mere GDP growth, and where the illusory promise of ever more expansion will no longer provide an excuse for ignoring compelling social needs. A postgrowth society will involve less consumerism and higher prices; quality of life will improve in ways too long neglected.
>
> (Speth, 2009, p. 19)

CHAPTER THREE

Gaia living with AIDS: towards reconnecting humanity with ecosystem autopoiesis using metaphors of the immune system

Peter Chatalos

The most important characteristic of an organism is that capacity for internal self-renewal known as health.

—Aldo Leopold

While health is a desirable condition for humans to achieve, it is increasing being used as a metaphor in conjunction with ecosystems. This paper argues that this "health" metaphor can be developed further, to state that the planet's ecosystems work as an immune system, protecting its biotic community from disease/ illness. It is further argued that without realizing their interconnectedness within the planet's ecosystems, humanity is increasingly straining this immune system, which is detrimental to the health of humans and ecosystems alike. The metaphor that the planet's ecosystems are suffering an autoimmune disorder may have a place in helping humanity to realize its embeddedness within nature and to recognize the consequences of its actions.

This paper comprises three main sections: the first looks at ecosystems' ability to maintain health, and the dynamic interface between disease, environmental degradation, and human behaviour. The second focuses on the role of humanity's mental and emotional disconnection from nature's self-renewal processes. The final section discusses how employing the metaphor of the immune system, to aid understanding and empathy, might ameliorate this.

Autopoiesis: nature's immune response

To begin with, I consider the validity of an immune system metaphor, arguing that the planet's ecosystems do actively sustain biotic health, and when damaged, biotic and environmental sickness proliferates. In this paper, health is conceived of holistically, rather than in isolation, especially when looking at ecological systems. Therefore, from the outset I wish to make explicit some assumptions implicit to this argument.

I am taking the ontological position of "the newly emerging paradigm ... [which] may be called a holistic worldview, emphasising the whole rather than the parts" (Capra, 1989, p. 20). This paper draws on insights from ecopsychology, systems theory, ecofeminism and deep ecology, which emphasize life's interconnectedness and critique the Cartesian duality that permits mind to be separated from matter.

> All natural systems are *wholes* whose specific structures arise from the interactions and interdependence of their parts. Systemic properties are destroyed when a system is dissected, either physically or theoretically, into isolated elements.
>
> (Capra, 1995, pp. 23–24)

This new paradigm employs organic and systemic metaphors, rather than the mechanistic metaphors still prominent in reductionist science where health is the property of the "well-made", as Descartes stated: "I consider the human body as a machine. My thought compares a sick man and an ill-made clock with my idea of a healthy man and a well-made clock" (quoted by Capra, 1995, p. 21).

This implies the existence of an external creator or agent, with nature as passive "object" devoid of its own agency (Merchant, 1983, Ch. 1), whereas the new paradigm conceives of nature as actively creating itself. This has lead to holistic or systemic views of "health" being increasingly used with regards to ecosystems, both as a normative concept and an endpoint for environmental management (Costanza, Norton & Haskell,

1992, p. 14). "Health" is seen as an integral property of the whole system, with the health of each individual "part" intrinsically connected to the system's processes and inter-relationships. "A healthy system must also be defined in light of both its context (the larger system of which it is part) and its components (the smaller systems that make it up)" (Costanza, Norton & Haskell, 1992, p. 240).

Subsequently, the larger ecosystems and their components are actively involved in their own "health" making-maintenance. General Systems theorists call this capacity for self-making/self-renewal/self-restoration "Autopoiesis". It is the ecosystem protecting and support-ing life, by organizing and adapting itself, becoming more complex and differentiated—a dynamic process of being healthy and increasingly creative (Bateson, 2000; Macy, 1991a, p. 186; Warren, 2000). It is this autopoietic capacity that is the crucial indicator of health—a process of actively protecting, maintaining, and sustaining ecosystem health defined as:

- Homeostasis
- The absence of disease
- Diversity or complexity
- Stability or resilience
- Vigour or scope for growth
- Balance between system components

(Costanza, Norton & Haskell, 1992, p. 239)

Lovelock's Gaia Theory (1995) is a well-known account of how ecosystems maintain homeostasis, which is vital for sustaining healthy life on earth. In addition, the planet's ecosystems synergistically sus-tain health by promoting "the absence of disease" (Costanza, Norton & Haskell, 1992). In effect, I suggest that the planet's ecosystems are anal-ogous to an organism's immune system, helping to protect against disease and illness.

Psychoneuroimmunology "reflects the interdependence of psycho-social processes, and nervous, endocrine, and immune systems" (Du Nann Winter & Koger, 2004, p. 123), so that in organisms, mental processes are intrinsically linked to the immune system. As we see later, as well as being physical and biological, autopoiesis is a mind-like process adapting and responding to stressors (Bateson, 2000). It is implicitly a holistic concept. Viewing the organism's immune systems purely, in terms of anti-body responses, is reductionist, whereas the organism's immune system can be viewed holistically.

Although, the immune system is inherent to organisms, its function is to prevent illness and protect the organism from *both* external and internal sources of disease. The survival of any part is dependent on fitting within the whole, so in effect, potential pathogens are adapted to or eliminated by other organisms and ecosystem processes, over time. While different "immune" processes are involved on this planetary scale than in organism immune systems, the overall effect is similar; the planet's ecosystems with their autopoietic processes optimize health and protect biota from disease. A clear example of external protection is the ozone layer, which protects against the sun's harmful radiation. As a direct result of human activity/consumption, the ozone hole has appeared leaving an area of the earth unprotected. This in turn has lead to an increase in skin cancers, which to my mind, is an example of ecopsychosomatics: a mental state causing physical disease through the environmental-human health interface. (For information on the ozone layer hole and skin cancers see: "The Ozone Hole" website, www.theozonehole.com/.)

Costanza et al. point out that health and sustainability are closely linked: "these [health] concepts are embodied in the term 'sustainability', which implies the system's ability to maintain its structure (organization) and function (vigour) over time in the face of external stress (resilience)" (Costanza, Norton & Haskell, 1992, p. 240). Increasingly unsustainable human activity is compromising ecosystem health, in turn damaging human health. Aldo Leopold describes disappearance of plants and animals "as symptoms of sickness in the land organism" (Warren, 2000, p. 164). There are ever increasing signs that globally ecosystems are sick—climate change, damaged aquifers, loss of biodiversity, acidification, desertification, ozone depletion, species extinction, as well as the increasing number of diseases, viruses, and plagues affecting life in the biosphere, may all be seen as symptoms of an ailing planetary ecosystem—a sickening world.

Environmental degradation is ecosystem "sickness", increasing diseases within the environment and diminishing ecosystem's self-restorative abilities. As a result of unhealthy ecosystems, there are an ever-increasing number of diseases, affecting both humans and other life forms, with a degree of cross infection (see, for example, Ecohealth on-line journal, http://www.ecohealth.net/).

"Zoonotic pathogens (those transmitted between humans and other animals) are responsible for 75% of the emerging diseases affecting humans" (Wildlife Trust, 2004). Global trade has been implicated with increased incidents of disease: "Kimball et al examine the phenomenon of trade-related infections; they show, through several case studies, the interplay between global trade in commodities and the emergence of new infections" (Wildlife Trust, 2004, see also Kimball et al., 2005).

In turn, human mental and physical health, including that of future generations, suffers through environmental stress/toxins/pollution and damaged ecosystems.

> The well being of an eco-system of the planet is a prior condition for the well being of humans. We cannot have wellbeing on a sick planet, not even with our medical science. So long as we continue to generate more toxins than the planet can absorb and transform, the members of the earth community will become ill.
>
> (Swimme & Berry, 2004, p. 146)

Pollution and environmental toxins that "can significantly impact neuropsychological and physiological systems" are damaging the health of both humans and the planet (Swimme & Berry, 2004, p. 139). The medical profession now recognizes "environmental illness" in humans, in the form of "various, allergies, chemical sensitivities and 'sick building syndromes' associated with air pollution" (Swimme & Berry, 2004, p. 127). "The relationship between environmental factors, stress and disease are complex. Environmental stressors can produce physical symptoms and directly cause disease; disease itself is a physical stressor" (Swimme & Berry, 2004, p. 139).

The psychogenic causes of ecosystem damage are at the heart of ecopsychology, informed by all branches of psychology (see Du Nann Winter & Koger, 2004). An example, from psychodynamics, is object relations theory. Here ORT emphasizes that unhealthy psychological development, can damage "the self-other split", impairing "our relationship with other people and the environment" (Du Nann Winter & Koger, 2004, p. 43). This can lead to neurotic behaviours, like narcissism, with likely environmental consequences: "Our inability to appreciate nature for its own complexity and beauty signals a deeply seated narcissism whereby we see the natural world only as resources .... At best, other species are considered irrelevant" (Du Nann Winter & Koger, 2004, p. 45).

There are far too many complex interactions and transactions occurring within human-environmental interfaces to describe in such a short paper but as Rapport states, "no single disease process has led to the current environmental predicament—unless one speaks of human imprudence" (Costanza, Norton & Haskell, 1992, p. 146). The growth of human populations, consumption, industrialization, transportation, and warfare are affecting ecosystems, wildlife and humans, with devastating results. As human activity damages the planet's health—stressors, illnesses, and diseases increase. Simultaneously, the restorative affects of natural environments are mitigated by the destruction and disturbance of those environments (see particularly Costanza, Norton & Haskell, 1992, Ch. 5).

So the smaller system of humanity is damaging the larger planetary ecosystem. "We are like the cells in the body of the vast living organism that is planet earth. An organism cannot continue to function healthily if one group of cells decides to dominate and cannibalize the other energy systems of the body" (Metzner, 1995, p. 67). Yet, ecosystems have autopoietic properties, and humans are part of these ecosystems. So why do "symptoms of sickness" exist? Why isn't humanity participating in the autopoietic, health-promoting, processes of the planet?

As long as humanity, as part of the planet's systems, continues to degrade the autopoietic capabilities that protect against disease it is, to further the immune system analogy, behaving like an autoimmune disease. An autoimmune disease occurs when the body's immune system reacts against its own components, producing disease or functional changes. I stress that an analogy is being made here, from the ontology of interconnectedness, where the earth is implicitly an extension of humanity's body, and humanity forms an element of the planet's autopoietic capability. As Kidner explains: "If the normality of our day-to-day lives depends on exploiting and degrading the natural order, then *psychological* 'health' will embody an intrinsic *ecological* pathology; and human life is defined as a form of parasitism" (Kidner, 2001, p. 69).

Autism: barriers to connecting with nature

The deep ecology perspective on this "*ecological* pathology" is that limited/unrealized notions of "self" as separate from the environment contribute to humanity's dissociation from nature (Du Nann Winter & Koger, 2004, p. 193). Mental and emotional boundaries between self and perceived "other" are creating human-ecosystem barriers, preventing humanity from fully co-participating in the autopoietic process. As we shall see, consequently, the human psyche does not fully integrate/identify with planetary ecosystem's psyche/mind-like processes.

Arne Naess coined the term the "ecological Self", for the fully self-realized individual, whose self-concept or sense of identity expands to include the biosphere and all its inhabitants (Naess, 1985, pp. 256–270). The individual's connection to nature deepens on an unconscious, cognitive, emotional and motivational level through an expanded identification with and realization of life's interconnectedness (Du Nann Winter & Koger, 2004, p. 193). The person's self-interest shifts from being egocentric to biocentric, integrating with Nature's psyche or systemic "mind".

Systems theorist Gregory Bateson explains in *Steps to an Ecology of Mind* (2000) that ecosystems exhibit mind-like properties. He understands "minds" as processes—rather than "things"—at many levels of being, not limited to association with brains or consciousness. These include all examples of systemic process, wherever there is an interaction between the parts triggered by difference, requiring energy and circular chains of determination. The term "mentation" is sometimes used to "describe the dynamics of self-organization at lower levels" (Capra, 1989, p. 315). Such "minds" would include organisms such as bacteria, parts of organisms such as individual cells or organs and also systems of multiple organisms such as social groups, societies or ecosystems. Each of these entities is mind-like in its activity and any given mind is likely to be a sub-system in some larger or more complex mind.

The mental is the subjective aspect of a system, so that each of the parts of the whole system has a subjective experience. Ervin Laszlo explains that "the world of inner subjective experience is accepted by systems theorists as a given that must be understood in its own right, and whose process can be made intelligible in terms of systemic self-regulation" (Macy, 1991a, p. 82). In other words, the autopoietic process of nature is mind-like, with its own agency and subjective experience. In this way, "all the phenomena in the world possess intrinsic ... subjective inner natures," states depth psychologist Stephen Aizenstat;

"these inner natures of the world's organic and inorganic phenomena make up the world unconscious" (Aizenstat, 1995, p. 96). These phenomena are experienced unconsciously in dreams and through our bodies. Ecopsychologists like Roszak, emphasize an existing unconscious connection between the human psyche and nature, which is usually repressed in the "unrealized" self. The "ecological unconscious" is the "core of the mind", where the earth can speak through us (Roszak, 1992, pp. 320–321). He argues that reconnecting to this ecological unconscious "awaken[s] the inherent sense of environmental reciprocity" which is fundamental to human sanity; contrastingly, its repression—a psychological barrier, is linked to humanity's environmentally damaging behaviour and "madness". "For ecopsychology, repression of the ecological unconscious is the deepest root of collusive madness in industrial society; open access to the ecological unconscious is the path to sanity" (Roszak, 1992).

What is emphasized here is the systemic intra-psychic context of individual human subjectivity. An individual's subjective reality is integral to, informed by and informing the wider system—with "a flow of information which both transforms and is transformed by the system's organization" (Macy, 1991a, p. 82). The system is in constant inter-communication with/within itself, e.g., through signs/signals (biosemiotics).

There is an ontology of interconnectedness here, where "the whole is always in a meta-relationship with its parts" (Bateson, 2000, p. 267), and where "the human experience exists in a field of psychic relationships" (Bateson, 2000, p. 267). The epistemological implication is that the people who perceive themselves as separate from the more-than-human world, *not* realizing their self-in-relationship or as interconnected, present psychological barriers against these relationships, leading to nature's signs/flow of information being ignored. This is tantamount to systemic or ecological autism.

Autism is defined as: "A disturbance in psychological development in which use of language, reaction to stimuli, interpretation of the world, and the formation of relationships are not fully established and follow unusual patterns" (Encarta World English Dictionary, 1999). My use of the word "autism" is inspired partly by Metzner (1995), and by Joanna Macy's observation: "Where minds interact, they mutually create. Only the autistic are independent" (Macy, 1991a, p. 186). In Object Relations Theory, according to Mahler (Mahler, Pine &

Bergman, 2000) there is "normal autism" over a child's first three to four years. The child experiences a "symbiotic unity", with its mother, which can be impaired, leading to developmental difficulties. This unity is centred on the child's sensations, with no sense of other/separate, so while there is unity it is without a concept of relation, and so autistic.

So to sum up, two connections with the ecosystem-mind processes are emphasized:

1. *The ecological unconscious: information is exchanged through bodily senses and dreams.* In the fully self-realized person, psychological barriers like repression are dissolved, uncovering the ecological unconscious.
2. *Conscious realization of the intrinsic interconnectedness of the individual with the biosphere and its participants.* The psychological process of "realization"—shifts the self-"other" psychological barrier within the human psyche so that notions (i.e., schema) of inside and outside merge. The realized individual awakens to a co-participatory reality—a shared earth-body, without separation from the surrounding world: "our relationship to the earth is that of a leaf to a tree ... we are participants in this planetary system, for good or for ill" (Reason, 2002, p. 9).

The previously external "other" becomes internalized as "self", while the "inner" world reconnects with the "outer", nature's psyche/mind/ systems through the ecological unconscious (e.g., Kidner, 2001). The result is a strong mental and emotional link with the planet, people defend ecosystems and the world becomes lover (Macy, 1991b). However, this reconnection also leads, to the ecological-self feeling the pain and despair of environmental degradation (Macy, 1991b).

Contrastingly, systemic autism results in alienation from nature (eco-alienation), as the unrealized self perceives itself as separate (alienated) from "other" life forms, leading to the various environmental problems occurring today (e.g., Metzner, 1995). The resulting lack of "holistic" or healthy realization can engender addictive and compulsive behaviours, such as addiction to technology (e.g., Glendinning, 1995; Metzner, 1995). But since the earth is an extension of physical body (from this perspective) and the root cause is psychological, the previously described ecosystem and human sicknesses/diseases and illnesses, can be viewed as psychosomatic or eco-psychosomatic.

Psychosomatic is a term that refers to the inseparability and interdependence of the psychological and biological aspects of humanity. This connotation may be referred to as holistic, in that it implies a vision of human beings as a totality, a mind-body complex immersed in a social environment.

(Ramos, 1984, p. 167)

Ecopsychosomatics extends this concept to include the earth-body and one's human ecology.

Unfortunately, there is insufficient space here, to cover the ecofeminist critique of the privileging of "self" as active-masculine, leading to the exploitation, oppression and domination, of "other" as passive—"feminine", which is entrenched in male-female power dynamics. While deep ecology critiques the perception of "other" as an exploitable/instrumental commodity, ecofeminism critiques patriarchal oppression, where perceived "other" is exploited/dominated as "feminine" (Merchant, 1983; Warren, 2000). This chapter focuses on connecting to "active" nature, with the deep ecological emphasis of "Other" as "Self". There is an implicit assumption that exploitation would not occur in self-self or subject-subject relations, that is, others are perceived as self with equal value and intrinsic worth. Although I recognize this as an important area, it is outside the scope of this chapter to debate how this might occur in practice, taking issues of control and power dynamics into account.

Metaphors that connect

The last section emphasized connection to nature through realization of interconnectedness, self-identification with ecosystems and the dissolving of psychological barriers. However, Bateson argues that human-consciousness with its goal-purpose orientation "(unaided by art, dreams, and the like) can never appreciate the systemic nature of mind" (Bateson, 2000, p. 145). Instead he emphasizes the role of metaphors for enabling human minds to harmonize with the mental processes of nature or to use a metaphor; metaphors allow humans to "read" nature. Bateson sees paradigms, worldviews and religions in terms of metaphors, or "the patterns which connects" us to the "bigger picture" (Bateson, 1980).

Metaphors We Live By (Lakoff & Johnson, 1980), concludes that metaphors provide "the only ways to perceive and experience much of the world. Metaphor is as much a part of our functioning as our sense of touch, and as precious" (p. 239). Metaphors are "how this whole fabric of mental interconnections holds together. Metaphor is right at the bottom of being alive." (Gregory Bateson in conversation, quoted in Capra, 1989, p. 79)—it "is the language of nature" (Capra, 1989, p. 84). Metaphors are therefore a vital way of understanding nature, developing empathy and engendering ethical environmental behaviour: that is, for engaging head, heart, and hand. The mechanistic metaphor of a machine world is unlikely to engender empathy, compared to the organic metaphor of a health sustaining nurturing and creative agent. "We can be ethical only in relation to something we can see, feel, understand, love or otherwise have faith in" (Leopold in Warren, 2000, p. 165).

Elisabeth Bragg's studies have shown that engaging the heart is a key to motivating environmentally responsible behaviour. "It seemed that caring about nature, for whatever reasons … was the essential motivator of environmental action" (Bragg, 1997, n.p.). Empathy harmonizes the part to the whole; it creates a "negative feedback loop" within a system to mitigate actions that are systemically detrimental.

I suggest that using the dynamic metaphor of the immune system allows the planet's ecosystems to be perceived as actively protecting life and preventing disease. As, from this perspective, the earth is an extension of the body, its autopoietic systems can be seen as extending personal immunity to disease, helping to develop ecological identification and realization, understanding and empathy.

> When people consciously understand that they are part of, and *intricately connected to,* the natural world, they will be able to expand their boundaries of empathy to include all.
>
> (Feral, 1998, p. 244)

GAIA's acquired immune deficiency

Perhaps using the immune system metaphor would be one way to help some minds and hearts grasp a multitude of variables within one concept, and to understand the autoimmune disease-like role of the "unrealized" human psyche. The metaphor can be developed further, to suggest that the planet is immuno-suppressed with human autism as an autoimmune-like factor, so that GAIA has its own version of AIDS. Such a syndrome with its psychogenic roots can be viewed as eco-psychosomatic.

This eco-psychosomatic syndrome does not need to separate between human and environmental degradation, such as increased pollution, species extinctions or asthma in humans. All are psychogenic symptoms of an ailing biosphere. This is a systemic metaphor, intrinsically incorporating interconnectivity. As an extension of the ecosystem/land health metaphor, it allows the various ecosystem sicknesses, and subsequent [human/wildlife/ecosystem] diseases, to be seen as a syndrome, affecting the overall health of the system or earth-body and its health sustaining capability.

It captures the sense of a system under pressure, which can continue to function for a while, until it rapidly collapses. In fact, Haskell uses the term "distress syndrome" to refer "to the irreversible process of system breakdown leading to collapse", and "a diseased system is one that is not sustainable, that will eventually cease to exist" (Haskell, Norton & Costanza, 1992, p. 9). It captures the parasitism of unsustainable, autistic, and oppressive human behaviour. This is not an attempt to emphasize a major ecosystem service, but to facilitate realization of humanity's embeddedness within the planet's systems, and to contextualize environmentally damaging behaviour within its autopoietic processes. This paper is emphasizing humanity's failure to *fully participate* within this "service", from a biocentric position. Humanity needs to realize its own place within ecosystem services, in order to "serve" or be "instrumental" to the system as a whole, not just for humanity's sake but the more-than-human too.

This could give a wake-up call to those who are open to the idea, encouraging a holistic/interconnected worldview and environmental reciprocity. Roszak argues that what is required is a positive vision of the future (Du Nann Winter & Koger, 2004, pp. 216–219). Perhaps people might turn off and be depressed by the metaphor of a planet living with a suppressed immune system. However, Macy believes it is important to get in touch with the despair of environmental degradation (Macy, 1991b). Yet there is a positive message here that the planet's ecosystems are working together to protect life, and that through understanding and empathy humans can benefit from their self-restorative capabilities. Using the compromised immune system metaphor can help people realize their own interconnectedness and the consequences of their actions, allowing them to consciously change their actions, so that a healing can be possible. It is time for humanity to heal, protect and fully participate in the planet's autopoietic processes.

Conclusion

For such a healing to be possible, I have argued that humanity needs to recognize and reverse its current autoimmune disease-like role, within the earth's immune system-like protection. We have seen that psychological barriers can be dissolved through realization of the ecological-self and extended empathy, breaking through humanity's ecological autism to reconnect with nature's psyche/mind-like processes. The connective role of metaphors was emphasized, and I have argued that the metaphors of the immune system and immune suppression, could help humanity to understand and empathize with a living earth that is actively protecting life against disease, sincep "seeing the earth as a living being helps us identify with its ... well-being" (Du Nann Winter & Koger, 2004, p. 196).

CHAPTER FOUR

Longing to be human: evolving ourselves in healing the earth

Paul Maiteny

Emerging humanness or instinctive emergency?

Every fifteen to twenty years since the 1960s, a wave of ecological anxiety has washed over "western" society. In the 1980s/1990s wave, Al Gore (1992) had already described our species as perpetrating "ecological holocaust" on planet earth. The focus then was tropical deforestation, the ozone hole, seal hunting, and whaling. Climate change was still taboo in mainstream scientific circles. Peak oil was hardly mentioned. Now, with these as the main anxieties, I see a similar sequence of reaction as before: "environmental" anxiety around a trigger issue followed by optimism about solutions and possible economic opportunities. Then, economic recession hits and takes priority, diminishing enthusiasm for pro-ecological action. Each time, discrediting of environmental scientists has also fuelled public scepticism and media shut-down on the issues.

This is disheartening. In each wave's wake comes despondency or exasperation about whether humans can ever change. Each time it comes a little deeper and darker, to the point where it is seen by some as a sign that *Homo sapiens* is an ecological aberration, an evolutionary dead-end.

A less pessimistic view is that our ecological emergency is rooted in humans having lost touch with our other-than-human origins in nature; to save ourselves we need to rediscover what we share with other species. Remoteness from nature is undoubtedly a major prob- lem, and recognizing our common evolutionary *inheritance* with other species is vital. However, I worry about highlighting this so much that we forget about, obscure or split ourselves off from the *particular* emer- gent nature of *Homo sapiens* that we do *not* share with other species, including emotional features (see Darwin, 2009/1916). Without these we could not reflect on our origins in the first place. Nor could we prac- tice compassion for other sentient beings, which Darwin considered the highest human virtue. Contemporary neo-darwinism tends to neglect capacities that only evolved with *Homo sapiens* and have important implications for *future* evolution.

I have been tempted by both humans-as-aberration and return-to- origins arguments, but they sit uncomfortably with me. They seem illogical in evolutionary terms. It is as unscientific to consider human emergent properties as irrelevant to evolution as it is to neglect those of any other species. Neither would we dismiss any other species as being irrelevant or redundant within the ecosystem. So why should we con- sider ours to be the only one that has no place in the web of life? I have spent many years pondering these questions, and seeking clues about them. Much of this chapter focuses on my explorations so far.

Working in ecological education and research since the late 1970s has often had a "Groundhog Day" quality about it—every few years, witnessing similar responses to peaks in anxiety about ecological breakdown. I am now convinced that the *particular* psycho-spiritual dimensions of our species (and therefore of the ecosystem) are (1) the key to bringing ourselves out of ecological holocaust and (2) the vital signs indicating our (and the planet's) possible evolutionary future. Essentially, the causes of our planetary crisis are emotional and spir- itual, rooted in our yearnings for meaningfulness in life and how we seek to satisfy them (Maiteny, 2009a, 2009b). Such aspects have been consistently ignored and tabooed in academic and campaigning cir- cles. The usual stock-in-trade of facts, information, and intellectual argument have never been enough to change deep-rooted behaviour. The decades-old assumption that they are is misplaced.

Consider your own experience of really meaningful periods (or moments!) when you have emerged significantly transformed, after which nothing seems quite the same as before and perhaps you wondered why you had not always seen things like this. Basic assumptions changed. You really *felt* the change emotionally in, as it were, your feeling body. Information and emotion came together as experience of deep meaningfulness. Crucially, this could not be forgotten or "unlearned". It was an epiphany, *kairos*, aha! moment.

Convincing, long-lasting behavioural *change* occurs when information or argument is "heart-felt". It *moves, motions and motivates* us so much that we *experience* meaningfulness. Resulting changes in behaviour are then inevitable, necessary, authentic, and emotionally sustaining.

What most moves us tends to connect with deeply held convictions and yearnings, but it is also what stops us changing and keeps us inside our comfortable assumptions. If we are convinced that our yearnings will be satisfied, and our anxieties quelled, by the same type of action but *more* of it, consuming, for example, then it is easy to see how deeply embedded are the *causes* of our ecological crisis in our emotions, yearnings and meanings.

We humans need to look deeply and carefully into which aspects of our psyche *really* motivate which aspects of our behaviour. When do we use the cognitive cleverness that evolved in us as a species to rationalize and justify behaviours as civilized, progressive or developed, when they are actually elaborations on instinctive urges that we share with other species. Though we often glibly say that emotions resulting in, for example, unrestrained consumption, exploitation, acquisitiveness, greed, are "only human", they may actually be "pre-human", that is, rooted in our other-than-human instincts (Darwin, 2009/1916). Our distinctly human cleverness, ingenuity, and technology—especially our use of fossil fuels—has *temporarily* freed us of constraints on our behaviour imposed by natural bio-ecological limits. Other species would also consume more than they need if they could, but they can't.

Looked at like this, it is the *pre*-human, other-than-human emotions in us, the instinctual ones we share with other species, that are fuelling ecological breakdown. To heal this and break through to something else, we need to contain these instincts by moving on from them and listening to urges that are distinctly of our species. To know and develop what is *only* human means coming into and living from those qualities that came into *existence* with the evolution of *Homo sapiens*— our *distinctly* human nature, true human wildness. It seems to me that human evolution of this sort is a prerequisite to healthy ecological conditions, to finding ways of sustaining ourselves emotionally that do not depend on over-consuming the planet. We are a species that can probably be more self-reflectively conscious than any other. As such, we are probably both (1) the only species that can be confused about our place (collectively and personally) in the ecosystemic scheme of things, and (2) for which finding our place within it requires a conscious process of discernment.

So, what is it that we might bring to the ecosystem by our membership of it? What might be our function or, to use ecological language, our *guild* (Volk, 1998)? How might realizing the distinct nature and wildness of our "own" species contribute to realising the possible evolution of the planet? Where might we look for clues or signs of such life?

Ancestral clues to possible human evolving

Clues to our possible evolution are closer than we might think, in the spiritual teachings of the world's religions. For millennia, we have found it convenient to interpreting them in ways that serve our self-orientated interests and that justify exploitation. We could, instead, read them symbolically, for the encoded meanings they contain and vital clues they give us about how to live in attunement with ourselves and the ecosystem.

For example, the Book of Genesis, shared foundation of the Abrahamic traditions (Judaism, Christianity, Islam), depicts human rejection of—or self-Exile from—our Origin, Source or Context, and the possibility of re-membering ourselves and consciously returning. The opening of our eyes in the Garden of Eden, can be understood as *Homo sapiens'* experience of "falling" from unconscious innocence into conscious choice, self-consciousness and apparent separateness from the rest of Creation. Consciousness and free will give humans the choice of remaining alienated or becoming fully human. This means choosing to accept the "role" of being the part of Creation through which It can become conscious of Itself. We have the option of refusing to accept or offer ourselves in this way. To do so is to refuse to evolve, as implied by the Creation myth in Genesis. There are countless other examples which I am in the process of gathering.

US Senator Al Gore (1992), in *Earth in the Balance*, highlights the importance of such religiously encoded messages. For some, Gore's insistence on the importance of religion may be his first "inconvenient truth". The ecological holocaust is, he says, caused by spiritual holocaust. To heal it, we must blow away the chaff of false, idolatrous religion that has been distorted to serve political, ego- and anthropo-centric, "diabolical" interests (see Buber, 1952; de Rougemont, 1944; Rappaport, 1999 on "diabolical lies"). On the other hand, we must, revitalize the true religious kernel, the purpose of which is to point humans towards their place and purpose in the context of what is Bigger than us—society, ecosystem, planet, and evolutionary process or "Creation". It is easy to blow too hard and lose the kernel when listening only to our prejudices against the chaff, politically correct prejudices though they may be. Ungerminated seeds still contain encoded beauty, truth, and wisdom. We would be foolish to throw this away because we cannot or will not see it. It may be the very guidance we need to emerge healthy and transformed from our eco-psycho-spiritual crisis.

> In order to change, we have to address some fundamental questions about our purpose in life, our capacity to direct the powerful inner forces that have created this crisis, and who we are … These questions are not for the mind or the body but the spirit.

> (Gore, 1992, pp. 238–239)

The true purpose of religio-spiritual teachings is to offer guidance on such questions. But they do not force us to listen or hold us to ransom. They contain clues to reconciling ourselves to our contexts (including each other), and have done for millennia. They are signs of life, vitality, pointing us to re-sources of meaningfulness and experience that are already germs within us.

Gore distinguishes germ from chaff when challenging the interpretation that, in Genesis,

> (God) delegat(es) … authority over nature to human beings … sanction(ing) as ethical all choices that put a higher priority on human needs and desires than on the rest of nature. Simply put, according to this view, it is "ethical" to make sure that whenever nature gets in the way of what we want, nature loses.
>
> But this is a cartoon version of the Judeo-Christian tradition … (A)ll of (the world's major religions) mandate an ethical responsibility to protect and care for the well-being of the natural world.

> (Gore, 1992, pp. 242–243)

To construe ourselves as the only species on earth that occupies no functional place or role—in ecological terminology, no niche or guild—in the ecosystem defies scientific logic. It is to split, fragment, distort, and exclude ourselves from the ecosystemic scheme of things. The psycho-spiritual aspects of ourselves are evolving emergent properties but, often in subtly prejudicial ways, we dismiss millennia of religious-symbolic clues to how we fit. In denying this we assault the deepest and most complex expression of nature and so all of other-than-human nature too. This also wastes time. We will eventually have to re-invent the wheel whose design blueprint we are arrogantly, though unwittingly, destroying.

Homo sapiens: evolutionary meaning-makers

Homo sapiens are the meaning- and purpose-makers of the planet. So far as we know, we are the only species the universe has evolved that can do this with such complexity. It is an evolving emergent property and integral *part of* the ecosystem. There is no getting away from this except by denying it. Complex choice is another emergent property. We can *choose* to deepen our creative meaning-making capacities, or not.

Symbolic understandings of religion are the result of our ancestors' explorations into what it means to be human. They are still available to us, containing clues and methods to entering more deeply into the "psychology of possible evolution" Ouspensky (1950). These spiritual traditions are eco-systemic in insisting that we are aspects of a greater whole. They indicate clearly how we *could* choose to resolve our entangled inner- and outer-sustainability problems by consciously finding and accepting our roles—both collective and individual—within this greater whole—our home (the meaning of Greek *oikos; ecos*).

Choosing not to explore this route means continuing to use our intellectual cleverness, combined with dexterity, to create ever more elaborate technological ways to try and satisfy other instinctive urges. As already mentioned, we often see the ecologically destructive results of this justified with the illogical "it's *only* human!" In evolutionary terms, it is pre-human. As far as we know it is *only* humans who can consciously experience and face or ignore the difficult questions and answers: Why am I here? What am I here for? Why do I do what I do? What impels me? What's the point of it all? What's my place in the ecosystemics of things? What can satisfy my yearning? Religio-spiritual teachings are the fruit of others exploring such questions. They help give shape and form to them, framing, interpreting, and making meaning in myriad ways so we can better navigate towards discerning our place in the bigger context where we live and move and have our being.

The various spiritual teachings describe two basic orientations through which humans seek to quell existential anxiety and experience meaningfulness and purpose. I term them "consuming" and "contextualising", or "contexturing" (Maiteny, 2009b, 2009c).

Wanting what has never been there: the consuming orientation

Consuming is akin to specializing, simplifying and splitting, an essentially instinctive orientation to context as a resource to consume. For all species, consuming ensures survival and quells basic survival anxieties. For humans, a nagging emotional-existential lack adds complexity to the mix, spurring us into a never-ending, addiction-like search for *something or someone* that will satisfy. Physical survival is not enough. We want more, to "survive in style" (Shea, 2004). We might see this promised by countless things: a product, a substance, place, pastime, fitness, wealth, greatness, fame, other persons …. We can also have a *consuming orientation* towards beliefs, ideologies, good causes like environmentalism, social justice, even seeking spiritual experiences. The Buddhist teacher, Chögyam Trungpa (1973) warned about meditation and prayer becoming spiritually camouflaged materialism when practised solely with the aim of *acquiring* peace, wealth, or happiness. The Christian priest Teilhard de Chardin also warned, "development in the spiritual life (is a) very delicate matter, for nothing is easier than to pursue one's selfish interests under cover of growing and of loving God" (1960). Satisfaction sought through the consuming mode always needs topping up with the next object of desire. Disappointment is inevitable yet, even *knowing* this, one can continue trying for a lifetime (see Žižek, 1989, for a Lacanian perspective on this).

Ecological and cultural constraints

Lacking our techno-ingenuity, other-than-human species are constrained from excess consumption by bio-ecological boundaries. We cleverly circumvent these constraints, apparently finding ways to increase populations and consumption without limit. The extra sunlight energy we access in fossil-fuels is not available to other species. Ours can only be temporary. When fossil-fuels run out, either we find new fuel or we revert to population and consumption levels of other, solar-fuelled species.

It is hard to accept that biologically rooted drives we share with other species are undermining the planetary life-support systems we depend on. All species seek to grow and consume, focusing attention, and activity on those aspects of their environments that are most relevant to them. We also do this, although we have the capacity to *know* we are doing it and to choose to do differently. Yet, we humans remain so addicted to our this consuming orientation we deny possible *non-consuming* ways to find meaningfulness and satisfaction. We deny our possible evolution out of breakdown and into sustainability, ecological, and emotional.

For most of human history, older, more sustainable societies than ours (Hartmann, 1998) existed without exceeding ecosystemic constraints. It is often presumed that pre-fossil-fuel peoples were somehow free from the instinctual desires of other species and present-day human excesses and/or had an inherent wisdom that kept them consciously in tune with their ecosystems. We do not know for certain if such universal eco-spiritual sensibility was true, or wishful thinking. Many civilizations have succumbed to ecological excess.

We do know that a combination of religio-cultural beliefs and corresponding emotions played a role in constraining behaviour that could be ecologically damaging. Reverence, fear, respect, etc towards God(s), Ancestor(s), Origins, Context and the otherwise Holy, plus behavioural taboos, effectively protected the systems on which human depend from degradation and desecration. Humans were even construed as serving the divine (Maiteny, 2004; Rappaport, 1999). Our society is run on beliefs that put *us* in the position of the gods/context. We seem to believe that everything is subservient to us. Along with species and habitats, this has pushed most ecologically functional cultures to extinction.

Cultural- and bio-ecological constraints cannot prevent individuals from *desiring* more. But, as long as economic security depended on social relations, and people honoured and respected the sanctity of Context (God, Ancestors, Holy ...), fearing the consequences of breaking taboos, such destructive behaviour was contained within sustainable ecosystemic limits. Cultural beliefs had a regulating, adaptive influence on human-context relations.

Dominant culture today encourages exactly the opposite. It *inverts* the relationship between social and economic, and collective/contextual and individual. It generates ecologically maladaptive and dysfunctional relationships. The free-market of beliefs and products disconnects individual economic welfare from its dependence on social cohesion, neighbourhood and community. Customs and beliefs no longer limit and constrain behavioural impacts on context. Culture no longer influences society and individuals to be integrated into the systems of which we are members. Our weak and impoverished symbolism reduces everything to a quantified and therefore oversimplistic "context" of economics and consumption. Everything qualitative is squeezed into the quantitative. Everything is simplified to fit into monetary terms. This is commodification. Everything, even emotions, become commodified. To pretend that ecological and emotional essentials can be converted into tradeable quasi-commodities like "ecosystem services" or "carbon credits" unavoidably devalues them. When qualities are force-fitted into quantities, our imaginations make them equivalent, comparable and apparently substitutable. What is necessary to existence—ecosystems, forests, air, water, soil, food, life—can magically be traded for what is desired—money, timber, concrete, cars, oil, shares. We are killing ourselves trying to feel better.

Humans are reducing and simplifying ourselves and everything else on earth (Totton, 2011). We achieve this suicidal feat by inverting the ecological order necessary to our existence so as to live instead in a fatal lie created by our own imaginations (Wilden, 1987). It is named a "diabolical lie" by both cultural ecologists (Rappaport, 1999) and religious philosophers (Buber, 1952). Mystical Judaism considers it the egocentric and, therefore, diabolical (*Qliphothic*) adversary of the Tree of Life, that is, the Tree of Death. We are using our species' distinct complexity, diversity and richness to desolate effect.

The main contemporary instruments used to constrain behaviour—legislation, policy, punishment—carry little emotional weight, meaning or legitimacy. They do a poor job of convincing people in comparison to the sanctity and taboo-based regulators of earlier cultures. Legislation and policy are rarely experienced as positive incentives. On the other hand, attempts to engineer a return to past cultures will always be futile. The genie cannot be put back in its bottle. Arguments as to why we *should* believe or do such-and-such will never catch on unless they are *experienced* as more meaningful than other options. Before this post-modern world of pick-n-mix belief systems, the one people were brought up with tended to be the lens through which they viewed the world. Nowadays, it is hard to settle on one particular worldview. Consequently, we have to look beyond engineering new cultural forms to find a way forward. It seems to me, we need to consider how we might evolve as humans. Looking to our ancestral traditions for sym-bolically encoded messages that we have not wanted to see before may provide us with some clues.

Seeing what has always been here: contextual participation and service

There is nothing new in what I call the contextualizing (or contextur-ing) orientation. It corresponds to the ancient *inner/alchemical* tradi-tions of most, if not all, religions. It describes and guides exploration of our inner natures, individual and collective, in the context of the Whole (i.e., Holy). Although more sustaining emotionally and ecologi-cally than the consuming orientation, it has often been appropriated to consuming ends. I believe that drawing on the deep experience and insights of these traditions provides us with clues to emerging from our ecological and spiritual holocausts. It would also be an important evolutionary step since we are a species that could, so far as we know for the first time, be in conscious, meaningful and intimate relationship with the contexts from which we have evolved. Maybe other species could too, but what is more important for us is knowing that we can.

Noted evolutionists and theologians agree on this, in principle if not in the details, amongst them Barlow (1994), Hardy (1975), Huxley (1957), Teilhard de Chardin (1960, 1969 and others), Wilson (1978).

> As a result of ... evolution, the universe is becoming conscious of itself, able to understand something of its past history and its pos-sible future. This cosmic self-awareness is being realised in one tiny fragment of the universe—in a few of us human beings. Perhaps it has been realised elsewhere too, through the evolution of conscious living creatures on the planets of other stars. But on this, our planet, it has never happened before. ... It is thus part of human destiny

to be the necessary agent of the cosmos in understanding more of itself, in bearing witness to its wonder, beauty, and interest ...

(Huxley, 1957, p. 121)

To live in contextualizing mode is to experience oneself as an aspect of a bigger whole, perhaps with a sense of purposeful role or niche within it. Other species, so far as we know, cannot reflect on their ecological niches. Humans can. We cannot *not* be part of the whole, but we use the evolutionary gift of our minds—consciousness, free will, intellect, imaginations—to insist on behaving as if we are not. We could use them differently. In these fragmentary times, we urgently need to discern what parts we play, as species and persons, for the adaptive, healthy, and holy (words with same origin) functioning of the ecosystemic whole. Our imaginations: What can our imaginations come up with as to why we are here; what ecological niche(s), guild(s), and purpose(s) we occupy in the eco-system? To repeat, to consider ourselves as having no place either because we are a superior species or an evolutionary aberration is an arrogant position. We are here and have a place, like any other species, albeit more complex.

Neither is such a complex species merely a planetary cancer. It is more logical to think of ourselves as an evolving aspect of the Whole. Yet, contemporary neo-darwinism has next-to-nothing to say about distinctly human qualities and their implications for future evolution. It only considers our *origins* and what we have *in common* with other species. It excludes questions of psycho-cultural evolution and, as it were, the purpose or niche this might serve in the whole. This is not just a dangerous omission, but one that unscientifically and illogically splits *Homo sapiens* off from the rest of life, the planet and their evolutionary process. It cuts us off from both external nature and our inner nature, and avoids the question of human responsibility; with dire consequences for our emotional, existential, and ecological health.

Sir Alister Hardy (1975), a cetacean specialist, was dedicated to understanding the adaptive significance of religious and spiritual experience, and of our capacity to construct complex, symbolic meanings in religious stories and mythologies. He wondered about our purpose in the Universe. The human yearning for such meaningfulness and relatedness is perennial. It resists attempts to ignore or destroy it because it is part of our inner nature—an emergent property of evolution. Spiritually orientated religion tells us, through diverse symbolic languages, that we are here to evolve conscious awareness of, or orientation towards, the Context and connectedness of all things, including our place within it, and to live accordingly. Putting ancient teaching into modern words, Huxley says this is to be an "agent of the cosmos in understanding more of itself" and in "becoming conscious of itself", as far as we know, for the first time in the history of the universe. That is an inspiring thought, awe-inspiring.

Put in still more contemporary terms, Huxley was suggesting that, just as there are ecosystemic functions—termed ecological guilds—such as pollinators, decomposers, and photosynthesizers—the guild of our species may be conscientizers and harmonizers. We differ from other species: we have to *choose* and consciously evolve our guild. We can choose to live in role and service to the whole or as if separate from it.

Spiritually orientated religion today is still eco-systemic and offers the contextualizing mode as a route to well-being and sustainable integrity. Some quotations follow which, though paradoxical, describe such spiritual-ecosystemic linkage.

Hindu perspective:

> It is said in the *Bhagavad Gita* (3:10–12) that … the Lord of Being brought forth creatures with sacrifice (*yajna*) and instructed them that "it is with sacrifice (*i.e., making sacred*) that you shall sustain the gods so that the gods may sustain you; by this reciprocal sustenance you shall attain the highest good. Sustained by sacrifice the gods will give you the food of your aspiration. He who enjoys their gifts yet gives the gods nothing in return is verily a thief." The greatest sacrifice is that of the self, which must be left behind … Otherwise, one makes oneself into a black hole of greed, stealing and hoarding every good for one's own egoistic purposes.
>
> (Ravindra, 1990, pp. 122–123)

> One can come to God following one's own deepest calling, and by that alone. … "Better to follow one's own *svadharma*, however humble, that to follow another's, though great. By engaging in the work prescribed by one's own inner calling, one does not miss the mark" (*Bhagavad Gita* 18:47).
>
> (Ravindra, 1990, p. 27)

Sufi perspective:

> The fulfilment of this whole creation is to be found in the human. And this object is only fulfilled when humans have awakened that part of themselves which represents the Divine.

> (Inayat Khan, 1999, p. 1)

Judaic perspective:
Humanity and nature. Ecological necessity:

> Putting themselves in relation with all things, humans can remember that in the deepest being of all that exists is hidden the Divinity to which they themselves feel "connected" and by which they are conscious of being inhabited. They can feel that the *Shekhinah*, the Divine Presence, desires to dwell in them ... When humble in front of their Creator and recognising Its goodness, humans regard nature with respect and come close to it without expecting gifts ... In contemplating these wonders, humans can sense their Creator who reminds them: "See how beautiful is My work! ... Be careful not to corrupt it ... because if you corrupt it no one after you will be able to repair it!"

> (Safran, 1998, translated from Italian)

Christian perspective:

> As the reality of God (*ie Source and Context*) has faded from so many lives in the West, there has been a corresponding inflation of expectations that personal relations alone will supply meaning and happiness in life.
>
> The spiritual life grows as love finds its centre beyond ourselves .... the more we give of self, the richer we become in soul; the more we go beyond ourselves in love, the more we become our true selves and our spiritual beauty is more fully revealed (as) we are seeking to bring one another into fuller life.
>
> (B)y making this new relationship, you have aligned yourselves with what we believe is the way in which life is spiritually evolving, and which will lead to a creative future for the human race.

> (Chartres, 2011, n.p.)

Re-orientating ourselves from addictive, self-destructive consuming mode towards contextualizing mode requires a learning process that is, in many ways, equivalent to individuation and the Work of alchemy: the symbolic Lead of pre-human instinctual drives and attachments, which weighs on and dis-integrates us, is to be transformed into the symbolic Gold of re-integration and Service to Context (see also Maiteny, 2003, 2009b).

The instinctual magnetism of the consuming orientation is hard to resist. Our ecological and psycho-spiritual health requires that we do. Finding our place as ecosystemic persons is an individuation process of discerning personal meaning (Self/Niche) and purpose (Will/Role) in the Contextual scheme of things. To the extent we do this, we also participate in evolving the ecosystemic Role of *Homo sapiens*. This does not mean being merely stewards looking after the Planet, which still implies a subtle arrogance and split. Ecological guild-ship involves accepting ourselves more as members than stewards. Were this to feel more meaningful than pursuing satisfaction by consuming the Whole, levels of consumption and ecological impact would lessen. We would not feel like consuming so much. Relationships with other people and other-than-human members of nature would also be less consumer-orientated and more intimate.

Our own collective religio-symbolic imagination has contained contextualizing signs of life for millennia. We have not yet noticed them enough. Hopefully, we are more likely to the more urgently we feel the pressures of ecological holocaust and psycho-spiritual malaise. We certainly need to for, clever though they may be, none of our other tired, tried and tested ways are succeeding in turning the tide.

Acknowledgement

I am grateful to Rebecca Hazell for inspiration, morale-boosting, discussion of ideas and help with editing this chapter. I would not have finished it without you.

PART II

OTHER-THAN-HUMAN
AND MORE-THAN-HUMAN

CHAPTER FIVE

The ecology of the unconscious

Margaret Kerr and David Key

The sun shines not on us, but in us. The rivers flow not past us but through us.

—John Muir (1911)

Introduction

From many years of professional practice leading groups, it is obvious that taking people into wild areas can improve their psychological health. This is now well supported by research (e.g., Davis-Berman & Berman, 1994; Kaplan & Talbot, 1983; MIND, 2007). Other research also suggests that these experiences can lead to "pro-environmental behaviour" (e.g., Palmer et al., 1998; WWF, 2009). Our intention here is to offer a deeper understanding of how experiences of wild and green spaces can heal the self as part of our larger ecology.

We believe that at the heart of this healing process is our capacity to open up both *ecologically*, as we realize our biological interdependence with the rest of nature, and *metaphysically*, as we go beyond our narrow egoic sense of self. In emphasizing interrelatedness and immanence, our practice is aligned with feminist (Wright, 1998) and "descending" strands of transpersonal theory (e.g., Sabini, 2002; Washburn, 1995) rather than with the "ascending" perspective of Wilber (Daniels, 2005). It is also informed by Taoist and Buddhist approaches (Preece, 2009; Prendergast, 2003; Watts & Huang, 1975) and the shamanic practices and worldviews of indigenous cultures (e.g., Brody, 2002a; Celi & Boiero, 2002; Siri, 1998; Williams, 2007).

Some transpersonal psychologists have explicitly acknowledged the connection between transpersonal experience and ecological awareness. However, traditionally much of Transpersonal Psychology has been centred on the human realm, so to make sense of our experiences we need a wider theoretical frame. This is provided by Deep Ecology, a social movement which emerged in response to growing evidence of our ecological situation (Naess, 1973); Transpersonal Ecology (Fox, 1990a); and Ecopsychology (Roszak, Gomes & Kanner, 1995). These disciplines present a model of a transpersonal Self as part of the entire body of the earth, both physically and metaphysically. This is especially clear through the notion of the "ecological Self" which aligns our psychological sense of *who* we are with the biological reality of *what* we are (Naess, 1986). (We have used the capitalized form of the words "Self" and "Being" to indicate a wide, interconnected, open transpersonal sense. This is in contrast to experiences of "skin-bound" self or being, which are centred on the personal ego.)

We use these diverse perspectives as a framework to facilitate journeys into wilderness areas. In essence, we lead people on a healing "descent" into the wild territory where personal and planetary health become synonymous. It is on this ground that we find a more complete, ecological, sense of Self. When we feel healed as part of nature, the motivation to live in more ecologically sustainable ways emerges spontaneously. Traditional ethics, positing a moral obligation to act out of duty, become obsolete. Instead, we act as part of nature protecting itself. As Arne Naess so clearly puts it, "If reality is as it is experienced by the ecological Self, our behaviour naturally and beautifully follows strict norms of environmental ethics" (1986, p. 236).

Wilderness as unconscious space

The ecological Self model suggests that we are deeply woven into a complex web of physical and metaphysical relationships. We are constantly in this web. We are in it now as we write, you are in it now as you read. With each moment, the pattern of the web changes, shifting our experience of "now"—sometimes this is a small shift, sometimes it is cataclysmic and life changing. Being in this web is called by Naess (1989) "gestalt ontology." The web's pattern is a gestalt: the whole is greater than the sum of its parts, and each part is experientially greater as a result of the whole. For example, a tree in an indigenous forest offers us a different experience from a tree in a city street. The tree's context changes our experience of it. Often we are unaware of the additional qualities that come with being part of a gestalt, but, if we are sensitive to them, even a mundane situation can be deeply affecting.

Experiences in gestalt ontology are "nondual", going beyond our habitual perceptions of self and other as separate: beyond, or perhaps before, dualism, in the "forestructure" of reality (Heidegger, 1996). We often try to abstract them into dualistic forms, for example through language (Abram, 1996). But the map is not the territory—or, as the Zen teacher, D. T. Suzuki wrote, "A finger is needed to point at the moon, but what a calamity it would be if one took the finger for the moon!" (Suzuki, 1969, p. 74). The nondual nature of gestalt ontology takes us beyond language—deep into the realm of Being.

Experiences of gestalten cannot be validated by positivist science, which relies on a dualistic paradigm; they do not have to be understood logically—although they are sometimes shared and therefore can be "validated" as a consensual or intersubjective reality (Husserl, McCormick & Elliston, 1981; Merleau-Ponty, 1962). But more important than the "truth" of these experiences is their outcome—they have personal and social meaning that can be translated into everyday life. They have gravitas. And they form a nucleus which can attract new personal behaviours.

For us, wilderness describes places where we can experience our self as part of the "primordial gestalt". Being part of that wild pattern changes our sense of self. "I" as a "part" becomes different because of the whole. Previously frozen self-constructs can start to thaw, and the possibility of transformation and greater authenticity naturally arises. It is here that we can experience a wider, deeper, reality where phenomena never encountered before present themselves to our conscious mind. Our journey into wilderness becomes a journey into the unconscious (see e.g., Snyder, 1990). The personal unconscious contains elements particular to each individual, whereas the collective unconscious is an immense store of psychological material shared by all of humanity and, we believe, beyond (Daniels, 2005). Under favourable conditions, we can experience a therapeutic opening to both the personal and the collective unconscious: new seeds of meaning are planted and take root, deepening our compassion and understanding. Less afraid, and more aware, we are free to become our true selves. Experiences of wilderness can provide the conditions for this process to unfold.

In what follows we explore our own wilderness experiences of self opening out to a wider reality, of encounters with the unconscious, and—within the vast "primordial gestalt"—of healing the ecological Self. We also explore how, in wilderness, the metaphysical and the physical may become inseparable. While our own stories are the touchstones of our work, such tales are common—shared by the groups we have facilitated, and throughout human history across many cultures (see e.g., Campbell, 1949). To maintain confidentiality, we have chosen to not draw upon the many unpublished stories told to us by those we work with (we do refer to one client's published story). At the same time, we recognize it is important to put our own experiences into a wider context, and to do this we will explore the writings of others.

Opening out

> As I was sitting beside the fire on the shore of Loch Ericht on Saturday night, a feeling of something about my dad came up. It was scary, like a faint echo—an association triggered off by something in the place we were camping, a sound, the smell of the mosquito coil—I don't know what. As I let it come more, I realised it was to do with my dad's experiences in the war—the unspoken fear that had been around as long as I can remember.
>
> I could feel myself starting to contract and become isolated. I talked to J about it as best I could. It eased a little, but it was really compacted—and too early to find words for it. The next day, the feeling was still there, and the first five or six hours were a real struggle, physically and mentally. But as the day unfolded, the feeling—and that part of me—started to open into the landscape. Like it was dispersing into something much more spacious. I started to become part of the vast wild place around me.... and my whole self could relax and open up into this. And it felt like coming home.

> (Kerr, 2010, 2009)

This experience shows how being in a wide open wild place can help us open out to unconscious parts of ourselves—things from our personal past that are locked away, or things we are carrying for other people. Ultimately this allows split-off, scary, shameful, helpless or grief-stricken parts of the psyche to be compassionately held in something much bigger than self (Bache, 1981). Prendergast (2003) describes how something similar can happen in a deeply attentive therapeutic relationship—he calls it "sacred mirroring". This non-dual state arises when client and therapist consciously engage with silent, unconditional presence; open and receptive to each other's Being. This experience "often evokes the sensation of a vast space" (2003, p. 103), and for some clients can simply be liberating—an experience of interconnectedness, wholeness and homecoming. However commonly the initial encounter with the vastness is terrifying—a fear of losing all reference points, of falling infinitely. Often in this type of encounter, unprocessed emotions and needs from early life emerge. Resistance to relaxing into this space shows up as bodily contraction, fear of loss and ultimately, fear of annihilation. As Prendergast notes, "it is not uncommon for clients to experience the vastness as alternatively [sic] terrifying and comforting, often in rapid succession" (2003, p. 104).

However, if clients can tolerate this upheaval, "their experience over time takes on a positive valence and the vastness is increasingly welcomed as their true ground" (Prendergast, 2003, p. 104; cf. Washburn, 1995). Prendergast describes opening to the vast ground of Being as a process that happens in the relationship between two people. It is perhaps a common assumption of psychotherapy that the relationship between people is the primary crucible where psychological wounds can be healed. However, for millions of years we have been held in our early life not only by our biological human family, but also by the whole gestalt of plants, land, trees, rivers, earth, and creatures. In the beginning, the void was a fertile void. When we got cut off from this gestalt by the "evolution" of our culture, the void became sterile, and a vital part of that holding environment was lost. It all became the responsibility of whatever human being was there in the role of Mother. Psychotherapy has tended to focus on early relational wounds between people, which we try to heal in the therapeutic relationship—and often this works. But we would suggest that this healing is incomplete, because there still remains the primal deficit of the whole wild gestalt.

Just as sitting silently open to another human being can be initially terrifying, silent unmediated contact with wilderness can also be very frightening. We are not used to that kind of contact in our culture. Separated from our original natural gestalt, we may sense that something is missing, but project our inner deficit onto the wilderness, and experience it as a vast, frightening emptiness. We try, in vain, to fill the emptiness with mass media, celebrity culture, consumerism, alcohol, and drugs. We have become afraid of the fertile darkness. And, as a culture, our fear is threatening to destroy the ecological ground that sustains us. Unconditional presence, in wilderness, or with another human being, brings us right up against the terror, power and love which is in Being. But Being in our original gestalt of plants, land, trees, rivers, earth, creatures ... we can slowly relax, and then be held—and feel the echo of that wider, ancient holding environment, which can help dissipate the terror and allow the power and the love to emerge. We are held in the mind of nature, and in nature's physical body. This is not to idealize nature as the perfect parent; but the depth of intimacy engendered by this kind of work allows us eventually to drop through the veil of projections. It allows us to relax and expand beyond the fear that creates dualisms of "good" and "bad" parent, "good" and "bad" self, and "good" and "bad" nature.

Richard Tarnas relates a story from Joseph Campbell, which suggests that this understanding has been known for a long time:

> Rasmussen, in the course of his explorations through the arctic regions of the North American continent, had conversations with a number of old shamans. One of them told the story of his own initiation as a young boy. He said that he was taken by an older shaman out on a sled over ice, and placed in a small igloo just big enough for him to sit in. He was crouched on a skin, he was left there for thirty days with just a little water and meat brought in occasionally during that period. He said, "I died a number of times during those thirty days, but I learned and found what can be found and learned only in the silence, away from the multitude, in the depths. I heard the voice of nature itself speak to me, and it spoke with the voice of a gentle motherly solicitude and affection. Or it sounded sometimes like children's voices, or sometimes like falling snow, and what it said was, 'Do not be afraid of the universe'." This discovery, Campbell goes on, became a point of internal, absolute security for

THE ECOLOGY OF THE UNCONSCIOUS   69

the initiate, and made possible his return to his community with a wisdom and assurance that was unmatched by everyone there, so that he could help others from that inner place.

(Tarnas, 2000, p. 261)

The most complete setting for us to encounter and heal our psychological wounds combines an accepting, holding, human presence with wild nature. This context is the most "ecologically valid", in that it has predominated in human societies for millions of years, before the advent of our current civilization. It is also ecologically valid, in that the way of Being that emerges from this ultimately healing encounter with the "vastness" can lead to pro-environmental behaviour by activating a personal realization of the ecological Self (Naess, 1988; WWF, 2009).

Time in the wilderness can equip us to return to our communities and take compassionate action from an increased sense of inner security, born of ecological Self-confidence. Opening to a wider sense of Self in wilderness then, can offer great potential for healing. However, it can also be a powerful and sometimes painful experience in which unconscious contents emerge in a variety of forms. This is a delicate process. To work with it sensitively we need to have insight—to hold a steady course, moving with the ebb and flow of trauma and breakthrough around us. Knowing the nature of the journey enables us to stay present, to witness and hold these experiences compassionately in ourselves, and with our clients. We can illustrate this with some of our own experiences.

Individual, collective, and intergenerational trauma

Over twenty years ago, when I was at medical school, I spent some time working in a Burns Unit. For about six months after working there, I suffered flashbacks, and feelings of isolation, guilt, fear, helplessness and sadness. Last Tuesday evening, I watched a TV programme about surgery for people who had suffered severe facial burns. Watching the programme, those old feelings came back, but I was able to talk them through over the rest of the evening. I felt more peaceful for this—a deeper understanding and some resolution.

Two days later we set off to climb Braeriach in the Cairngorms … we scramble through the Chalamain gap, over all the giant boulders. It feels like a good day. There's a bit of a slog up to the Sron na Lairig Ridge, but we reach the top of the ridge quite easily. And suddenly, I'm back in all that fear and sorrow and loneliness. I can't stop thinking about the horror, the trauma of severe burns. And I keep thinking "why again now?". My chest is tight. There's a lump in my throat. I feel overwhelmed with pain and darkness and grief. And finally, as we climb the last few metres of Sron na Lairig, I start sobbing. J holds me. I can't stop. The plateau is absolutely desolate, like I feel inside. It is so painful. The sky is stormy, and filled with wind and rain. Gradually the sobbing subsides and I'm left feeling empty.

We press on to the top against a strong wind. Stop for about thirty seconds on the summit cairn and turn back down again. Below us in the corrie, Lochan Uaine is dark and contained. On the way down the ridge, we pass a heap of metal poles ... wonder what they are. Back along the ridge, my thoughts are still pulled to the trauma. The strange thing is, I realise—it feels like I'm inseparable from all people who suffer this trauma, and at the same time, it's not mine. I go back in my mind on the way down, layers of free-association. Pushing through the thick heather. My father's war experiences, both grandfathers witnessing deaths from burns. The darkening sky. A story about me almost pulling a pan of boiling milk over myself when I was two. A wee boy I met when I was 12—his face scarred with burns. We jump over streams—in Scotland, they're called "burns".... Burning witches ... I'm starting to think, what happened in this area? We wade through some more thick heather and bog. Exhausted. Something's gradually clearing. Moving off ... opening out.

A couple of days later, feeling rested, and no longer possessed by all of this, I think of the pile of metal on top of the mountain, and google "Braeriach Crash". And there it is. During the Second World War, two bombers crashed into the Sron na Lairig ridge. The wreckage was spread over to dark little Locahn Uaine. So ... that was the crack that opened up in time! It was like somehow I connected with the spirits of the men who probably burned to death on that mountain with their friends ...

Since this experience, I feel that I have laid something to rest. Some parts of my experience after working in the Burns Unit were appropriate resonances with what I had witnessed. However, some parts were of my own unconscious making—the fear and guilt that came from making "people with burns" into something alien; the isolation that came from being ashamed to speak of the trauma; the helplessness that came from my disconnection. Now, when I think of this trauma, and that part of myself, it is inextricably woven into the landscape of Braeriach. I feel connected to the suffering, but not overwhelmed by it. I no longer feel alone with it, and the guilt and shame are gone. I'm left hoping that I was able to give something in return to the ghosts of that place.

(Kerr, 2009)

This illustrates the layered and interconnected nature of unconscious contents in the psyche and in the land. Personal history opened out to intergenerational residues of trauma, and right out to collective trauma—contained in the land, imprinted on that place (Irwin & Watt, 2007; Roll, 1997; Sheldrake, 2006). If trauma is near the surface of the personal unconscious, it seems to act like a resonator for physical and psychological wounds held collectively in the land. Understanding this and being receptive to its meaning offers the potential for healing personal, and perhaps even collective and ecological, trauma (see e.g., Bache, 2000).

Images and symbols

The resonance of unconscious and ecological elements can arise spontaneously, as described above, or can be more deliberately sought. We have often found that during solo time in wilderness, group participants discover symbolic forms in the landscape, mirroring their individual and collective situations. Rivers, trees, dense areas of scrub and clearings in forests, reflect stages in both the psychological and the physical journey. Gavin, a participant in a recent project, described this experience in one of his blogs:

This tree was not well. Up above me was a resplendent rowan tree, nestled next to a waterfall showing off its clumps of berries like Christmas decorations. But here on the ledge things were sparse, spindly and sickly. Moving under it I could see how growing out of the top of the rock cleft gave it limitations; a misshapen gravity defying U-bend trunk, stunted branches, a smattering of leaves and shrivelled fruit. Like our treatment of the planet this tree was trying to sustain itself but drew too much on limited resources. I imagined cutting the tree down and counting its rings. Its thickness suggested several decades, I fancied it, like me, being about 40. How had our lives compared? What seasons, weather, colours had it seen pass? How many birds had visited and taken rest in its branches? Straining towards sunlight, pushing roots in tight gaps for nourishing soil, scattering seeds? Whose life was the more life affirming?

(McLellan, 2009)

Through guided imagery, storytelling, and contemplative work outdoors, we invite participants to step into the space where landscape and psyche meet in symbol and metaphor. Gavin describes this in a later blog:

Frequently I am at the summit ridge, possibly over the horizon, away working, providing for my family in the forest brook. The glade spoke to me about home, a place of canopied security, sheltered, a source of comfort and nourishment, yet I wasn't within sight of it often enough. I need to find a way to stop ascending ridges of work pressures and pressing on to the next career summit and find the will to stay closer, within sight and calling distance of the valley, the tree line, and the homely bank.

(McLellan, 2009)

Myth and archetype

While some experiences bring individual and collective trauma to consciousness, and others find symbolic imagery mirroring unconscious material, the following stories describe encounters with local mythological, and more widely known archetypal forms.

I was alone camping in the Sant Aniol valley in the foothills of the Spanish Pyrenees. Being in the bottom of a deep, steep sided gorge, the only flat area to sleep on was a gravel bank in the dry river bed. It was a crystal-clear night and as I lay out under the stars I could see a thin strip of the dark sky marking out the edges of the gorge high above. Either side of this strip, the rock walls of the gorge were an intense ink-black. I fell asleep.

I awoke suddenly, as if I'd heard a noise, but there was complete silence, not even a breath of wind. I looked up and realised I could no longer see the sky which had now clouded over. As I tried to find the edge between the gorge walls and where I knew the sky was, I saw something in the darkness. Right there, like an image on a cinema screen, I saw a man with short black hair, deeply lined and tanned skin, dressed like a shepherd in a sheepskin gilet. I thought I was dreaming and there was a moment of confusion and panic as I realised I was in fact wide awake, lying on my back on the gravel bank in my sleeping bag. The man was bending over and reaching down, struggling with something at his feet. I could see he was pulling at something that was pinned underwater by a huge boulder in a river pool. As I looked I realised he was pulling at a corpse. The face of the corpse became clearer and I could see a young man with long thin blonde hair, his face was emaciated and drawn, his eyes closed. The corpse looked like it had been trapped for some time. Before the man could drag it free of the water the image disappeared. I scrambled out of the confines of my sleeping bag frantically looking up at the darkness but I couldn't see anything. I found my head torch and shone it around the gorge walls to the depths of its power, but could see nothing except towering rocks, trees, shrubs and shadows. It took me several hours before I could get back to sleep and when I awoke in the morning the image was very clear in my memory.

The following week I was waiting for a lift in Girona, an hours drive away from the gorge. I had some spare time and was exploring the mediaeval city walls with a friend. As we descended a stairway, I noticed a barred alcove high in one of the walls. In it was a figure carved from wood, underneath it was a brass plaque engraved in Catalan. The figure was the dark-haired man who had appeared in the gorge. I was so shocked I couldn't move or speak and it took me several minutes to gather myself. My friend asked someone if they spoke Catalan and asked them to translate the plaque. The carving is, they said, of the "god of the Sant Aniol river".

It wasn't until several weeks later as I was describing the vision to a friend that I realised, with a shudder of goose bumps, that the corpse was me. I had witnessed the recovery of my own dead body from entrapment under rock and water. I had been discovered and rescued by a mythological figure. I now believe this vision was a glimpse into my condition at the time, it was an affirmation that

I was going through some kind of psycho-spiritual death and rebirth, and it also felt like a warning, like the vision had come to make sure I didn't let this opportunity for renewal be missed in the profanity of everyday life.

I had never had a "vision" before and, to be honest, was sceptical about them. They must be something from the imagination surely? The discovery of the wooden figure in Girona soon dealt with this cynicism. There was my vision in material form—as real as a piece of wood.

(Key, 2008)

Describing a vision he'd experienced Carl Jung wrote, "At first I could make out nothing but then I saw that there was running water. In it a corpse floated by, a youth with blonde hair and a wound in the head" (1963, p. 203). He describes this as "a drama of death and renewal". The comparisons with the story above are obvious and we were shocked to find Jung's account while researching this chapter. But in exploring the collective unconscious, it is not surprising that parallel experiences and meanings arise.

Interestingly, the form experienced in this story was located in a specific geographic area, embedded in the stone and water of a particular place. We believe this distinguishes it from more widespread archetypes that can be found across diverse geographic and cultural space. The following journal entry of a dream, and the wilderness experience where the dream character re-emerged in the physical world, describes an encounter with one such widespread archetype:

I had a dream featuring a frightening character who ate the flesh of children. The character was dressed in a cloak, had a long thin white beard, carried a walking stick as tall as himself and, very distinctively, had a patch over his left eye. A skinny grey dog curled subserviently around his feet. The dream was very detailed, vivid and deeply disturbing. I awoke fearful and shocked at scenes and images that I had never knowingly experienced. Where had they come from?

After the dream I searched on the internet for the character I'd seen. I came across a text on Norse mythology and there he was! Staff, eye patch, beard and dog—Odin, the "All Father" (Harrison & Svensson, 2007, p 63.). Suddenly, I realised the dream was about my recent experience of fatherhood, the fear of failing as a father—of consuming my daughter in my own fears and doubts. It also brought up many realisations about my own father—perhaps where my fears about fatherhood had themselves been seeded.

Some months later on a night solo in an ancient woodland, I met the character from my dream again. I knew I would, and had prepared myself for him—cutting a long staff of my own from a hazel tree, barring the door of my shelter with it to protect myself, and lying in wait deep into the night. Of course, I could have made all this up! A fantasy … but whatever it was, for me, that night, Odin was right there in the darkness and when I jumped up and ran at him, my staff held out horizontally in front of me, he withered, fearful and lonely, and disappeared off into the beech trees. He was the vulnerable one, not me. It was his own fear that made him consume the flesh of children and the message was clear.

(Key, 2009)

What we need is here

What if you slept, and what if in your sleep you dreamed, and what if in your dreams you went to heaven and there you plucked a strange and beautiful flower, and what if when you awoke you had the flower in your hand? Ah, what then?

—Samuel Taylor Coleridge (1817)

The stories we have told suggest that psyche and matter are immanent in each other. Whichever direction the journey goes—into the psyche or out into material nature—it leads to the same territory, a territory which opens to us only if we open to it. The parapsychology researcher William Roll points to a tendency of the skin-bound self—the "small body"—to split mind from matter. "Matter feels different from mind to the small body, heavy, recalcitrant, immune to command, and so we place it in another part of nature" (Roll, 1997, p. 64). Connecting to a wider sense of self, elements of the physical world are seen to be "permeated with meaning and memory; they are as mental as they are material" (Roll, 1997, p. 64; cf. Dunne & Jahn, 2003). At this depth, psyche and matter seem to infuse and illuminate each other. As Robert Romanyshyn, the Jungian analyst and researcher, writes:

> The soul of the world, then, is the light of nature, a dark-light, a luminosity in the darkness of matter …. At the deepest level of the unconscious, the unconscious is nature. The consequence, of course, is that as the psychologist probes deeper and deeper into the psyche, he or she descends into the soul of the world … He or she discovers that the unconscious is not just in us, but that we are in the unconscious of nature, and that at the deepest level of our psyches, we retain some dim remembrance of once, very long ago, having been a part of the world's dark-light.
>
> (Romanyshyn, 2007, pp. 38–39)

Our stories provide some empirical support for this. However, the main thing that these stories illustrate is that taking the outcome and meaning of this kind of process seriously is more important in our lives than proving the "reality" of phenomena per se (Daniels, 2005). In the end, to argue over the objective "validity" of the stories themselves is, as Alan Watts (1957, p. 13) so eloquently puts it, "to eat the menu instead of the dinner". The experiences and insights described in our stories were, and still are, important in our lives. Without these journeys into what Romanyshyn calls "the soul of the world", we could have become entangled in serious psychological, spiritual or existential problems. Essentially, these were wilderness experiences that healed us. But this is not only a personal healing. It is clear to us that in transformative journeys such as these, wild nature holds us through the whole transformation, and we begin to experience nature as the core of our identity—the ground of our wisdom and personal meaning.

> As I relax into this place, I feel at the centre of my chest, a deep tenderness—like I'm touching something right at the heart of my own Being. Like I'm held in the heart of this place, and it in me …. and I would do anything to protect this place. The pine branches, feathery in front of the moon. The curve of the mountain. The intense cold. All of it is in me. I am in all of it. I am so grateful.
>
> (Kerr, 2010)

Our wilderness experiences embed us in the heart of nature, our own primordial heart. From this core of tenderness and joy, emerges compassionate action, beyond moral obligation, ethical duty or rational debate. We realize we can take action—we do not need to search for a "magical solution" outside ourselves, outside of nature, and "pray ... for new earth or heaven". What we need instead is,

> to be quiet in heart, and in eye, clear.
> What we need is here.

> —Wendell Berry (1998/1973)

Making the journey wholeheartedly, we return with insights that are profound and, most importantly, useful. We find ourselves changed—interconnected, healed. We become conscious of, and resilient to, the divisive illusions of industrial culture. The perceived separation of self and nature dissolves and, at last, we arrive home.

CHAPTER SIX

Remembering the forgotten tongue

Kelvin Hall

In folktales throughout the world, humans and animals converse, exchange pledges of mutual assistance, even take on each other's form. In an old Hungarian story, a peasant saves a snake from the flames, and in gratitude he is granted the power to understand everything that the creatures around him are saying. In contemporary Britain, many individuals have discovered a fluency in their communications with other creatures which enables smooth co-operation and safe intermingling. They testify that this offers humans access to some previously buried part of themselves. This phenomenon is part of a spectrum of intimate connection, which can include that with plant-life, landscape, and the elements. Within the psychotherapy profession, a version of this has also been arising. A growing number of therapists have been incorporating the intervention of, say, dogs, horses or wild creatures into their work, and the richness and resolution this has uncovered for some clients has been striking. A profound but hidden need seems to be met in all this. Indeed, the frustration of that need is a major factor contributing to our cultural discontent, sense of impoverishment, and drive to consume. When the yearning for connection is met the hunger to consume is less. Identifying this need offers the possibility of a nourishment which may be much needed in turbulent times to come. It may also be one of the less widely recognized tasks of therapy.

In childhood, certain people know a profound bonding and ease of communication with other creatures. One mother described to me the discovery of her daughter standing next to a massive bull alone in its field, stroking it fondly. On being told to carefully edge away, as the creature *was* a bull and not a cow, the child answered. "Yes, but it's a *nice* bull ..." Another woman remembers going into a stable alone as a child, and spending a long time talking peacefully with the horse within, to be surprised by the alarm of adults, who, arriving on the scene, whisked her angrily away, since this was the horse known to be a danger to anyone venturing into the stall. "The animals," she said, "were more 'real people' to me than the people were." A third woman, for whom a dog was a major caregiver in her infancy, describes the state of mind in which she and the other shared mutual understanding, as like "the use of a particular muscle."

Two points can be conceded to sceptics here. One is that such closeness often occurs when the bonding with the human caregivers is lacking, and that it can have a compensatory element. The other is that mutual affinity between children and animals is far from universal—witness the attacks on infants by savage dogs or the findings of Kellert (1996, p. 47) who deduced after years of research in many cultures that "children under six years of age are egocentric, domineering, and self-serving in their values of animals and nature ...". I submit that those points do not refute the validity of my respondents' recollections, but instead deepen the mystery of what differing circumstances produce such contrasting perceptions and occurrences.

In a newly emerging view of human evolution, our "domestication" of animals did not originate from some clever and deliberate manipulation by humans. Instead it arose from moments of meeting in which the curiosity, initiative and playfulness of animals has as much a part as the ingenuity of the human. Temple Grandin writes, "When wolves and people first started keeping company, they were on a more equal footing than dogs and people are today" (Grandin & Johnson, 2005, pp. 304–305). She even puts forward the idea of the wolves as *teachers* of humans, something close to the version presented in some Native American tales. "Wolves had complex social structures; humans didn't. Wolves had loyal same-sex and non-kin friendships; humans probably didn't, judging by the lack of same-sex and non-kin friendships in every other primate species today …. By the time these early people became truly human, they had learned to do all these wolfie things. When you see how different we are from other primates, you see how doglike we are …." (Grandin & Johnson, 2005, pp. 304–305). In a similar vein, Robert Miller (2005, p. 19) writes, "The first human to ride was probably a boy, mounting a foal he had befriended and bonded with." We have fostered a version of history which, in losing sight of the richness of animal soul-life, silenced their conversation and dulled our connection to their world. In the seminal volumes of Abram (1996) and Jensen (2000) they propose that there is a continuous conversation in progress between us and other life, awareness of which is largely repressed. Jensen presents this as the major difference between post-industrial and indigenous man. This conversation takes place through subtle responses of the body, of which our reliance on verbal communication renders us unaware.

Nevertheless, there are many examples of individual adults from "civilized" society who discover ways to mutual and lucid partnership with other creatures, and for whom this becomes their life's meaning. Sean Ellis (2010), for instance, has studied the culture and signals of wolf packs to the extent that he can intermingle with a pack, adapting the role of mediator in disputes between individual wolves. In the case of bears, the contrasting subjectivity of human perceptions is amply illustrated. Where one human sees attack as likely, another sees conversation as an option. Dr. Lynn Rogers in Minnesota has for forty years been learning how to keep the company of wild bears with whom he exchanges signals, goes on treks and makes physical contact. Many television viewers will have seen the incident in which wildlife photographer, Gordon Buchanan, who had been tutored in bear etiquette by Rogers, suddenly found a mother bear's jaws clamped round his thigh. "I knew it wasn't an attack," he says on film (www.bearstudy. org), "she was having a conversation with me, and telling me I'd gone too far." And indeed, responding to his composure, the bear very soon resumes her accepting behaviour. On the other hand Guy Grieve (2006), in his record of a winter in Alaska, assumes the likelihood of attack and the necessity of carrying firearms. His encounters with bears are tense and wary. And a third variation is provided by Timothy Treadwell who, confident of his rapport with bears after twelve summers in their company, was attacked and devoured in the ghastly circumstances narrated by Werner Herzog in his film *Grizzly Man*. (2005).

What I am emphatically *not* suggesting, therefore, is that nature automatically presents a sweet face if only humans cast prejudice and assumed superiority aside. I fully accept that it *is* often "red in tooth and claw". But to conclude it to be either chiefly one or the other is to become like the Kleinian child who splits "good mother" from "bad mother" when they are in fact one and the same person. Indeed, some commentators (e.g., Taylor, 2005) conclude that there was a moment of disenchantment when the human species lost its trust in the earth— and that we are still struggling our way towards an "adult" perspective beyond either idealization or distrust. The challenge for us is to come into a mature and authentic relationship with nature—but a relationship none the less. And this means facing the huge question of what it is in us that elicits from other creatures a particular response rather than another. In other words, what are the animals telling us about ourselves?

An acquaintance related the time when he lost his clearly defined managerial role on the farm where he continued to work. Until the change, the cows would go through the gate for him with no difficulty. But from then on, their co-operation vanished—as if they picked up his sense of loss of role. A different kind of reflection was narrated to me by a social services executive: "Colleagues sometimes find me ferocious, when I'm just focusing on the matter in hand. Afterwards I feel miserable about that. Then I saw a falcon on a handler's wrist. It was so superbly made to swoop and grasp, and it was utterly beautiful. Then I cried. I felt I could accept that I was just like that. It was what I was made for."

Animals' capacity for reflecting back to humans that which they may not be fully seeing has provided a rich vein of learning for a sector of the equestrian world. The last decade has seen a significant culture shift, which, Robert Miller (2005) has argued, amounts to a "revolution in horsemanship". Partly due to modern media, the skills of some particularly gifted and empathic individuals (e.g., Bill Dorrance, Buck Brannaman) have become more widely known and passed on. These skills are based on recognizing the messages we unwittingly transmit, and learning to read the messages the horse both sends and understands. Before absorbing them, I was an enthusiastic recreational rider like many, managing to take part in varied equestrian activities and "getting by", in spite of my horse frequently shying, pulling away and showing various nervy signs considered normal among confident riders with a "spirited" horse. But afterwards I was able to earn calm and willing responses which defied my previous expectations and astonished some observers. A nervous horse would come to me from the field rather than having to be "caught". A skittish horse would stand perfectly still to be mounted rather than stirring restlessly. And loose in the field together (me on foot) we could twist, turn, follow and chase in a way more akin to the sport of young animals than the conventional model of the horse/ human dyad. I also realized that the horse's previous nervy behaviour often embodied my rampant anticipation of high octane excitement, my disowned expectation. Many riders who have followed this path testify to the subtlety with which horses seem to pick up our very thoughts, even when we consider them hidden.

Certain principles emerged from this experience which suggest the beginnings of a new model of partnership with nature. The first is the acceptance that other life forms have their own agenda, and we have to understand it and recognize its validity. For example, horses' reactions are based on their survival strategy as a wild prey animal, and many human movements and gestures will confirm to them that we are predators, so the horse will be anxious in our presence. This isn't, in spite of the customary comments of many horseowners, "silly" or "stupid". For a creature relying on speed and alertness to survive, it is eminently wise. (Indeed, if the hegemony of the human species collapses under ecological strain, and predators again roam unchecked, horses will be proved wise to have maintained their tried and tested means of survival.) A second principle is to be clear about our own intentions, because otherwise the other cannot respond clearly. Furthermore, these must be put across in the other's language—a matter of breath awareness, body position, gesture, timing, and more. The difficulty here is that the animal often responds to our mixed messages and unconscious impulses. I have watched a woman who wishes to earn a horse's co-operation walk towards it with a pugnacious and combative gait of which she was quite unaware—and the horse shied away in alarm. So again we encounter the central principle that the other often reflects to us that which we disown.

This new approach, then, requires learning a different body language to that of civilized humans; a precise negotiation of spatial boundaries; a split second timing of response; recognizing the instincts of the wild herd animal in the horse; learning its particular body language of movement and gesture; a realization of just how subtle are the signals which other creatures pick up. I still cannot quite account for an incident I witnessed while watching Leslie Desmond (www.lesliedesmond. com), an exemplar of these methods, who argues that these creatures always register our fundamental intentions—and that therefore we need to be honest with ourselves about what they are. With her back to a group of loose horses, all new to her acquaintance, she announced to the watching humans that she would ask the horse on one side to lift its head, that on the other side to move its foot. In the next moment (with the woman still turned towards her audience) this happened. I checked with my two companions if that's what they both witnessed and this they confirmed. The marvellous reward for this approach can be moments of mutual trust, tenderness and affirmation that are heart-melting. For example, the sound of welcome on my arrival at the field, such as is usually only afforded to another horse. Such moments of mutual recognition have a completeness far transcending their practical context. Beyond that, there can arise moments of fusion that challenge rational explanation. In a celebrated passage, the poet Kathleen Raine (1975, p. 119) described an extraordinary experience when, seated before a hyacinth, she "became" the plant. "I was no longer looking at it, but I was it .... I dared scarcely to breathe, held in a kind of fine attention in which I could sense the very flow of life in the cells. I was not perceiving the plant but living it." Such moments also occur between human and animal. Indeed it is pivotal to some shamanic cultures that beings from different species can exchange form, and such occurrences as Raine's Hyacinth event verge on that territory.

This kind of partnership opens doors within the human. The mutual attention to a non-verbal conversation brings an awareness that is pure, entirely in the present moment, all-absorbing, tingling with aliveness. It awakens a sense of the invisible threads between us and other living things all around us. For some, the discovery of those threads has the impact of profound healing. Geoffrey McMullan was a soldier in the First Gulf War, witnessing grim scenes of combat, who found that the presence of birds offered a solace which preserved his emotional health. After leaving the army, he adopted an eagle owl as his companion and dedicated himself to introducing tracking skills and wilderness awareness to others for whom this marks a radical shift— for instance young people with histories of addiction and abuse (www. pathfinder-uk.com). Others have found that this particular client group are decisively helped by the company of horses. The clarity, for instance, with which these animals confirm the firm assertion of boundaries, enables some people to have their first experience of this.

Within psychotherapy theory and training the anthropocentric strand has been subtly pervasive (albeit with notable exceptions such as certain passages in Jung or in Freud's last diaries). Carl Rogers, (1951, p. 489) for instance, considered the independence and autonomy of humans to be a key feature of their position "high on the evolutionary scale", compared to "lower" creatures". Irwin Yalom (1989, p. 11) sees "fusion" as a flight from acknowledgment of our fundamental isolation. Fritz Perls defined maturity as "the transition from environmental support to self support" (Yontef, 1988, p. 55). More recently, Sebastiano Santostefano (2008, p. 514) wrote, "In spite of its popularity and momentum, I disagree with the basic premise that nature automatically has the power to enhance and heal a person's mental health." Such emphases veer away from a more intersubjective encounter with other life, or a sense of bonding or interpenetration between human and other.

However, some therapists have allowed the forgotten tongue to be heard within their practice, with a profound significance for clients. This has often occurred when they relaxed the frame that had hitherto characterized their work. Anita Sacks (2008) published several case studies following her accidental inclusion of her dog into the consulting room. She was adamant that the animal responded with great accuracy to the differing needs of her clients—offering one a light touch of the paw when they shed tears, but keeping distance with another client when they did the same, in a way that was entirely appropriate to the individual case. She argued strongly that the dog's contribution was catalytic in ways which her presence alone would not have been. She also argued that animals could be crucial figures in early biography, even the vital "hidden relative", the recognition of whom was crucial to a successful analysis. She also indicated that they could offer major relationships in current life situations, but that clients needed their therapists to be able to recognize this. She thus emphasized how far the therapist's picture of reality can restrict or liberate the process.

Whereas her approach became quite deliberate, and based on the well-established and intentional partnership with her dog, other therapists have welcomed the unexpected intervention of wild creatures. When one client sat down in the room and launched into a long but fruitless complaint against all those impeding her life, then just outside the window a feral tomcat began a long, loud, unrestrained yowl of displeasure. It seemed to resonate exactly with the client's state of mind, but expressed with less inhibition. The therapist fought back his laughter, but in the end gave into it and said, "Well, that says it all, doesn't it ..." The client also laughed, and this event marked a new facility in their alliance. With one of my own clients, a moment came when she was struggling with the discomfort of intimacy in the therapeutic partnership, and unwilling to let its reality be acknowledged. Just at the moment when she said "*relationship* is not a word I'd use for *this*," a fly began to whiz rapidly between us, making a figure of eight in the air above our two heads. We exchanged eye contact and I felt we were both aware of the symbolism, as if the fly was saying, "But this *is* a relationship." I decided not to speak, feeling that this would have been experienced as a disregard for my client's statement of discomfort with the notion. The fly did the work for us, taking our communication as far as it could go at that moment. Later in our partnership, when open verbal communication had become more comfortable, my client confirmed this version of events, *and* that she already had a particular affinity for flies and would often speak to them.

The field of equine-assisted therapy has been expanding at a rapid rate. In this, the response of loose horses to the client's presence is treated as the main intervention. Both clients and practitioners have recounted the accuracy with which the horse's behaviour can refer to the issues the client has brought; for instance, offering, withdrawing or resuming contact to someone who believes they are "poisonous to relationships", or displaying ferocity towards someone carrying great but disowned anger—which subsides as the human allows that anger. One client had years of different therapies in an effort to combat persistent depression, but found the interplay with horses was the only approach which shifted it decisively. Rupert Isaacson's story of the effect of horses on his autistic son has had such an impact that the monthly training courses in his methods are continuously full and the work arising from them steadily expanding (www.horseboyfoundation.org). Of course, all this raises the question of whether it simply represents a new version of the one-sided use of animals for human benefit. The degree of regard and respect for the creatures, the extent to which their needs are listened to and what understanding we have of those needs—this is precisely where the greatest exploration needs to take place. Various individuals active in the field, for instance Tricia Day of the Equine Assisted Qualifications organisation, are already pursuing this. These transactions with other creatures seem to include two distinct but overlapping phenomena. In one, the animal is like a messenger bringing us news which we need to hear—whether we see it as coming from our unconscious, or from the wider universe to our narrower awareness. In the other phenomenon, the animal calls us to encounter it as a fellow being in its own right, which can be healing for both parties.

It may seem as if I advocate here a model of relationship based solely on softness and openness. My experience, however, is that, partners in all intimate relationships require at times to be able to display a hard edge. This is clearly the case among animals themselves, who do not hesitate to bare their teeth when trespassed upon by fellow herd or pack members, let alone their territorial rivals or predators. However, when my human partner becomes resolute in confrontation there is also a relief—I know we have fully met; I am clear about what she wants. It often seems to be like that for horses, who seem to become at peace when clear leadership is shown. This is utterly different from being bullied, cowed or antagonized. Indeed, consummate horseman Mark Raschid asserts that true herd leaders are often quiet, unobtrusive, trusted—rather than the pugnacious individuals who may be more visible. As we reassess our relationship with nature and reject domination or objectification, this grittier area of emphatic assertion is easily avoided. I more often hear ecopsychologists avow their cherishing of the earth than I hear them recognize the tensions inherent in any partnership with her. But accurately used, this part of the vocabulary increases the fluency in the forgotten tongue rather than negates it. In her exploration of this theme, applied to the human/dog partnership, Margot Lasher (2008, p. 108) urges the use of a new word for this state of connection. She calls it *thirdness* because in it, competition for power has become irrelevant since a third entity has been created, beyond the two individual creatures involved.

Attending fully to the conversation in the forgotten tongue which is the language of such states, we can also recognize our transference—both negative and positive—onto other-than-human life. We can find moments of awesome mutual encounter. We can find the invisible threads that join us to the life all around us. We can begin to understand the assertions of Bateson, Jung, and others—including all those ancient storytellers I mentioned at the start—that mind and soul, rather than being confined within us, permeate the earth. And this also, rather than just human transactions alone, becomes the substance of therapy.

For it offers us a homecoming, all the more poignant because the danger of losing that home is becoming so imminent. In some visions of sustainability, animals are virtually eliminated from Britain. James Lovelock (2010) proposes that only a rigorous use of space for crop production and human habitation will ensure human survival. But this sounds to me like the old mentality in which the important thing about us is our particular species identity and its welfare, whereas actually it may be our quality of relating to, and belonging with, other life. I suggest this is at least as essential as our species survival itself.

CHAPTER SEVEN

Restoring our daemons

G. A. Bradshaw

Out of my experience ... one fixed conclusion dogmatically
emerges, and that is this, that we with our lives are like islands
in the sea, or like trees in the forest. The maple and the pine
may whisper to each other with their leaves, and Conanicut and
Newport hear each other's foghorns. But the trees also commingle
their roots in the darkness underground, and the islands also hang
together through the ocean's bottom. Just so there is a continuum
of cosmic consciousness, against which our individuality builds
but accidental fences, and into which our several minds plunge
as into a mother-sea or reservoir. Our "normal" consciousness is
circumscribed for adaptation to our external earthly environment,
but the fence is weak in spots, and fitful influences from beyond
leak in, showing the otherwise unverifiable common connexion.

—William James (1911, p. 204)

Physical fences were no accident in James' world. The psychologist and his brother Henry and sister Alice were raised when the American wilderness began to be stalked in earnest. Miners, hunters, and settlers poured across the continent in the last half of the nineteenth century. Ax blows and saws silenced Longfellow's murmuring pines and hemlocks. Miles of fences rapidly converted seamless landscapes into complex quilts of ownership. By the time James had died on the eve of World War I, the American wilderness was well underway to domestication.

My awakening to James' idea of cosmic consciousness occurred in another land, far away, in Africa, where humanity itself is said to have emerged. The African wilderness has also been beaten down by colonial possession. The damage there is pervasive. In the southern and eastern regions the most noticeable impact is the wildlife. Elephants, lions, and other iconic species teeter on the edge of extinction (Bradshaw, 2009). Compared to times before occupation, wildlife now is but a tiny fraction. However, western civilization seems to have a harder time retaining its mark on the African landscape compared to its American counterpart. There is something formidable in Africa's nature that defies complete surrender. Trucks fail to withstand penetrating red dust and piercing rocks and ruts of African roads and try as they might, western styles lose their identity of origin. Baseball caps and t-shirts reduce to mere accents when adorned. Yes, as innumerable travellers attest, Africa is powerful magic.

As often the case, revelation came through a seemingly unremarkable encounter. It happened one afternoon, while staying at a resort in southern Africa. A group of us sat in desultory conversation. The gusto of lunch had passed and day hung in the golden hours between morning's vigour and the wary vigil of night. Lions slept, baboons groomed, and wildebeest tails switched idly. The low laughter of maids and gardeners carried across spacious lawns. I left to fetch a notebook, but distracted, ended up wandering to the gift shop.

A young woman in her early thirties sat, legs crossed, on a stool at the lintel of the shop door. Her eyes flashed fresh white against a dark brown face. She wore a scarf of pale yellow turban-style that matched her dress. We exchanged smiles and she gestured to come into the store. There were the usual carved elephant statues, hippo bedecked t-shirts, postcards, maps, and trinkets for tourists eager to possess a piece of Africa. I spied a wooden rhino standing defiantly on the shelf. Head turned slightly toward the viewer, his armoured body was painted in bright lacquered colours of South Africa's flag: red, green, blue, gold, and black.

I bought the rhino and paid in fumbling currency, making an offhand remark about the beautiful countryside. The woman asked where I was from and within minutes, we sat beside each other, laughing in touch and voice. Perhaps it was just the relief of being with another woman after travelling for so many days with men. I have no recollection what we talked about, but she pressed me to come by the kitchen for tea later that day. Her name was Ngina.

By now my companions had emptied their glasses and stood outside the waiting truck and we were soon off in Land Rovers to look for lions. We were part of a group of scientists who were looking into the effects of a large-scale wildlife reintroduction process. After being extirpated, lions and other animals were being imported into the country to stock the parks for ecotourism. Post-apartheid South Africa was once again a popular destination for those eager to see its wild sights.

The truck made its way along brush-lined dirt roads bumping along until arriving at a nobby kopje, a small hill bedecked with jumbled boulders and prickly bush. We pulled over, jumped out, slammed the car doors shut, and headed up the hill. Finally making the top, the veterinarian with us handed me binoculars and pointed out over the plain to a pair of eagles circling above. There they were, looking larger, darker, more entitled than our North American Golden and Bald-headed cousins. I breathed in a deep lungful of the open blue sky, content and awed once again with Africa's wilderness.

It wasn't the time or place for lions so we turned back for dinner. Returning to my room, I threw down my pack and dug through the suitcase for clean clothes. Washing off the dust, I pulled on a fresh shirt, and hurried down to the kitchen. Ngina ran up with a big smile and clasped my forearms pulling me into the rondoval. Banging pots and clattering ladles intermingled with music blasting from a small radio on the window shelf. Faces looked up and hands waved as Ngina introduced me to the kitchen staff, then led me to a small table in the corner where we sat for tea.

She told me about her father who had gone to work in the mines, her mother who had stayed with the four children, waiting for his return while she did laundry sent down from the big house, and about her brother who was killed in the streets. "Times were hard," Ngina said. The conversation stopped, kitchen sounds dinned on. She stirred her tea and offered me more. I asked: "How did you manage?" Ngina put down her cup and dipping her head to catch my gaze, held my hands in her own, and said, "It was difficult. But I chose life over survival."

Time suspended and for a moment, fences dropped. Then, just as suddenly, we materialized back into separate shells of reality with the bark of laughter from arriving guests. Someone called to Ngina and she slipped from serious to gracious warmth. Excusing herself, she got up, gave me a strong embrace, and, looking back with a smile, went off to help serve cocktails. I joined colleagues under the African sky awash with stars.

The next day we were gone. I had looked for Ngina and asked of her whereabouts to say good-bye, but the kitchen staff said that it was her day off. I never saw her again. Her story stayed with me. Every so often, I would think back to what she had said about her choice of "life over survival." It wasn't until years later that I fully understood what she had meant. Unsurprisingly, insight came out of Africa as well, from the stories of compatriots.

Over the past decade, my work has focused on humanity's wild victims, individuals suffering from the west's hunger for possession (Bradshaw, 2009). There was the African elephant matriarch Echo striding across Kenyan plains with her kin struggling to avoid guns made greedy in the race for ivory. There were other mothers under siege (Bell-Scott, 1991): such as Dame Daphne Sheldrick, a survivor of attacks on the wildlife orphanage she founded outside Nairobi. For over half a century, she has pulled infant elephants from the oblivion of droughts and machetes. Dame Daphne and male Kenyan Keepers take the place of elephant allomothers, the kernel of aunties and siblings who rear generations of young pachyderms. These humans work diligently to hold the fences down and revive the psyches of elephants who must live in increasingly restricted patches of land surrounded by an ever-consuming human population.

Then there are the captives: animals forced behind physical barriers to stem their wildness. While stories of free living elephants often end in violence, almost all captives begin in violence. Medundamelli (also known as Dunda) provides an example of what goes on behind fences. At age two, the baby Dunda was captured after her family was slaughtered in Africa. She arrived at the San Diego Wild Animal Park and Zoo on September 18, 1971. One day, eighteen years later, the head zoo elephant keeper and four other men beat the female elephant with wooden axe handles while all four of her legs were chained to the extent that she was nearly prone. They sought to "discipline" her. Their actions were considered by authorities to be an "accepted technique": "You have to motivate them and the way you do that is by beating the hell out of them." Only after the second day, when Dunda accepted an apple did her punishment cease. A senior trainer described what he heard from one of the perpetrators.

> I asked how badly Dunda was hurt, and [he] replied, "Well, she rolled over on her side and moaned." I was appalled when I heard this and I still can't get it out of my mind. Lou described the area around Dunda as covered with the horrific flow of liquid feces. This condition of excessive elimination is a sure sign that the animal was in a state of fear and is easily recognized. An animal being disciplined for aggression would not do this until it had been frightened by the disciplinary action and would understand what was happening. Dunda was defecating and urinating profusely from the beginning .... This frightened, cornered animal was in a state of panic situation and had no idea what was happening to her. She was fighting for her life, and she must have felt it was over.

> (Quoted in Bradshaw, 2009, p. 193)

Ray Ryan was also a zookeeper at the Wild Animal Park but did not participate in Dunda's beating. He underscores the link between internal violence and that against nature.

> It's hard to describe, but when you eventually get control over someone who has no natural control and is so big, well, it makes you feel big. It is a real display of machismo .... You could show you were a real man if you could beat down a big powerful animal. And I could always tell who had had a fight with their wife the morning or night before. We have not changed much since cave days. Men are still beating up women, still trying to run the world with domination. And if you notice, all the elephants we work with are females.

> (Bradshaw, 2009, p. 167)

This theme of gender, sexuality, and violence is found elsewhere more explicitly.

An elephant keeper at the Oregon Zoo arrived under the influence of alcohol and chased Rose-Tu, a female child elephant of the age of five to six years. According to testimony, he swore at her and stuck an ankus (a metal pronged tool used to punish and control elephants) into her anus and pulled hard, after which she crumpled to the ground. He was eventually stopped but not before Rose-Tu was wounded more than 170 times. Her physical scars traced those inside. After being mated with a bull elephant and giving birth, Rose-Tu trampled the infant pachyderm. The baby survived but infanticide is not uncommon in captivity (Bradshaw, 2009). Other practices banned by the Geneva Convention are routine in zoos.

Nonconsensual captive breeding is increasingly common in zoos for the purpose of replenishing their "stock". Wildlife progeny are born into concrete jungles through masturbation by humans or other methods that "train" orcas and elephants to yield semen for artificial insemination. Chai, an Asian elephant at the Woodland Park Zoo, Seattle, has been inseminated 57 times. "Experts" from Germany were brought in to perform the procedure in 2005. To execute the insemination:

> A scaffold was erected at the business end of Chai so Dr. Thomas Hildebrandt, from the Berlin Institute for Zoo Biology and Wildlife Research, had easy access. Hildebrandt was covered in plastic protective gear and sporting a bike helmet he had equipped with ultrasound imaging goggles. Beneath Hildebrandt, his colleague Dr. Frank Goeritz sat on a stool in front of a bank of computer screens, electronic equipment and a tangle of computer and power cords. Tended by six or seven keepers who were there to keep both the Germans and Chai happy, the procedure involved Hildebrandt inserting an ultrasound probe into the elephant's rectum while Goeritz fed an endoscope (a light-emitting tube that allows visual inspection internally) into a larger catheter that had been inserted into Chai's "vestibule." The vestibule is just one feature of the animal's 10-foot-long reproductive tract that makes artificially inseminating this creature a challenge. An elephant's vaginal opening is not external but located inside this chamber called the vestibule. The vaginal opening is about dime-sized with two false openings, or pockets, on either side. And the bladder's opening is also nearby, and much larger, within the vestibule.
>
> (Paulson, 2005, n.p.)

The Zoo's general curator, Dr. Nancy Hawkes considers that "artificially inseminating an elephant is a technique that enhances animal welfare .... It's enriching" (PhinneyWood, 2011). Bruce Bohmke, zoo Chief Operations Officer points out that forty-eight of the total were "inseminations were done more than ten years ago. They weren't real inseminations. They were attempts to just inseminate by putting semen into the elephant, which was not, as we know now through studies in captivity, an effective way to inseminate them .... We have an effective way to inseminate them now and we have had at least one pregnancy because of that, which unfortunately ended up in a miscarriage" (MyNorthwest, 2011). According to Hawkes, the last two decades of failed inseminations occurred because "they were usually just insemi-nating the bladder" (Paulson, 2005). One can be sure that Chai knew the difference.

These survivors attest that nature has a face, wilderness is ensouled. They are testimony that cosmic consciousness still pulses. *God is alive, magic is afoot* (Cohen, 2001). Their power to move and live beyond the body speaks of a different consciousness, a consciousness that lives beyond survival. While some cry anthropomorphic tres-pass when Jeannie's or Chai's experiences are referred to as rape and Black Diamond's as slavery and torture, the truth cannot be denied. Science itself has dismantled the accidental fences (Bradshaw & Sapolsky, 2006; Marino, 2011) and opened the future to a new concept of consciousness.

Philosopher-cum-neuroscientist Alva Noë and others have given technical form to a Jamesian consciousness (Noë, 2009). This new con-ceptualization heralds a radical paradigm that upends conventional wisdom. According to the Berkeley professor, neuroscience made a wrong turn when it claimed that the cogs, bells, and whistles of the brain are what make us who we are. According to conventional wis-dom, consciousness—felt existence and experience—is produced by the machinery inside our heads.

Not so, insists Noë. What we thought was inside, is outside. Similar to how attachment theorists discuss psychological development, where how we think and feel is now understood to be the produce of a part-nered dialogue between parent and infant, consciousness is not a tape playing inside our heads but rather is created out of our minds with others. "Consciousness is not something that happens in us. It is some-thing we do" (Noe, 2008, n.p.).

In lieu of the idea of consciousness as by product of an industrious brain, Noë likens consciousness much like a dancer in dialogue with his or her environment. What we experience and what we know forms in tandem with and through the matrix of relationships in which we are immersed. We are not only what we eat, but who we see, touch, smell, taste, and hear. *The life is not inside the animal. The life is the way the animal is in the world* (Noë, 2008). James' fences—the perception and belief that each of stands separate from the natural matrix we call life—are indeed accidental, illusory, and ephemeral.

Noë vanquishes the ghost in the machine by elegant discussions of experiments on perception and things neurological. Yet there is much more. This theory of consciousness coalesces with many more concepts and experience to have emerged in the west since the turn of the twentieth century. Elsewhere, science has provided ample conceptual mortar and empirical bricks that give Noë's vision tangible form.

Over the years and in various fields, science has readjusted the theoretical lens it uses to examine nature. Instead of reductionism's method of divvying up the world into smaller and smaller pieces like so many matryoshkas, current theories have reversed this conceptual meiosis and reconciled differences. Nature is no longer pitted against nurture in the battle to determine who we become. Genes and the environment converse as we age and traverse the relational map of the world. Biological consciousness resonates with theories from other hyphenated neuro-fields.

Until recently, neuropsychologists and others who study human and animal behaviour pictured the mind as a something "owned" individually. What we think and feel are uniquely ours, indeed make up our personal identity. But over the past two decades, this school of thought has given over to a different understanding. How we develop from birth through adulthood, how and who we become who we are, depends not only on what we inherit through genes but on the people and things we experience. Each of us is still unique, but we take a little of the others whom we know with us—the good and the bad. Early relationships are most influential and if a child experiences abuse or premature separation from their parent, they can become traumatized, emotionally insecure, and psychological vulnerable. Our brains, our minds, and sense of selves are created through relationships. Our sense of self is relational.

Expanding even more, neuroscientists finally acknowledge Charles Darwin's thesis conceived over 150 years ago that root ethological observations in neurobiological models. What is observed on the outside plays out inside. All vertebrates, humans included, share common structures and processes that govern emotion and cognition. As a result, human identity is no longer calibrated by how different we seem to be from other animals; animal and human natures have merged into the new field of trans-species psychology, where study of human and animal is conducted via a unitary model of brain and mind. Fences erected separating species are, like consciousness, accidental. Even mind and body have signed a truce, agreeing to share territories. The result is that dualism's edgy divisiveness has been replaced by warm, fuzzy holism with Noë's model of biological consciousness providing a nice clean wrapper around these reconciling pieces.

On the surface, this out-of-the-box vision of consciousness merely appears to add one more item to an ever-growing list of new scientific theories. But it is much more grand. Biological consciousness has brought down the entire House of Descartes by showing that life itself, how we know it, and how we experience it, is relational at heart. In so doing, a new theory of life is born.

What we live is made up of moments, such as those shared with Ngina, collected and made meaningful over time in partnership with whom we interact. The cavalcade of relational moments gathered over a lifetime—a snippet of conversation, the flash of an image when eyes meet eyes, the sensation evoked when scent meets sensor—come together like so many water lilies in a painting by Matisse to create a single coherent narrative. It is this experience that we call consciousness. Life is not distributed in neat little organismic packets. Life is the hyphen between matter and spirit, the intake of breath between the bodily-shared world and inner essence and it happens out of our heads.

This alternative understanding of consciousness puts the stories of Ngina and the others in a completely different frame. Broken in body and scarred in mind, Jeannie, Dunda, and the others are not survivors. Yes, they had survived, but they chose to live. Their stories are not chronicles of survival eked out from misery, but a fierce embrace of life. Life. Life was the common thread linking Ngina and Noë's neuro-philosophical thesis. Life as relational existence, the drive to continue for someone or something and oneself that was not defined within the confines of a single mind. Whereas survival telescopes motive and meaning into the confines of the single social cell of the individual, the choice to live is the celebration of connection. I is we (Bradshaw, 2010).

The answer had been there all along, but western culture has generally focused on suffering through the lens of survival. A glance around at other cultures suggests that this is not a universal. Collective, interdependent cultures present a different psychology. In contrast to western human individualized, independent-based values, elephants, orcas, birds, reptiles, insects, and others indifferently labelled as "bio-diversity," as well as tribal humans who doggedly refuse to embrace "civilization"—lack the symptoms of moral decline now gripping industrialized society (Bradshaw, 2011; Narvaez & Gleason, 2011). Their reality does not seek to sever the thread of life. Their life is not inside; their life is the way the animal is in the world.

This understanding of connection comes not a second too soon. Members of the modern-postmodern era have become prisoners of sur-vival, transfixed with the struggle to withstand what humanity has cre-ated and memorialized in the litany of genocides, wars, and ecological destruction. Modernity is the recipient of that mixed blessing, "May you live in interesting times." Interesting indeed, if its definition includes environmental collapse, nuclear war, and psychological estrangement so profound as to make Post-Traumatic Stress Disorder (PTSD) epidemic. Even in the reassuring presence of thermostats to ward off climatic stress, refrigerators to smooth out erratic supplies of food, and other conven-iences that earmark modernity, life feels fraught with uncertainty.

Family intimacies and the loving embrace of a schoolteacher are corroded by suspicion of sexual abuse. The aspirin that relieved mus-cle pain and stuffy heads may cause death if poisoned by an angry employee. Blessings of harvest celebrated on Thanksgiving reveal as symbols masking violent appropriation of indigenous land and the recapitulation of past human genocides is diverted to millions of tur-keys. Wine, timeless juice of the earth, seemingly unburdened by wor-ries that beset other foodstuffs, has vanquished the cork that has graced Mediterranean soils even before the ancient Greeks. Almost every aspect of modern living seems to be fraught with contradictions. We cannot seem to escape existential quandary. Even while standing at the grocery checkout, we are faced with deciding the planet's future: "Plastic or paper?" No matter where we turn, what right we seek to amend, there seems to be a dark side that counters what good was intended. As a result, reality distorts in this cultural house of mirrors and we become strangers in our own home.

All these everyday inconsistencies and paradoxes overwhelm. Exter-nal guideposts—the ideas, beliefs, cultural practices, and pundits that have provided the psychological, political and practical architecture for knowing how to live—no longer align with what we experience or know.

Which is why a new paradigm, a new way of seeing, understanding, and living in the world is so desperately needed.

That is exactly what biological consciousness offers. An idea organically grown in the same minds and culture that created the problems to begin with. An idea that resonates with other philosophies that reigned before when the world was not darkened with the shadowy threat of nuclear war and animal kin did not flee at the sound of a human voice. A new concept has brought the possibility of consilience with life.

A new theory of mind is not an attempt to render matters of conscience and ethics into equations and numbers—far from it. Further, it would be folly to regard science as a knight in shining armour. As psychological seer C. G. Jung observed half century ago, science has cut both ways, offering ingenuity on one hand and a Faustian price on the other.

> As scientific understanding has grown, so our world has become dehumanized. Man feels himself isolated in the cosmos, because he is no longer involved in nature, and has lost his emotional "unconscious identity" with natural phenomena … Thunder is no longer the voice of an angry god, nor is lightening his avenging missile … No voice now speaks to man from stones, plants and animals, nor does he speak to them believing they can hear.
>
> (Jung, 1964, p. 95)

Noë's theory of biological consciousness brings welcome cheer that stones, snakes, and thunder have not stopped talking: we have stopped listening. While humanity may not wish to hear, nature is speaking loud and clear in the language of drowning polar bears and anger of unseasonable weather. Science's new understanding of consciousness and psyche is significant because it offers a way to connect what we knew to what we will discover. The ability to articulate the relationship between something as intangible as a worldview and the hands-on operations of thinking and method in customary symbols provides a reassuring cognitive trail of bread crumbs leading from the known world to an unfamiliar land unencumbered by past assumptions.

If we listen carefully to those forced by circumstance to relate to life through experiencing near death, such as Ngina, the elephants and chimpanzee survivors, it is possible to grasp what the difference between life and survival might look like. In writer Primo Levi's moving tribute to a camp worker at Auschwitz (Levi, 1995), there is a suggestion of what transformation from survival to life might be.

Lorenzo was a mason employed in France when his firm and its employees including himself were swept up by the Germans in 1939 and transferred to Upper Silesia. Primo Levi was selected by his Kapo to assist Lorenzo and another man to rebuild mortar and bricks walls that had been damaged by bombs. At first the two men did not recognize that they were both Italian, even neighbours from the Piedmont, one from Turin, the other from Fossano. Despite the possible lethal consequences, they spoke together. Levi describes how his life was saved with hidden soup and slices of bread and how he and his companion were astounded that in "the violent and degraded environment of Auschwitz, a man helping other men out of pure altruism was incomprehensible, alien, like a saviour who's come from heaven" (Levi, 1995, p. 113).

Levi tried to compensate Lorenzo for his help, but the man refused. "I offered to have some money sent to his sister, who lived in Italy, in exchange for what he did for us, but he refused to give us her address." He later learned that Lorenzo had helped several others but did not mention for fear of seeming to brag. Lorenzo was, indeed a saviour, but a "morose savior, with whom it was difficult to communicate" (Levi, 1995, p. 113).

When the war ended, Lorenzo made it out and walked for months to Turin where Levi's family lived. He lied to Levi's mother saying that all prisoners at Auschwitz were dead thinking that in all likelihood this was the case and that it would be better for her to resign herself to his death. Levi's mother offered Lorenzo money so that he could take the train. But again he refused.

After release from Auschwitz and five months in Russia, Levi returned home to Italy. He went to Fossano where he found Lorenzo living a nomadic life as a mason and sleeping in the out of doors even in the bitterest cold of the 1945–1946 winter. "I found a tired man; not tired from the walk, mortally tired, a weariness without remedy" (Levi, 1995, p. 117). The writer had secured a masonry job in Turin for his comrade, but Lorenzo would not take it. Soon thereafter, he became ill and with assistance from Levi's physician friends, was hospitalized. However, Lorenzo ran away and died a few days later. Levi closes his story with these words: "He was assured and coherent in his rejection of life. He, who was not a survivor, had died of the survivors' disease" (Levi, 1995, p. 118).

Levi makes the point that the man he encountered after the war was "mortally tired" someone who succumbed to "survivor's guilt" symptomatic of many who managed to endure whilst their loved ones and others did not. Later in his book of essays on the camps, Levi writes that "the worst survived, that is, the fittest; the best all died" (Freilander & Landau, 1999, p. 564). Himself beset with depression and memories, Levi's death forty years later is officially considered a suicide.

Despite the despair that possessed them both, the two men ultimately chose to live, not just survive. Levi captures it best with a tribute to his saviour friend when he wrote: "Lorenzo was a man; his humanity was pure and unblemished, and he was outside this world of denial. Thanks to Lorenzo I happened not to forget I myself was a man." It may be that past horrors and what they revealed about present-day humanity became too much to bear and overwhelmed, that life reduced to survival. But, at one point, Ngina, Lorenzo, and Primo Levi all chose to live. They lived because they dared to live for someone or something outside themselves: meaning and life sprang from the space in between.

Let us visit another story, *The Golden Compass* by Phillip Pullman (Pullman, 2003) to illustrate this natural alliance.

> In the magical world of the Golden Compass, every person has a life companion in the form of an animal called a "Daemon." A Daemon is a cross between the soul and a best friend. The animal form it takes is a manifestation of the host's true personality.
>
> (Dopetype, 2008)

This fantastic story tells of a young girl, Lyra, undertakes a journey with her daemon, Pan (short for *Pantalaimon* which is Greek for all compassionate), in a mysterious and dangerous parallel universe. There, in this strange but familiar world, everyone is born with a daemon. This soul-friend may take multiple forms. Pan morphs from moment to moment from delicate moth to mighty eagle to tiny mouse. But all is not well for girl and daemon. There are dark forces at work that threaten.

Lyra discovers that members of the General Oblation Board are conducting nefarious experiments that entail severing the daemon of kidnapped children. Violently separated from their daemons, the children, and their allies, wither and die. Along with her daemon and others including a giant polar bear king, Lyra rushes through diverse adventures to save her friends and allies.

Pullman lyrically paints the bridge towards the new, relational science and, intentionally or not, identifies the source of post-modern destruction in this beautiful but haunting tale. The present-day near-epidemic trauma gripping human and animals across continents, has grown from acts based on human-nature separation. Trauma emerges not only through the rampant spread of asocial, amoral behaviour and violence experienced at the hands of others, but as a self-inflicted embrace of western thought and action. Just as surely as the blade sliced through the gossamar connection of child and daemon, the concepts and agenda defining western society cuts humanity from its life source, its daemon, nature. The daemons that populate the natural world, those who make the untrammeled forests and mountains tingle with life and mystery wither and die. The world has been fragmented into brittle edges and wounded psyches by humanity's contraction into the bare bones of survival. Images of drowning polar bears, tribal Nukak suicides, and dolphins gasping for air in the wake of the Gulf oil spill remind us that extinction involves more than physical loss. A soul does not die alone.

The cure for society's malaise, wildlife extinctions, and environmental collapse will not come, as many argue, by *re*-connecting. One of ecopsychology's pioneers, Robert Greenway, points out that this goal is based on an implicit misconception because "the existence of a relationship implies separate entities or processes". Congruent with a number of other cultures, this premise maintains that humans and their minds have never been disconnected from nature and to imagine so is artificial. "Reconnections between mind and nature ... such as gardening, diet, natural dwellings, nature study, ... transformation via vision quests and long-term wilderness immersion, though often beneficial (usually pleasurable as well) are still based on the illusion—the initial distortion—that *minds* can be separate from *nature*" (Greenway, 2009, n.p.). Greenway's observation underscores something key, namely, that the present planetary state that we seek to heal has been achieved by *denying connection*. A false conceptual separation has cultivated perceptual and ethical distancing that has legitimized profound psychological dissociation as normative.

Now when learning of Harp seal mothers who have no ice upon which to give birth and garbage islands the size of states floating in the Pacific ocean, we understand that their plight is intimately linked with the hand that tosses away the plastic bag. When we bulldoze the earth to build a house, bear, deer, and squirrels watch *their* homes disappear under concrete. Their trees, their berries, and their bushes are appropriated with fence construction. We see wildlife through windows, thrilled to be so close, to feel *connected to nature*. Yet this yearning has not brought us closer after all. Suddenly, action made possible through psychological dissociation is no longer anonymous or blameless. Global collapse is personal.

The lesson: Life is only possible when lived in relational health. Saving nature comprises a radical conceptual and ethical transformation to embrace a relational living with nature, a trans-species paradigm. Only then will our daemons revive or have the possibility of revival will we as a species live.

This is not an easy process. The psychological mechanisms that permit a strident claim of love for nature to exist side by side with violence against wild flora and fauna, express deep archetypal conflicts precipitated by a crisis in human identity: an identity, Becker maintains, that is constructed by the denial of death (Becker, 1997). The crisis in ego-human identity manifests in violent eruptions such as those that have marked genocides of indigenous and animals. "The uprush of dark forces deployed itself in the individual … eventually breaking through the individual's moral and intellectual self control … [and] there was often terrific suffering and destruction" (Jung, 1946/1970, p. 242). This psychological crisis translates to the righteous battle for land and space leaving elephants, tigers, and other wildlife refugees in their own homes.

Nonetheless, if wilderness is to live inside and out, if we are to move from the isolation of survival to the inclusivity of life, then humanity must be willing to relinquish the protective shield that Cartesian privilege provided. The question is, will we let down our accidental fences, make ourselves vulnerable in the nakedness of unity, and join animal kin in life?

CHAPTER EIGHT

Ecopsychology and education: place literacy in early childhood education

Inger Birkeland and Astri Aasen

Introduction

This chapter will explore how ecopsychological ideas are relevant in educational settings. It is co-written by Astri and Inger together. Between 2005 and 2009 Inger was doing collaborative research on sustainable place planning in Tinn municipality in Norway. One part of the project focused on place-based learning with two kindergartens and four primary schools in the rural areas. The starting point for the collaboration was the question: What happens when we see schools and kindergartens as resources for the local community, and not only the local community a resource for children's learning and development? Through a focus on learning in, with, and for place, the research aimed at strengthening children's and adults' ties and relationships to each other and to the place and local community where they live.

At the time of research, Astri worked as a kindergarten teacher and department leader in Vesletun kindergarten, a private kindergarten that participated in the project. Astri had also enrolled on a further education course in pedagogical development for kindergartens at Telemark University College. She decided to use the project in Vesletun to write her project report. Astri received much praise for her work, which explored pre-school children's place-making activities in an innovative way (Aasen, 2007). Inger invited Astri to join in the writing of this chapter; Astri's contribution is mainly the section that describes how Moss Cottage was created as a good place to be for the three- and four-year-olds at Vesletun kindergarten. She documented the activities in the project and explored those aspects she saw were important for the children's play and well-being.

Ecopsychology has much to offer early childhood education. In this chapter, we will shed light on how we might educate young people for another way of living sustainably by developing place as a tool for education for sustainable development based in ideas from ecopsychology. We will elaborate on the connections between children and play in outdoors places, in particular in terms of attachment to the more-than-natural world. We suggest such play fosters the development of *place literacy*, which we understand as a particular competence, an ability to learn from direct experience to create meaningful understandings of what it means to be (in) place and what it means how to know our place and other places.

We start with a clarification of the relationship between place, education and ecopsychology. We will then turn to Vesletun kindergarten and the empirical example. Finally, we explore the theoretical implications and show how children's play may foster the development of place literacy.

Place, education, and ecopsychology

One way to talk about the valuation of nature and the natural environment in society is to talk about place. Place is a concept that mediates between body and mind, nature and culture (Birkeland, 2005, 2008). Humans are created from place, live and think with place and act towards place. As a meaningful location, place is related to the subjective and emotional attachment people have to places, understood in everyday life as particular and bounded areas of the surface of the earth (Cresswell, 2004). From an experiential and existential perspective, place is condition for being, it is often more lived than known, both tacit and discursive at the same time (Casey, 1993, 1996; Tuan, 1977).

As a condition for being, place acts as a condition for learning and development (Løvlie, 2007). Place is important for education through its constitutive role: place makes and teaches humans

(Catling, 2005; Gruenewald, 2003a, 2003b). An international social movement called place pedagogies sees place as important for working locally and connecting globally in order to develop place-responsive education for sustainable development (Gruenewald, 2003a, 2003b, 2005; Gruenewald & Smith, 2007; Somerville, 2007; Somerville, 2010). Local places are particularly effective tools for exposing children and youth to learn and think productively about different issues connected to sustainability, like diversity, equity and intercultural understanding, climate and environmental change, economic globalization and development.

Practitioners of place pedagogies have much in common with ecopsychologists by being interested in the way psychological and ecological worlds are related. Ecopsychology brings psychological principles and practices to the study of socialization, individuation and development in ways that avoid making the human being the single object and aim of psychology (Abram, 1996; Fisher, 2002; Kidner, 2002; Rust, 2004). Both ecopsychology and education are tuned towards change and development. Educationists and ecopsychologists agree that a transition to a sustainable future must include change, and in particular change of human beings' lives, values and practices. Such change must start in early childhood, for several reasons, but most importantly because values, attitudes, behaviours, and skills for sustainability acquired in this period may have a long-lasting impact in later life (Premling Samuelson & Kaga, 2008). Whereas psychotherapy and counselling concern development that has failed or gone wrong in some sense, education concerns facilitation of healthy development and can provide a wide range of possibilities for application of ecopsychological ideas since all children have a right to education.

Vesletun kindergarten and "Vassreisa"

The activities at Vesletun kindergarten are built upon three values: the natural environment of the local community, its traditions and its culture. As part of the research project, Vesletun worked with the three and four-year-olds with a focus on water. The adults named their project Vassreisa, which translates as the Water Trail and which is the end result of the project, as they created a public trail along the river Gøyst. The adults working in Vesletun kindergarten had much experience with outdoors work with pre-school children. In this project they wanted to focus on the three- and four-year-olds' exploration of some of the close surroundings of the kindergarten that had not been used before.

The starting point was to make a path along the river Gøyst involving different activities. The adults had agreed beforehand to let the children lead the way as much as possible and had planned that each group of children should find a place where they felt ownership and belonging. From previous experience the teachers in Vesletun knew that children did find good places to play in nature. Now, Astri thinks this is a competence the children in Vesletun have gained from playing in nature as soon as they could walk, which means that we think that three- and four-year-olds are old enough to identify a good place to play. Vassreisa was made by taking walks every week during one whole year. Vassreisa is now a popular outing for families, which takes about half an hour in all.

The trail has signposts with posters and other documentation of the work. There are displays of what was found and what can be done along the way: rocks, plants, places for rest, fishing, and having lunch, places to listen, wonder, and philosophize. There are particular areas for development of motor skills (like balancing, climbing), and there are connections to the camping grounds for youth organizations 4-H and the scouts. A version of a Herbie car was even made of scrap and things they found in the area, with a bit of help from the adults. The signposts were of course made by the adults and parents.

The making of a good place: Moss Cottage

Philosopher Martin Heidegger uses the term "clearing" in order to express how something can come into being. The clearing is where things and people can make themselves meaningful and significant. It is world-disclosing. It is not that we as humans produce the clearing, but that the clearing produces us as human beings, according to Heidegger (1996). The clearing is a place for self- and world-making, a process. Becoming a self can only take place in the context of a clearing.

Mosestua, or Moss Cottage, is the name of a good place, a clearing in the woods that was created by the three- and four-year-olds. Moss Cottage was also the name chosen by them. Moss Cottage was made in one day when the children started to walk down an old tractor road that led to a sandy opening, which had been cleared for laying down a cable. This was the place they called the Sand Castle. This day two adults went walking further towards the river together with three children. A few days later they went with the whole group to have a closer look at the area by the river. It was difficult to walk there. Some of the girls walked first. All manoeuvred a way through bush, branches, and grass.

Suddenly a nice, moss-covered field showed up with large, old trees along the river Gøyst, and without any of the adults saying anything some of the children stopped up and started to play, while others started to clear away twigs, sprigs and branches. The next time they came to this field the same things happened: some of the children cleared the area while others began playing. Tree roots became houses and buses. Some of the children found a tree that lay on the ground and started balancing upon it. What surprised the adults was the peace and serenity the children found. Without conflicts the children regrouped into smaller groups. Play lasted for a long time. When it was time to walk back to the kindergarten, they said they wanted to stay. After this first day, the adults saw that the children looked very much forward to coming back to this place. They had not yet found a name for the place, even though they had come up with many suggestions.

The making of Moss Cottage was not finished on this first day. What happened over the next week and months was a continuing creation of a place that simultaneously gave an opportunity for the development of young children's selves.

We will now look at some aspects of the children's play there that we think are important for their self-making. The children behaved in particular ways when they arrived there. They started to play and explained that they wanted to be there, play there, sleep there, and eat there. It had secret places: behind trees, roots, and pieces of wood, and it had place to be together: one can walk there together, play together, and eat together there.

It was obvious that it facilitated safety and security. An example of this is that the area could be used for naps. One of the girls in the group used to sleep for some time during the day. One day when she was asked whether she would like to go to the kindergarten to sleep or whether she would like to sleep in the forest, she said "sleep in the forest". She had a jacket tucked around her and she slept so well. The feeling of belonging and security was also demonstrated in other ways. The three- and four-year-olds got quite astonished one day when they found that some other children were playing there. "There's somebody in our place", someone said. At this point the place had been made "theirs".

The children always stopped when they arrived at Moss Cottage. It seemed they had no need to go further down the river. The area was perceived as a separate place with boundaries and content. Mosestua was perceived as having a start and an end: children were not sure where it started but had a clear perception of where it ended. Astri invited the children to talk about how they understood it. They did not give any meaningful answers as to where Moss Cottage started. When Astri asked where it ended, they gave more clear answers: "It ends in the dump over there", someone said. It was clear that the river was part of Moss Cottage. In addition, the place had a centre: the spot where they all had lunch.

At Moss Cottage the adults observed a variation of play that contributed to a variation of sense impressions. They saw that different sense impressions complemented each other and contributed to an integrated set of experiences of a situation, and of its meaning. Walking to Moss Cottage provided stimulation of the primary senses. Climbing on a root of a tree, picking a rock and throwing it in a river requires sense integration, or else the child will not master the activity. When the challenge is too huge, it will be overwhelming and uncomfortable for the child, and they would start crying, become passive or very dependent on support from one of the adults.

What about those children who did not have the motor skills to feel this much at ease, in being there, and playing? The adults of course wanted that the children should gain positive experiences from the trips to Moss Cottage. In the beginning, there was no path to Moss Cottage. It was a huge challenge for some of the children to walk there. Some days it rained, and there were bushes and grass clinging to their faces. There were insects, they slid on slippery rocks and got water in their faces. The reward was to participate in the play and camping life at Moss Cottage, have lunch there, and go to the river to drink water or throw sticks and stones in the water. Children who struggle in this way seem in Moss Cottage to use all their attention on mastering the terrain, but they will soon turn their attention to play when mastery is achieved.

For these children it is important to pay attention to the role of attachment, to the need for a sensitive, responsive and consistent environment for the developing infant. It is important that the child has had time to create attachment to one or more of the adults. Plenty of time and possibility to wonder and get to know the environment is important for the child.

One example: There was one boy who was at the back of the group together with an adult. He wondered about everything he saw. When he was to walk on logs to cross over some water he just stopped, put his hands down into the water, stirred it with a stick, and tasted the water. He didn't say a thing—he was just sensing his surroundings. Luckily the adult didn't say anything either, just waited until the boy was ready to go on to have new experiences.

Another example: There was also a girl who had little experience walking on uneven surface. It was a huge challenge for her to walk on rocks along the river. In the beginning she just used her feet and hands and crawled to get down to the water. Here, she sat on a rock, and remained sitting there looking at the other children. Only after a few trips to the river did she dare to move closer so that her boots were down in the water. Suddenly she was into the water with both feet: "Look, I got wet on my pants!" she said and smiled. After more weeks she gained good motor skills, Astri recalls. She could even decide what kind of new experiences she wanted to explore, there were more than enough challenges, and with a little help she sought out these challenges, and experienced the feeling of mastery in a new environment. Astri says that it may be frustrating both for adult and child to go through such learning, but development of skills is not reached without bodily, sense-based experiences and testing of those skills.

Self- and place-making in early childhood

We find support for Astri's observations in Louise Chawla's (1992) work on what types of satisfaction the environment provides for children: security, social affiliation, and creative expression and exploration. Chawla noted that the environment supports the development of self-identity both by affording opportunities for children to try out predefined roles in conventional settings and by offering un-programmed activity space. The availability of undefined space for children and youth of all ages is very important, Chawla argues. The need for undefined space is like a basic need for place for children (Nabhan & Trimble, 1994).

We also find the work of Edith Cobb (1977) important. In a famous passage from the paper on which her book was based, she wrote: "what a child wanted to do most of all was to make a world in which to find a place to discover a self" (Cobb, 1959, p. 540). Cobb writes that the world of the imagination for children is related to the biophysical, external world. The imagination is the starting point for the ability to act creatively, for creative acts and thoughts. The reality of the child is in itself interplay between inner and outer worlds, with the imagination as a driving force for development and social interaction. In this sense, all children are makers of their own places and worlds. Cobb describes such activities as world-making activities, and argues that it is crucial for these to be developed.

Even if there are many studies that focus on the role of place for children (Chawla, 1999, 1992; Hart, 1979; Nabhan & Trimble, 1994; Olwig, 1989, 1991; Rasmussen, 2004; Scourfield, Dicks, Drakeford & Davies, 2006), most do not problematise a dualist construction of place where place is object and not subject: place as not me. From our observations of children's play at Moss Cottage, we see that place appears as a relationship and process, neither totally subjective nor absolutely objective (like topological location). Our example shows how Moss Cottage is a part of the children's everyday world, their place-world, where place is more like a dynamic interplay—a relational phenomenon—between the developing children and their environments.

We are interested in using this observation to develop a language for describing small children's learning and development in relation to places in nature. We know that children's interaction and play in undesigned nature positively influences their motor skills (Fjørtoft, 2001, 2004). In our research, we have seen that play in undesigned places in nature affords children's development of sustainable selves, which we locate as a relational field, not completely subjective and not completely objective. We have observed that small children form relationships to their significant others. Small children are able to form sustainable relationships to their others, human or more-than-human, through play, and early childhood is thus very important for the overall work for sustainable development. The children who developed Moss Cottage were ready to become and to be place. But they were not making Moss Cottage with a dualist sense of place in mind. We think that place is something that becomes for and in children in the field in between the children and their environments, that field D. W. Winnicott (1971) describes as transitional space.

According to Winnicott, it is genuinely human to work and rework inner and outer worlds, in terms of a "perpetual task of keeping inner and outer reality separate yet interrelated" (Winnicott, 2007, p. 3).

This work does not consist of the same thing throughout the course of life. All humans begin in formlessness and all humans need to gain the feeling that they exist in their own right as whole human beings. For a newborn baby it is perfectly normal that there is no differentiation between inner and outer worlds. Transitional space is not an inner world, which can be studied only subjectively, nor is it an outer world, which can be studied objectively. In the journey from subjectivity to objectivity, so to say, transitional objects are very important, and the whole transitional field is important, as a place of self-making for the child. Moss Cottage is providing a multitude of transitional objects: it is a transitional space.

We would like to connect the idea of transitional space to the concept of nature as a holding environment for the child, with some perspectives on attachment. We think that attachment is important for the development of sustainable selves. It seems that the children at Moss Cottage create attachment not only to care-takers and adults, but to the more-than-human world. In attachment theory it is generally assumed that things or material objects are of less importance than people. This is what Harold Searles, the psychiatrist, is questioning when he talks about the non-human environment as meaningful for attachment. Marianne Spitzform has shed light on Searles' writings (Searles, 1960, 1972; Spitzform, 2000) with the term "ecological sense of self", which refer to the unfolding human experience of self in relation to the non-human world.

The non-human environment is there, it moves and changes through its own life process, and provides a secure environment. We use the term "more-than-human" instead of "non-human" as Searles did, in order to rethink the premise that psychology begins and ends with the idea of the human being as this has been understood in a modern and dualist sense, apart from nature and the world. Ecopsychology can and should begin with human becoming alongside the becoming of many other terrestrial beings and agents in a more-than-human world. Such reflections are based on the questioning of the human that happens within post-humanism (Haraway, 2008), which is a way of dealing with the relationship between humanism and the figure of the human. Human beings are created through social relationships that are both human and more-than-human.

The child needs to feel the environment as trustworthy and safe, as being able to 'hold' the child, and this environment's stability makes a difference for the continuity of experience and a developing sense of personal identity for the child. Things in the natural environment can be simple or complex, they can be manipulated, provide practice ground, offer relief from certain tensions, and can be a source of solace and companionship. Sometimes such a stable environment provides a refuge from a social environment that is more unstable and manipulative, and less trustworthy. The more-than-human world may sometimes be free from some of the pressures of social interaction or the effects of society.

We do not want to idealize nature. Ideas and interpretations of nature are not reducible to the "real" nature they depict or refer to (Castree, 2005). As adults, we are not free from human projection of meaning upon nature and our socialization into interpreting nature in particular ways that are culture-specific. Nature, or what we think nature "is" and how nature is experienced, differs very much around the world. Humans, communities and their environments are connected and have developed within different technological and social interventions in late modernity, and this means that it is important to contextualise educational work based in ecopsychological ideas. We do want to stress, however, the ways in which nature plays an important role through its bare being and becoming, as it is there, always, relatively constant and changing at the same time. It is the lived nature of place that should be in focus.

Place, learning, and development: place literacy

In early childhood education, global issues and environmental problems do not make sense in the same way they may do in primary, secondary or higher and adult education. Early childhood pedagogies are well aligned with education for sustainable development (Pramling Samuelson & Kaga, 2008). Place is often an integrating framework for teaching and learning in terms of working with the outdoors environment. Use of interdisciplinary approach, holism, use of the outdoors for learning, integration of care, development and education, learning through concrete experiences and real life projects, and involvement of parents and communities are core ideas in education for sustainable development in early childhood. In early childhood education, we think that the most important insight is to provide children with opportunities to become fond of nature and to develop emotional and positive attachment to the natural environment. This can be done in a variety of ways.

Environmental educator David Orr has used the term "ecological literacy" to pinpoint one of the failures regarding the environment (Orr, 1992). Western society is not literate regarding the natural environment, according to Orr. Literacy in its narrow sense is becoming increasingly important today because education plays a particular role today for creativity, innovation, and new economic growth. There is a danger that one forgets to ask what literacy, what competences and skills, are essential for meeting future challenges. Literacy is recognized as important in development and for development, but whose development are we talking about? Are we talking about business-as-usual development or sustainable development for humans and communities? And what kind of literacy? How can attachment to place be important in literacy? Margaret Somerville argues that place literacy could be very important for a sustainable future. Place literacy is not another subset of multiliteracy. It is an approach to literacy that should be underpinned "by a new epistemology and ontology, a new way of understanding what it means to be (in), and to know our places" (Somerville, 2007, p. 162). This is in my view literacy for sustainable self-making.

The term "place literacy" is an attempt to open up a meaningful discourse for the role of the more-than-human in children's self-making. We understand it as a particular competence, the ability to learn from direct experience of place and create appropriate responses towards place. It is a way to address a shared human condition so that we teach each other adequate responses to the environment. Place literacy is a concept that relates well to Unesco's aims for education for sustainable development. By looking at self- and place-making as interrelated, we can develop relevant and authentic learning arenas for pre-school children. We want to be able to talk about the big issues, like climate change and environmental destruction, as something that concerns children's self- and place-making. But we want to do this by working locally to cater for healthy, caring and positive experiences. It is our view that for many adults concerned with environment and environmental policies, a horizon of disaster, doom and gloom has eclipsed a healthy cultural response towards climate change issues. The future is not about doom, but about creating the conditions for development that is sustainable also in a culturally and self-sustainable sense. Place-based work in early childhood education is in this way one of the important uses of ecopsychology.

PART III

THE VIEW FROM POSTMODERNISM

CHAPTER NINE

The ecology of phantasy: ecopsychoanalysis and the three ecologies

Joseph Dodds

Dreaming at the precipice

We are in a planetary pyramid scheme, getting into an ecological debt from which there can be no bail outs. We live on a finite planet with an economic system predicated on unending growth. Scientists estimate human demand already exceeded the biosphere's regenerative capacity in the 1980s (Wackernagel et al., 2002, p. 926), yet somehow this just doesn't hit home, our behaviour doesn't match our knowledge. Why? I draw on ideas from my recent book (Dodds, 2011) to explore the possibility of a nonlinear ecopsychoanalysis with which to respond to a climate at the edge of chaos.

The current crisis is not only an ecological crisis, but a crisis of theory. While our fields of knowledge continue to fragment into ever more narrowly defined subjects, climate change embodies a world of unpredictable, multiple-level, highly complex, nonlinear interlocking systems. There is a need for a "meta-theory" able to integrate the disparate strands: not a "master-theory" so distrusted by postmodernists, but rather what Bion (1984) calls the work of linking, which he connected with the alpha function and the dreamwork. Bion describes the building of links between mental objects, and the attack on linking characteristic of psychosis. When "alpha-function" is compromised, we are left with undigested fragments of experience or "beta-elements" incapable of being woven into the tapestry of our psychic landscapes. From this perspective academia has divided human thought into a schizoid fragmented space. We require a means of linking diverse elements together without losing their specificity.

The ecopsychoanalytic approach argues that we need the new sciences of complexity and the philosophy most suited to deal with this often counter-intuitive way of thinking: Deleuze and Guattari. I argue that there is as much a need to bring nonlinear and ecological thinking into psychoanalysis as for a psychoanalytic approach to ecology, taking seriously the possibility of thinking in terms of what Guattari (2000) called in his final book, *The Three Ecologies* of mind, nature and society.

Science has developed with the concept of linear systems but is increasingly realizing that these represent a special case in a fairly nonlinear world. We can think about this using the concept of *attractors,* points towards which a system tends to converge. Any variation in starting point within the *basin of attraction* is cancelled out by the powerful pull of the attractor. Within limits as our global climate temperature increases, *negative feedback* processes act to draw the system back to a more central point, the *point attractor* (other more complex attractors include "periodic" attractors, and "strange" or "chaotic" attractors). However when moved towards the edge of the basin of attraction we reach *bifurcation* points, where non-linearities rule as the slightest difference in starting conditions or tiniest fluctuation causes a radical shift, a *phase transition* to a new attractor or set of attractors.

Scientists suggest that our climate may well be approaching such a tipping point, with potentially lethal *positive feedback* processes no longer capable of being damped out. A nonlinear perspective is crucial not only for climate science (Anisimov, 2007; Sawaya, 2010) but also for the psychology of climate change. Our familiar ways of thinking imagine there must be a linear relationship between CO_2 emissions and warming, that warming will happen at a measured pace, and there will always be time later to turn it around. This is a failure in our mental ecology which leads, via pathological forms of social ecology, into a potential catastrophic collapse of natural ecology.

Psychoanalysis and climate change

Freud (1927) claimed civilization arose to defend us against nature, but that the aim of achieving total control over either our inner nature or the outer world was a dangerous illusion, an illusion of control and mastery to protect us from feelings of helplessness and fear in the face of the awesome power of mother nature, our fear of acknowledging dependency on this largest of "holding environments", the ultimate "environment mother" (Winnicott, 1987).

Freud's "eternal adversaries", Eros and Thanatos, are unfortunately unlikely partners in their destructive effects on nature. Both aspects of Thanatos feed into our destructivity, the active destructive desires and the desires for non-existence and annihilation. We can see the "nirvana principle" in our virtual indifference towards the world's sixth great mass extinction, and in the apocalyptic rhetoric of the environmental movement and recent "eco-disaster" films. For Žižek (2007, n.p.) "'The world without us' is ... fantasy at its purest: witnessing the earth itself retaining its pre-castrated state of innocence, before we humans spoiled it with our hubris". Eros, through over-consumption and overpopulation, also works towards the potential collapse of the biosphere (Bigda-Peyton, 2004, p. 251). However, in the form of "biophilia" (Wilson, 2003) Eros can work to reinvigorate our love of nature. This may be crucial if we are to turn back from the brink (Weintrobe, 2010).

Climate change is deeply threatening and involves irreversible loss not only of natural ecologies, but also of social ecologies. Terror Management Theory (TMT) (Becker, 1973) suggests world views function as cultural-symbolic defences against death anxiety. The ecological threat would therefore lead us to cling more tightly to our world view, but the latter is also threatened by climate change, leading in turn to greater death anxiety. It is always difficult to let go of a way of life, especially when it is most required. To explore climate denial further, we can turn to a joke Freud (1905, p. 62) used to illustrate the logic of the unconscious. When a man is told he should replace a pot he borrowed and returned damaged, he refuses, claiming: 1. I returned it undamaged. 2. The hole was there when you gave it to me. 3. I never borrowed it! These mutually contradictory answers alert us to unconscious processes united by the motivation to remove the blame and prevent need for action. The joke's formula corresponds well to many arguments against action on climate change (also often argued simultaneously).

1. *There's nothing wrong with the climate kettle*: The first set of phantasies are basically paranoid (the UN destroying our freedom, capitalists trying to stop poor countries developing). The second claims "the evidence is not conclusive" (the IPCC's "unequivocal" is not unequivocal enough)

appears more logical, but when compared to other risk evaluations the irrationality becomes apparent. Few would agree to play Russian Roulette without suicidal inclinations even with 90% certainty of not getting the bullet, yet we are playing Russian Roulette with the entire planet with far worse odds. 2. *There was a hole in the planet when you gave it to me.* Here there are two contradictory claims. Either "it's not humanity's fault" or "it is caused by *other* people (e.g., India, China), not me, so there's nothing I can (or should) do about it". Both support unconscious deflection of guilt but do nothing to stop the disastrous consequences of climate change so we would still need to take urgent action. One psychoanalytically interesting conclusion is at times people can fear guilt more than their own, or everyone's, destruction. Finally, 3. *There is nothing we can do about it* is also found in burnt out environmentalists filled with feelings of despair and disempowerment, the "we're completely fucked" defence (Rust, 2008), allowing us to give up thinking.

The different arguments relate to defences against specific anxieties. *It's not happening* involves more psychotic defences against paranoid-schizoid anxiety (extinction, annihilation). *It's not our/my fault* involves neurotic defences against depressive anxiety (difficulty in acknowledging human culpability and guilt). *There's nothing I/we can do about it* is closest to recognizing the problem but without realistic reparative possibilities the individual is stuck with the despair and pain of the depressive position without hope. As Searles (1972, p. 366) put it, "instead of feeling isolated within emotional depression, one feels at one with everyone ... in a 'realistically' doomed world." Such defences need to be understood not only individually, but as involving unconscious alliances (Kaes, 2007) created socially, through small interactions at all levels giving rise to *social phantasy systems* (Jaques, 1955). In complexity theory this is an example of *self-organization*, where lower levels interact to form higher level structures embodying emergent properties which then feedback to lower levels in a process of ongoing recursivity.

Object relations and ecological relations

Object relations, emphasizing the self as constituted in and through relational webs, moves psychoanalysis in an ecological direction, since ecology is above all the science of relationships, interactions, and interdependencies. The object relations model of development means moving from "absolute dependence" (or "symbiotic unity") to "mature dependence" (Fairbairn, 1992), suggesting an ecological vision for a more mature culture, which sees the self as inextricable from its relations to other beings, to ecological webs, and to the earth. For Searles (1972, p. 368) "an ecologically healthy relatedness to our nonhuman environment is essential to the development and maintenance of our sense of being human" which has become "so undermined, disrupted, and distorted, concomitant with the ecological deterioration, that it is inordinately difficult for us to integrate the feeling experiences, including the losses, inescapable to any full-fledged human living".

Traditionally, psychoanalysts would analyse environmental concern as reflecting "deeper" feelings relating to human "objects", internal and external. But human conflict could equally be a displacement from anxiety concerning the environment. If we broaden Winnicott's "holding environment" to include the holding environment of the earth, we can understand how realizing the enormity of the crisis can threaten psychological disintegration and collapse. Not only is environmentally damaging behaviour a form of addiction (e.g., consumer items functioning as Kohutian selfobjects to shore up a fragile self), but addictions can also arise to deal with anxiety concerning our damaged world (Bodnar, 2008; Randall, 2005; Rust, 2008a). Psychoanalysts need to recognize that engagement with ecology is not only for "applied" psychoanalysis, but is crucial to its core clinical domain.

Since early attachment processes powerfully affect later life (Bowlby, 1988; Green, 2004), we might understand the phrase of "Mother Earth" as indicating that our experience with the planet relates in some way to our experience with our (m)other, not only involving feelings of love and being held. A Kleinian perspective might suggest a phantasy of an infinitely giving earth-breast we feel entitled to suck on with ever increasing intensity without limit. Unable to tolerate weaning, our response to the ecological crisis includes rage, envy and destructiveness. Mishan (1996, p. 59) claims when we defend against "recognition of our relationship to the natural world, the consequences … are manifest in the external world in continued environmental destruction, and in the internal world in the form of persecutory guilt". This can take the form of hatred and omnipotent attacks and spoiling of the earth-breast. Meltzer's (1967) "toilet-breast" concept is useful here: the breast is not only a provider of nutrition, but a place into which we expel unbearable states of mind.

Various developmental levels may intersect with our problematic relationship with nature. In terms of Klein's (1987) paranoid-schizoid position (PS) the paranoia surrounding climate change allows the "bad sadistic enemy" to be fought against "not in the solitary isolation of the unconscious inner world, but in co-operation with comrades-in-arms in real life" (Jaques, 1955, p. 483). The apocalyptic threat of climate change may evoke extremely primitive persecutory anxieties leading to omnipotent defences to protect against feelings of helpless and fragmentation (Jordan, 2009a). Searles (1972) points out there is now a certain objectivity to schizophrenic "end of the world" fantasies. This can lead to many intuitively feeling ecological warnings are "crazy" and we shouldn't listen to them, partly out of fear of contamination, and partly because they touch a "crazy" part of all of us. The ecological version of Klein's (1987) depressive position (D) involves mourning for environmental destruction, guilt for the damage done, a growing awareness that the lifestyles and civilization we are so proud of are also causing such damage to planetary ecosystems, and a reparative drive to restore, repair and recreate the lost and damaged world (internal and external).

At the phallic-Oedipal level, Searles (1972, p. 364) identifies phantasies of eliminating Oedipal rivals (including our children and future generations) and the "moralistic" tone of some ecological writing, involving the projection of the writers' Oedipal guilt, accusing us of raping mother earth "and now we are being duly strangled or poisoned ... for our sin". Through relentless advertising, possessions such as cars have become a symbol of genital achievement (Randall, 2005). Relinquishing such symbols of (male) genital primacy feels like castration.

The environmental crisis makes us face the traumatic aspects of transience, that nothing is permanent. Drawing on Freud's (1915) concept of anticipatory mourning, we might expect individuals and societies to adopt positions of consciously not caring about the environment or even our species survival, or becoming actively destructive and self-destructive, as a defence against the mourning yet to come. Alternatively we may engage in a premature anticipatory mourning, falling into a despair preventing the very action which might avoid the feared loss, while there is still time.

Freud (1916, p. 306) urges us to face with honesty and courage the fact that a "time may indeed come when the pictures and statues which we admire to-day will crumble to dust … or a geological epoch may even arrive when all animate life upon the earth ceases". In the face of the enormous pain and fear the ecological crisis evokes, we need to find effective means of reparation, to restore and recreate the damaged world inside, and out. Without hope that meaningful, as opposed to manic, reparation is possible, we have only the choice between denial, madness, and despair. As psychoanalysis opens itself up to a greater awareness of the web of life, the object-related self and the narcissistic self needs to be viewed as developing alongside the ecological self.

Dark ecology

Ecopsychology's rhetoric of overcoming alienation through reconnecting with nature and allowing ourselves to feel "our pain for the world" (Macy, 1995, p. 241) is very appealing, but there are dissenting voices. Morton's (2007) call for an "ecology without nature" uses ecocriticism to deconstruct the ecological imaginary, including concepts of "Nature" held within parts of the ecology and ecopsychology movements. This approach can lose sight of how the ecological crisis ultimately reaches beyond any linguistic constructions, and is not itself a "text" which can be "deconstructed", but is a "Real" beyond language, traumatically rupturing the Symbolic order.

Environmental and ecopsychology writings often emphasize alienation from nature and call for psychological and spiritual renewal through reconnection with natural "life-worlds". Žižek (2007) interrogates this claim, arguing that it is our very embeddedness in our life-world that prevents us from seeing the problem. When we flush the toilet, subjectively the waste simply disappears through the u-bend from our reality, into a non-space, or that fecal space Meltzer (1992) calls the "claustrum". Our sense of immediate living prevents us seeing the effects of our waste or the complex paths into which it flows. Žižek argues we therefore need more alienation from our immediate "life-world" in order to better grasp the complex abstractions that we are involved in.

Žižek additionally argues that our very idea of "Nature" is a problem: nature as a homeostatic, harmonious Gaia where all parts fit and interact perfectly with the whole, disrupted and destroyed through techno-industrial hubris. This vision of nature, he argues, is "a retroactive projection of man … 'nature' is already, in itself, turbulent, imbalanced"

(Žižek, 1991, p. 38). According to Žižek (2007), we need to "accept the utter groundlessness of our existence". Nature is thus "deprived of its impenetrable density, of what Heidegger called 'earth'", appearing as "a fragile mechanism which, at any point, can explode in a catastrophic direction." This doesn't mean humans have not caused immense damage, but that the idea of a holistically pure "world without us" is false, and dangerous. For Žižek (2007) "there is no big Other (self-contained symbolic order as the ultimate guarantee of Meaning); there is also no Nature *qua* balanced order of self-reproduction whose homeostasis is disturbed ... by imbalanced human interventions ... what we need is ecology without nature: the ultimate obstacle to protecting nature is the very notion of nature we rely on."

Morton (2010a) relates a common situation, reflecting the fate of a traditional part of social relations, "the weather conversation", in the light of global warming. The weather, "that nice, neutral backdrop that you can talk about with a stranger ... has taken on a menacing air" producing a "failure of the normal rhetorical routine". The weather (as background to our lives) no longer exists but is now felt as merely a symptom of a more disturbing phenomenon, "climate". Furthermore, once the seemingly stable background we call "environment" has dissolved into all too contingent accident, the foreground itself disappears. Rather than retreating into the comforting fantasy of Hobbit-like Heideggerian "life-worlds", Morton (2007, p. 186) encourages us to embrace *dark ecology,* based on a "melancholic ethics", with interesting potential connections with a Kleinian ecopsychoanalysis shorn of certain of its ontological pretensions.

Of course simple disillusionment is not the answer (Winnicott, 1987), and there is a real danger that ecocritique can remove a primary motivation of the environmental movement. Talk of "nature no longer existing" may feed into psychological defences by arguing that as "nature" is already so altered by human activity that "wilderness" in a pure sense doesn't exist, there is no reason to protect a nature which has no substance. Despite this, ecocriticism crucially helps us become more aware of how we use 'nature' psychologically, so our projections and phantasies don't get in the way of more genuine environmental practice.

One fundamental problem with ecocriticism lies in the difficulty of deconstructive or postmodernist approaches in giving ontological space to nature and the material as anything other than an effect of language, or its negation as the "Real". With their mixed semiotics, Deleuze and Guattari—whose strange assemblage will be written here as Deleuze I Guattari, following Herzogenrath (2009)—offer a way out. Herzogenrath (2009, p. 3) claims a Deleuzo-Guattarian ecology "allows for the incorporation of the workings of the 'repressed' of representation... of the 'real', of 'nature' ". According to Bonta and Protevi (2004, p. 4), Deleuze I Guattari's political engagement with complexity theory "helps break free of the postmodernist trap by rethinking sense and reference, and in so doing shatter the postmodernist equations of signs with signifiers". This provides a vision of sign systems beyond the linguistic register, where "at critical thresholds... physical and biological systems can be said to 'sense' the differences in their environment that trigger self-organizing processes" (Bonta & Protevi, 2004, p. 4). A non-linear reading of Deleuze I Guattari offers not a flight into mysticism, or a naïve positivist reductionism, or even a postmodernist play of signifiers, but an "intelligent materialism", a "geophilosophy".

Complexity theory and ecopsychoanalysis

Deleuze I Guattari (2003a) describe two kinds of science: *axiomatics* (royal science) and *problematics* (minor—nonlinear—science). *Axiomatics* approaches matter through the linear stratified forms of equilibrium (*stratas*) which can be studied through the "molarizing" process of averaging. Problematics concerns "intense" morphogenetic processes operating far-from-equilibrium, involving lines of flight, bifurcations or becomings, which open the system's creativity. Complexity and chaos theories have strong implications for psychoanalysis (Piers, Muller & Brent, 2007), and have "changed the basic concept of the human mind itself" (Guastello, 2004, p. 4), providing a new way of thinking about the three ecologies.

Phase space represents all possible states of a system, definable by its *attractors* (see above) and its *dimensions* representing the degrees of freedom or ways of changing a system. In Deleuze I Guattari an *abstract machine*, or *virtual diagram*, is the phase space portrait which "lays out what an assemblage can be made out of and what it can do" (Bonta & Protevi, 2004, p. 48). Psychoanalysts might consider how dreams draw a virtual diagram of the psyche, a fractal graph of the mind.

Self Organization (SO) occurs when global patterns *emerge* from interactions among lower level components rather than being imposed from the outside. For Palombo (1999, p. 24) SO is "the most significant missing ingredient in psychoanalytic theory", and shows how small pieces of insight self-organize into ever larger structures. SO functions as an *abstract machine* (Deleuze I Guattari, 2003a, p. 514) embodying a structural pattern of relationships in many separate domains, including all three ecologies: "Every abstract machine is linked to other abstract machines, not only because they are inseparably political, economic, scientific, artistic, ecological, cosmic—perceptive, affective, active, thinking, physical, and semiotic—but because their various types are as intertwined as their operations are convergent".

Chaos theory portrays chaos as far from the opposite of order and structure, undermining this fundamental binary of our civilization (Freud, 1930). This is consistent with Deleuze I Guattari (2003b, p. 118) who see chaos as productive, "defined not so much by its disorder as by the infinite speed with which every form taking shape in it vanishes ... not a nothingness but *a virtual*, containing all possible particles and drawing out all possible forms". Chaos is a feature of all nonlinear systems. As a system's randomness increases in the "march to chaos", it moves from a point attractor (a stable value to which the system returns), through periodic attractors (where the system oscillates among a number of fixed values), to a chaotic or strange attractor where predictability breaks down. Chaos is essential for SO as the latter involves the amplification through positive feedback of random fluctuations.

Living systems attempt to occupy the *edge of chaos*, the fractal borderzone between stability and instability providing maximum *ecological flexibility* (Bateson, 2000). A healthy mind can be defined as "an open, complex, dynamical system" which self-organizes and evolves towards the edge of chaos so that it is "capable of flexible reorganization in response to unpredictable social and environmental contingencies" (Marks-Tarlow, 2004, p. 311). Busch (2007, p. 429) describes pathological infantile attractors as "*black holes in psychological space*, sucking everything in that comes near its orbit, remaining outside of awareness and thus unable to be modified by other structures." Iwakabe (1994) suggests the psychoanalytic process therefore works through "destabilization", changing point attractors and limited periodic attractors to strange (chaotic) attractors. While most psychoanalytic change is confined to the local level as it is absorbed by wider psychic defences, as the system reaches *self-organized criticality* the tiniest local shift can precipitate "a cascade of disorganization throughout an entire system"

(Miller, 1999, p. 364). Such models are crucial for understanding the dramatic psychological and social shifts involved in human responses to climate change.

Moving towards social ecology, Stacey (2006), argues that Bion's (1961) work group and basic assumption groups interact to create regions of stability and disintegration, with potentially creative fractal regions of bounded instability at the edge of chaos between them. Nonlinear fractal geometry undermines any clear line between inside and outside, providing new ways to think about the individual and group as a multidimensional fractal borderzone. Similarly, Jacques' (1955) *social phantasy systems* can be understood as emerging through the self-organization of individual defences, with global patterns feeding back to effect lower levels recursively. Nicholson (2003) suggests that unconsciously, American group cohesion is connected to a continuous sacrifice of nature. Unless the group fantasy can move to a new basin of attraction it is likely to remain dangerously stuck in its abusive relation to the natural world.

For an example of a nonlinear social phantasy ecosystem we can turn to Randall's (2005) discussion of the non-active majority who project their environmental concern onto activists who function as containers for the split-off collective environmental superego (supereco). A nonlinear social systems perspective lets us explore the feedback loops which are carried around the circuit with complex social and psychological effects, reverberating back and forth in new iterations as the system moves forward in time, and as other individuals and groups get drawn in, either damping-out the mad oscillations (Bion, 1961), or getting swept up in nonlinear amplification effects. As collective guilt becomes more shared, it becomes "less persecutory and destructive" and can "be managed in more creative ways" where projections are reduced and a larger non-psychotic space created for reparative action (Randall, 2005, pp. 176–177). This embodies a system of multistability, with complex shifts between basins of attraction as internal objects and affects flow through the network, with major shifts between states, sometimes after long periods when the system seems stuck despite the best efforts to destabilize it by pushing it towards a bifurcation.

We can draw on the evolutionary model of a "fitness landscape", where each helpful mutation lets the species move closer to a local adaptive peak, while the fitness landscape itself constantly shifts in new directions with the ebb and flow of evolutionary and geological time. One consequence is that a species can get "stuck" at a local optimum.

In psychoanalysis, patients can become similarly stuck, unable to make the temporary regression required to find new more creative ways of living (Palombo, 1999, p. 114). The analyst's task is to help deform the fitness landscape, through shifts in the analyst's behaviour, to facilitate further movement. This is a novel account of "resistance" in psychotherapy and deadlocks in the wider culture concerning climate change, suggesting an inability to leave a local peak even when long term consequences may be disastrous.

Using complexity theory, we can see our current period as showing disorder and instability in some areas, while being apparently stuck and frozen in others. The first can feel frightening, the latter deadening and demoralizing. Periods of instability are "natural and necessary stages on the path toward greater self-organization" (Eidelson, 1997, p. 68) but with no guarantee that what emerges will be more adaptive. In a highly complex and interconnected system, relatively small changes of one parameter can have disastrous (and unpredictable) effects on the whole. Diamond's (2006) research on the collapse of civilizations suggests the importance of the interaction between systemic social interconnectivity, environmental damage, and climate change. Many past societies entered a rapid period of catastrophic collapse shortly after reaching their peak, which should invite deep reflection for our own society.

Complexity theory lets us understand how psychological, natural, and social ecologies are organized, and how fragile they can be. It also shows how in certain conditions, even minor changes can produce dramatic effects. The task then becomes experimental, including the search for "lever points" to open up the possibilities of more radical transformation. As Deleuze I Guattari (2003a, p. 161) write, "This is how it should be done: Lodge yourself on a stratum, experiment with the opportunities it offers, find an advantageous place on it, find potential movements of deterritorialization, possible lines of flight, experience them, produce flow conjunctions here and there, try out continuums of intensities segment by segment … It is through a meticulous relation with the strata that one succeeds in freeing lines of flight".

Geophilosophy and the future of the three ecologies

DeleuzoGuattarian philosophy is one of becoming rather than being. DeLanda (2005, pp. 258–259) points out that on a sufficently long time scale, "the rocks and mountains that define the most stable and durable traits of our reality ... merely represent a local slowing down of this flowing reality ... very slow for rocks, faster for lava." Similarly, our own bodies and minds represent temporary "coagulations or decelerations in the flows of biomass, genes, memes, and norms". In this perspective, "it is the flow ... that matters, not the bodies and species that emerge from these flows". DeLanda's *assemblage theory* helps us orient ourselves here. Deleuze (DeLanda, 2006, p. 121) defines an assemblage as "a multiplicity which is made up of heterogenous terms and which establishes liaisons, relations between ... different natures ... it is a symbiosis, a 'sympathy'". Assemblage theory studies how structures at all scales emerge through their interacting components. Applied to social processes it offers a method which, "starting at the personal (and even sub-personal) scale, climbs up one scale at a time all the way to territorial states and beyond" (DeLanda, 2006, p. 6).

This model requires a "flat" ontology—as with Žižek's toilet, there is no ontological u-bend. DeLanda (2006, p. 119) claims this allows us to integrate insights from all spatiotemporal scales, forming "a chorus that does not harmonize its different components but interlocks them while respecting their heterogeneity." Assemblage theory provides a way to approach all three of Guattari's ecologies, in a dense heterarchy of connectivity, where a "territorial assemblage opens onto a social assemblage" which is also "connected to cosmic forces" and "pulsations of the earth" (Deleuze I Guattari 2003a, p. 549). For DeLanda (2005, p. 267), Deleuze I Guattari create a vision of a world where "geology, biology, and linguistics are not seen as three separate spheres" but as "coexisting and interacting flows" where "one stratum can serve directly as a substratum for another". As Deleuze I Guattari (2003a, p. 69) put it, "a semiotic fragment rubs shoulders with a chemical interaction, an electron crashes into a language".

Deleuze I Guattari follow Bateson towards an ecological view of mind, where fallacies in the ecology of ideas have direct and catastrophic results on the social and ecological registers such that "there is an ecology of bad ideas, just as there is an ecology of weeds" (Bateson, 2000, p. 492). The ecology of mind leads us to new ways of understanding subjectivity. For Deleuze I Guattari (2003a, p. 18), partial objects self-organize into larger assemblages with emergent properties below (larval subjects) and above (social machines) the traditionally conceived human subject. Thus the schizoanalytic unconscious is "an acentered system ... a machinic network of finite automata", a self-organizing swarm. This leads to an ecological conception of immanent mind where, as Bateson (2000, p. 492) writes, "'the eco-mental system called Lake Erie is a part of *your* wider eco-mental system ... if Lake Erie is driven insane, its insanity is incorporated in the larger system of *your* thought and experience".

In our current ecological crisis we must face the possibility that achieving the necessary ecological flexibility to survive requires a fundamental re-examination of many of the basic coordinates of our lives. Like the patient stuck on a local optimum, unable or unwilling to cross the threshold to a more adaptive peak, entire species and civilizations have in the past found themselves in dangerous dead ends; including those within the ecology of mind, ways of thinking and being that become pathological if they fail to evolve along with the constantly shifting relations in the constitution of natural and social ecosystems. The contribution of psychoanalysis is to help us overcome such errors of thought through investigating their unconscious roots.

Ecopsychoanalysis argues that our world is governed by nonlinear dynamics, to the extent that the prediction and control promised by Enlightenment rationality will always remain to some degree illusory. Instead, we need to engage with the creativity of the earth, and follow the lines of flight we uncover, exploring "the potential for self-organization inherent in even the humblest forms of matter-energy" (DeLanda, 2005, p. 273). Despite all the defensive reasons to *not* know, we are starting to become conscious of the enormity of the danger which now confronts us. The nonlinearity and chaos of nature, and the forms of thinking required to sustain our relationship to it beyond the limited horizons of our experience, are both frightening and liberating. Yet, despite the anxiety, guilt, and terror that climate change forces us to face, this crisis can offer us an opportunity for a more open vision of ourselves, as subjects, as societies, and as a species among the interconnected life systems of the earth.

CHAPTER TEN

Did Lacan go camping? Psychotherapy in search of an ecological self

Martin Jordan

This paper explores how psychotherapy might begin to facilitate the development of an ecological subjectivity in post modernity. I will take a critical look at the concepts of nature and subjectivity: my argument is that we need to start to re-imagine the ecological subject and how an "ecopsychotherapy" might help in facilitating the development of an ecological self. I will explore how the process of ecological communication occurs between mind and nature at the present time in history. We live in an age where the environment can no longer be positioned as a passive backdrop; climate change, species extinction, environmental degradation and potential catastrophe lurk both in the forefront and in the hinterlands of our consciousness. Nature and subjectivity are not static entities, both are in flux, multiplicities that assemble and disassemble in a process of becoming. The paper will explore how the human and the natural need to be re-imagined in order to understand and develop ecological subjectivities suited to merging and emerging postnatural contexts. I will not explore psychotherapy practice in natural environments in any depth, but instead focus on the subject at the heart of an ecopsychotherapeutic project: the ecological-psychological subject which ecopsychology aims to foreground in an attempt at reconnection to the natural world as a reciprocal process.

Introduction

If we attempt to understand human nature relationships in the form of ecological communication, we soon hit on the idea of *miscommunication* between humans and nature, leading to distress for humans, non humans, and ecological systems. One argument put forward by ecopsychology (Roszak, Gomes & Kanner, 1995) is that human psychopathology increases the more we find ourselves distanced from the environment. The longer this ecological miscommunication persists the more ecological systems seem to be in disarray, as evidenced by growing concerns about climate change and how this may affect (and is affecting) planetary ecological systems.

A number of writers (e.g., Boston, 1996; Greenway, 2010; Schroll, 2007; Scull, 2009) have articulated the field of ecopsychology. But I especially want to locate it within complex systems of thought which are emerging at this time in history. Ecopsychology will benefit from being understood in relationship to the pre-modern, modern and post-modern systems of thought which have forged its birth. But finding a "core" language to represent ecopsychology as a unified discipline is problematic, and it might best be seen as a location for thought, language and practical action that is attempting to articulate the human-nature relationship.

Roszak's initial vision for ecopsychology sought to place the psyche back in the context of the earth, "the physical matrix that makes living intelligence possible" (Roszak, 1992, p. 320). He outlines some of the principles of ecopsychology, arguing that life and mind emerge via evolution within an unfolding sequence of the physical, biological, mental and cultural systems. He proposes that the core of the mind is the ecological unconscious, a place where our inherent reciprocity and connection to the natural world exists as the centre of our being, and that through industrialization this has been repressed resulting in madness and rampant ecological destruction. Roszak acknowledges the idea is "speculative", but in his view no more so than the rest of the field of psychology (Roszak, Gomes & Kanner, 1995, p. 14). In linking ecopsychology to psychotherapy he states that:

> Just as it has been the goal of previous therapies to recover the repressed contents of the unconscious, so the goal of ecopsychology is to awaken the inherent sense of environmental reciprocity that lies within the ecological unconscious. Other therapies seek to heal the

alienation between person and person, person and family, person and society. Ecopsychology seeks to heal the more fundamental alienation between the person and the natural environment.

(Roszak, 1992, p. 320)

Although Roszak (1992) identified human alienation from the natural world as one of the causes of mental ill health, there has been little work in ecopsychology towards fully understanding alienation from the natural world as embedded in systems of thought at particular times in history. Historically, I believe, we are in a "complex present", where the subject in relation to nature can no longer be positioned a simplistically as it has within ecopsychology. Ecopsychology as a field also hasn't meaningfully thought itself out of epistemological dead ends, often retreating into ideas of nature mysticism, Gaian holism, and notions of nonduality (Davis, 1998, p. 2003). The problem is that in posing nonduality as a way of overcoming and resolving the problem of mind-nature communication, you set up the very binary dualisms you sought to overcome, by using duality of mind and nature as your starting place. By starting from the split between subject and object (humans and nature), you unwittingly set up the binary differences of subject and object found in disciplinary fields such as ecology and psychology. We need to start in a different place whereby nature, systems, culture and psyche can be re-imagined, and then locate the ecological subject within this matrix.

My argument is that we need forms of ecological communication which give rise to a clearer sense of ecological subjectivity. However in doing so we must engage with the complex present we find ourselves in, and not retreat to forms of splitting between damaged minds and a damaged nature. I will start by exploring the contentious argument that it is the very idea of a pure and holistic "Nature" out there that is getting in the way of being able to think and act ecologically.

Emerging post-nature

When we talk of the nature we have lost contact with, we are not just talking about a singular unified "Nature". Our understanding and perception of the concepts of "nature" and "wilderness" have shifted throughout history, especially in relation to culture and technological development. Recent writing contests the idea of nature as a uniform concept, stating that it is impossible to situate it as a singular entity (Mcnaghten & Urry, 1998). Nature has emerged historically through its articulation in the natural sciences (Latour, 1993) and through the practices and economic developments of modernity (Bluhdorn, 2001). It is clear that to use the term "Nature" unproblematically without some further elaboration and exploration would leave us with the fantasy of a singular nature.

It is in this sense that a "desire" for a pure unaffected nature and wilderness out there that we can connect to, is very problematic, as Morton argues: "Putting nature on a pedestal and admiring it from afar does for the environment what patriarchy does for the figure of Woman. It is a paradoxical act of sadistic admiration" (Morton, 2007, p. 5). Morton argues for an ecology without the romantic illusion of a singular nature that we have lost. He goes on to suggest that if we accept the radical premise of ecology that everything is interconnected to everything else, we have to forge links with everything: the rubbish dump, hybrid creatures created in laboratories, and technologies that distance us from the natural world and each other.

For Morton (2010b) the ecological thought starts at the centre and finds no edges; the idea that we cannot extricate ourselves from an ecological matrix that includes global warming produces a terrifying loss of bearings. If we accept this then ecological subjectivity needs to position itself in relation to everything else - the hybrid, the unnatural, not just the pure nature that we seek and believe we may have lost. We need to reconfigure how we emotionally and psychologically hope to survive such connections. Morton continues:

> If ecology is about radical co-existence, then we must challenge our sense of what is real and what is unreal, what counts as existent and what counts as nonexistent. The idea of Nature as a holistic, healthy real thing avoids this challenge.
>
> (Morton, 2010b, p. 10)

Exploring this tension, Dodds (2011 and this volume) has highlighted the problem of the "ecology of phantasy": postmodern deconstructive theories after Lacan (Zizek, 2007) and Derrida (Morton, 2007) argue that the vision of pure nature is itself an illusion, a desire to make up for our "lack" of a place in late modernity, a "big other" that will come and save us. However Dodds (2011) argues for a path in between, using a bifocal vision, which retains a material nature beyond the idea of a linguistic construction and more radical theories of complexity and chaos in order to understand how the three ecologies (Guattari, 2000) of mind, nature and society interweave and affect one another.

To explore the importance of reciprocity between nature and the ecological subject, I am going to use Anderson's definition of nature as an "emerging postnature" (Anderson, 2009). Following from Latour (1993) and Whatmore (1999), Anderson states that there has never been an ontological separation between humans and nature: the idea of "pure" nature outside of society is a fallacy. He argues that in a world of merging and emerging ontologies the concepts of nature, culture and mind can never really be positioned as distinct entities, separate from one another. The world and those who move within it, humans, places, natures and cultures, all change over time, simultaneously both immersed in one another and emergent. In these merging and emerging movements we do not find a distinct "mind" coming into contact with a distinct "nature" through a distinct "culture" (as some versions of reality would argue). Anderson goes on to to say:

> Postnature is therefore not simply a locking together of separate entities within a passive context rather it is a convergence of mutual interaction and interference involving humans non-humans and place. The meaning of any human or non-human species in this assemblage can thus only be marginally known if taken in isolation.
>
> (Anderson, 2009, p. 123)

Bonta (2005) argues that the post-structuralist idea that "nature" and "space" are fundamentally shaped by discourse, rather than by the experimentality and unpredictability of corporeal action and relationships between actors, fails to recognize the non human co-present with humans in all places and at all times. This happens not only through semiotics but also through a corporeal process which is both beyond or beside discourse.

I have written elsewhere about the practice of ecotherapy (Jordan, 2009b), and how the psychotherapeutic frame shifts when we move into an outdoor and natural environment (Jordan & Marshall, 2010).

As part of my therapy practice I have worked in the outdoors with both individuals and groups. The area where I see my one-to-one clients is within a park close to woodland. The space is interspersed with tracks, roads, fences and fields; in the background you can hear the distant hum of a motorway; part of the site is given over to horticulture and therefore the space is a managed environment. This isn't the pure nature that in one sense ecotherapy and ecopsychology might like us to connect back to, it is a merging and emergent space, that encompasses aspects of both natural, urban, unnatural and the hybrid that represents post-nature. When people venture out into this space they encounter these different processes and they bring them back as parts of stories that mirror and fuse with their interior worlds. I will turn next to these interior psychic worlds.

The non-unitary subject

Traditional phenomenological views of the subject have been used to understand how better to perceive and connect with the natural world (Abraham, 1996; Fisher, 2002). The classic Husserlian phenomenological subject positioned in these and other ecopsychological writings, is transcendent in its ability to view objects from the vantage point of a separate consciousness. This view of the subject, both explicit and implicit in a lot of ecopsychological theorizing, is problematic since again it sets up the very binary dualisms we might seek to dissolve in forming the ecological self. Psychoanalysis has formed a body of work in relation to psychotherapeutic practice that has re-imagined the subject as divided and non-unitary (Layton, 2008).

In particular, the relational turn in psychotherapy has positioned subjects in complex relational processes between bodies and environments (Mitchell, 1988). In his repositioning from within the field of psychotherapy of the psyche as a relational phenomenon, Mitchell argues that there is no "object" in a psychologically meaningful sense without some sense of oneself in relationship to it. There is therefore no "self" in a psychologically meaningful sense in isolation outside of a matrix of relations (Mitchell, 1988, p. 33). Mitchell argues that in developing a sense of self, the human being is faced with the difficulty of the temporality and complexity of our conscious existence. Mitchell sees human consciousness as operating in time and in a continual flux, a stream of thoughts, feelings, sensations and desires: from a relational perspective the self is a temporal and spatial entity in a process of continual movement.

Lacan's original work focused on a radical revisioning of the subject as fundamentally alienated from its own desires. Instead of being the subject of one's own desires, objects other than us become the cause of our desires (Fink, 1995). So instead of being conscious of our desires, we become more radically decentred in our subjectivity. Post modern writers have taken up the Lacanian position in order to demonstrate how discourses both shape and also construct the spaces of thought which we can inhabit. In this sense the other's desire, normatively in the form of the parents wishes and hopes for the child, start to shape the child's own subjectivity: the child wishes to please the parents and starts to inhabit a space created in the image of their desire. In this sense the desire for a pure nature "over there" to which we need to reconnect is a phantasy.

This starting point for understanding human-nature relations leaves us with the problem of how subjective interiors and objective material exteriors come into some form of communication. The question arises as to whether it is useful to think in these terms, as they set up the very binary dualisms which a psychotherapy in natural environments might seek to overcome. If we view the Cartesian self as an invention of the enlightenment, which drove modernism down the path of separating things out in order to get a better view of them, then it is quite a challenge to find spaces where we can view interiors and exteriors without setting up the same binary dualisms which positioned us in the first place. So for instance, to experience the therapeutic potential of a natural environment we either have to fall back on interiors, e.g., how do I feel about this? What psychological and historical frames do I bring to this contact with nature? What symbols and metaphors resonate with my personal emotional narrative? Or we move outwards contacting the environment through our senses, e.g., how does my body feel in this process? What visual and sensory stimulus do I encounter? Inside always relates to outside, or vice versa—how does the outside become the inside?

These questions also link to the therapeutic focus of the work. Does the therapist focus solely on the interior of the client and normative relational dynamics such as the client's developmental history and experience of relationships? Or do also they focus on what the client is experiencing in the moment of encounter with the natural world by provoking and exploring contact with the natural world? Each has different potential therapeutic effects and relies on different theoretical lineages in order to understand emotional distress. The way that different systems of meaning and experiencing communicate with one another becomes important for understanding the therapeutic work.

A recent book by Neil Ansell explores how his experience of living alone in a remote natural setting affected his sense of self and mirrors the points made above—that self is located in otherness, more a "space" than a unified entity:

> What I found was not what you might expect. You might think that such protracted solitude would lead to introspection, to self examination, to a growing self awareness. But not for me. What happened to me was that I began to forget myself, my focus shifted almost entirely out of the window. It was as if we gain our sense of self *from our interaction with other people: from the reflection of ourselves we see in the eyes of another.*
>
> (Ansell, 2010, p. 30)

I now begin to explore theoretical thinking which I believe offers a way forward in thinking through some of these difficulties. By relying on an ecological self as posited by ecopsychological writers who draw from a classic phenomenological position of subjectivity and consciousness in relation to a nature "out there", I believe we get stuck in epistemological dead ends. By re-envisioning self and nature as movement in flux we start to disrupt notions of binary opposition. I turn next to process thinker A. N. Whitehead.

Process philosophy

Process philosophy posits the processual nature of existence which cannot be downgraded to the materiality of things. It is a movement of stages and phases Rescher (2009). This idea of process has been linked to ontologies of movement in the form of "becoming" (McCormack, 2009). In relying on fixed notion of epistemology and ontology which become static reference points, we tend to get stuck in interior or exterior places: space becomes a static entity fixed in a material form. According to McCormack the problem with this view is that space exists as a fixed grid within which transformation unfolds, so that we become caught again within the Cartesian space of knowing subject viewing the world from an independent standpoint.

This notion of identity and space as fixed points doesn't capture the spatiotemporal flux of these positions within modernity, postmodernity and globalization, where self and space feel more fluid—a process. McCormack (2009) draws on pre-socratic philosophers Heraclitus and Parmenides to illustrate tensions in contemporary western thought around being and becoming. Heraclitus saw the world as flux and motion, a flow which is not uniform but a lively mix wof conflicting and contrasting forces. Parmenides, by contrast, in a pre-Cartesian move saw the world of being in which everything exists in a fixed eternal essence.

A. N. Whitehead (1920/2004, 1978) has articulated a process philosophical position in relation to nature. Whitehead (1978) presents a relational theory of matter, in which the "object" observes is the attributes it possesses in relation to space. Whitehead (1920/2004) proposes a revision of the subject object split into a process philosophy that sees things as existing in relationships within particular forms, which in themselves are context dependent on the perspective of viewer and relationships between attributes of substances, spaces and times. Thus his philosophy is a process theory of relationships between entities in time and space, viewed from the interpretive stance of the observer.

> Accordingly it would seem that every material entity is not really one entity. It is an essential multiplicity of entities. There seems to be no stopping this dissociation of matter into multiplicities short of finding each ultimate entity occupying one individual point.
>
> (Whitehead, 1920/2004, p. 22)

According to Whitehead we have become confused in our conceptions of nature: the modern account of nature is not what the mind knows about nature, but an inaccurate account of what nature does to the mind. He later says:

> Unless we produce the all embracing relations, we are faced with a bifurcated nature, namely warmth and redness on one side, and molecules, electrons and ether on the other side. Then the two

factors are explained as being respectively the cause and the mind's reaction to the cause.

(Whitehead, 1920/2004, p. 33)

Sense awareness becomes important in our relations to nature: it is both independent of, and related to, our thoughts about nature. Whitehead believes our sense perception about nature is disclosed as a complex set of entities whose mutual relations are expressible in the heterogeneity of thought and sense awareness. For Whitehead there is a problem of homogeneity in our relations with nature, which through our doctrines of science have caused a bifurcation of nature and mind. "Nature" is a heterogeneous experience of "events" in motion. Whitehead (1978) calls these events in motion "actual occasions", in that there is nothing behind things to make them more real: their reality comes through in the process of the becoming of actual occasions. So nature loses the static material quality attributed to it by dominant modes of scientific thought: Isaac Newton, argues Whitehead (1978), fell into the "fallacy of misplaced concreteness". The physical world is bound together not by laws, which Whitehead argues are not always followed clearly anyway, but by a general type of relatedness, a process of becoming, rather than the con-crete end point positioned as material reality. The world is self-creative, with actual entities part of a transcendent process of self-creation; the mind comes into relation with nature through the process of feeling, a complex of mental operations which go to create the actual entity, thus an actual occasion is affected by feelings through which objects enter into, in this sense feelings constitute things (Stenner, 2008).

In these terms we can understand nature as a series of unfolding events in process, not singular in form or location. The self, or subject, starts to mirror nature as a relational process, folding and unfolding in a spatial temporal locations, which are both interior and exterior. Recent developments in geography have explored these ideas.

Emotional geographies

In recent years geography has taken an "emotional turn" (Bondi, Davidson & Smith 2005; Smith, Davidson, Cameron & Bondi, 2009), locating the importance of emotions in relation to places and spaces and how affect positions the perceiver and place in a reciprocal feedback loop. Bondi, Davidson, and Smith (2005) argue for a non-objectifying view of emotions as relational flows, fluxes or currents, in between people and places rather than "things" or "objects". In doing this they want to position emotions "spatially".

If we link this back into counselling and psychotherapy, Bondi and Fewell (2003) see counselling as working at a "spatial temporal" interface which transgresses normal boundaries of care; in particular, issues of confidentiality and ethical boundaries are re-imagined simultaneously as being both concrete and specific, fluid and illusory. This dualism between what is real, material concrete space and what is imagined, fantasy symbolic space is played out in the counselling relationship via the contradictory positions of counsellor and client attempting to maintain what Bondi and Fewell term a non hierarchical and relational practice, whilst at the same time engaging with the positioning of their clients which is neither fixed nor easy to change. One of the most prominent spatial metaphors of counselling is the space between inside and outside. Bondi and Fewell (2003, p. 540) argue that counsellors conceptualize the interface between client and practitioner as a dynamic space within which these exteriorizations and interiorizations can be explored, thereby redefining the space and boundary between inner and outer realities.

Hence "space" becomes important in understanding subject and object.

Space

To locate space conceptually is a challenge, especially in that space always seems to relate to something. Space is normally filled with matter; solid objects inhabit space and give it a character and some objective sense of presence. But viewed from a materialist post-structural perspective, space is not located but understood as produced by an enfoldment of interiors and exteriors. In this sense space can be thought of as a process of becoming that does not separate space from time, so things can be understood as spatiotemporal unfolding on a plane of immanence (Deleuze & Guattari, 2003a/1980). Colebrook (2005) argues that the problem with the coding of space in Western thought is that it is always located reactively as one general territory. Rather than understanding space as a fixed location, a field upon which things are mapped, Colebrook proposes space is best understood as a plane of singular affects and events. Drawing heavily upon Deleuze l Guattari (2003a/1980), Colebrook (2005) argues that the Deleuzian concept of immanence is central to understanding how space is the different expression of life as it unfolds in different spaces, relations, fields and trajectories, "the immanent power of corporeality in all, matter" (Deleuze & Guatarri, 2003a/1980, p. 411, cited in Colebrook, 2005, p. 195). In this sense space can be understood both as a process and unfolding event. Colebrook goes onto to say:

> Space would, then, be the effect of a synthesis of points, not a container or ground. Space is the effect of relations. This would apply both to space in a metaphorical sense, such as the space or field of a grammar or social structure, and literal space. Geometry is not a pre-given and ideal order of a space that bears its own laws; rather, our space is constituted through the sense we make of it, the mapping of our field of orientation.
>
> (Colebrook, 2005, p. 195)

Conclusions: ecopsychotherapy and the ecological subject

I want to conclude this paper by positioning the subject and nature as a complex assemblage, and argue that this constitutes ecological subjectivity. In re-imagining subjects reconnecting to the natural, space is somewhere between subjectivity and objectivity, it is both internal and external, an in between zone, which is psychic, social, embodied, natural, and unnatural. Nature and subject are processes of becoming, always in movement and in flux; consciousness is not static, neither is the idea of the natural, which as Whitehead tells us is always an "event" not an end point. The ecological self is a fundamentally decentred space, located in a matrix of relationships.

How does this help us with the global and personal traumas that an ecopsychotherapy seeks to address? The trauma of the complex present invites us to simplicity, to go back to simpler times when there was a singular nature that was part of a singular culture in reciprocal interdependence. This is one part of the answer in the complex assemblage that ecopsychotherapy is. But however good it is to dig and plant my allotment, to walk in the hills, these are always transient processes, I am always returning to the urban that I exist within, shopping in the supermarket, having to drive my car, these complex ecological relationships that both jar and also form part of my late modern identity. It is in these movements that I have to negotiate the different geographical, emotional, cultural, and psychic spaces I occupy, these spaces are all relational and moving in and out of one another.

Rather than being something that transcends the dislocation of modernity by reconnecting to a pure nature we have lost, the ecological subject is a space moving in and out of different spaces and temporalities. The radical nature of ecology means that everything is interconnected, and it is the job of ecopsychotherapy to help humans negotiate the complex and interdependent present, not by romanticising the perfect ecological past nor predicting some future ecological catastrophe, but by bearing to stay with the temporal spaces of the complex present.

PART IV

WHAT TO DO—POSSIBLE FUTURES

CHAPTER ELEVEN

Ecological intimacy

Mary-Jayne Rust

The universe is a communion of subjects not a collection of objects.

—Berry (1990, p. 45)

Most people claim to love nature. Yet we all collude in seriously damaging the web of life we inhabit and depend on. In psychological terms, this would be described an ambivalent relationship between humans and the rest of nature; arguably this lies at the heart of our ecological crisis.

For those of us who have grown up within a Western mindset it is taken for granted that human welfare and human law should be prioritized over the needs of the nonhuman world. The earth has become a set of objects, a bunch of resources to be used for human purpose. These attitudes, which have been called "species arrogance" (Prentice, 2011) are in many ways enmeshed within Western philosophy, religion and the law, as well as how we live and organize what is often thought of as "our" world. This is a human-centric view.

Stepping outside this perspective is to go against the flow of two thousand years, or more, of western history. It is no surprise, then, that culture change takes time, and meets with plenty of resistance, even when we know the situation at hand is so urgent. It is a process of making conscious and understanding the old story we have been living by, while piecing together the different parts of an emerging new story about eco-centric living. Navigating our way through this liminal space can be turbulent, chaotic, and confusing as old identities and cherished ways of being unravel.

This old story, sometimes referred to as The Myth of Progress, describes the onwards and upwards rise of human civilization, from a primitive life in dark caves into the light of reason (Tarnas, 2006, pp. 11–16). This began as an understandable need to protect ourselves from the elemental forces of nature. From a psychological perspective, this has turned into, over time, the journey of a male hero who is trying to conquer nature, for whom nature has come to embody a number of things, including: nature as the all-powerful elemental enemy; nature as sensual temptress; nature as wild and out of control; nature as unconscious dark matter. The hero's solution is to tame, control and dominate the aspects of nature which are threatening, including his own human nature. He also tries to escape the struggles of being an embodied part of the ecosystem through transcendence, reaching upwards in search of a God in the sky. He does this by cutting himself *out* of the web, an image which appears in popular stories today. This is a very powerful story about how and where we find peace and freedom. Yet this withdrawal from nature leaves us in a place of feeling not so much disconnected, but once removed from the earth, as if living on top of the land rather than inside a living system.

There is also a new story emerging which is about coming back into relationship with the earth, returning to the joys and difficulties of embodiment and intimacy with the rest of nature. To live sustainably we must find a way of accepting the power and limits of the earth, respecting the needs of others with whom we share our home. How might this transformation take place?

In this chapter, I will explore some ways in which the old and new stories appear in our modern lives, both in our attitudes towards the other-than-human world, as well as towards our bodies and human nature. It will become clear that therapeutic attitudes have much to offer to the new story, but inevitably there are ways in which most forms of therapy and counselling are caught in a human-centric view.

From human-centrism to eco-centrism

I begin with a story which describes a pivotal moment in the life of Aldo Leopold who was a wild life manager in the early 1900's and one of the fathers of the modern ecology movement. As a man of his time, he was of the view that humans were superior to the rest of nature, and that it was morally right to manage and control nature to ensure human safety and well-being.

One day, Leopold and friends were out hunting when they spotted some wolves close to the river. They shot excitedly into the pack and Leopold rushed down to see a wolf as she was dying. He writes:

> We reached the old wolf in time to watch a fierce green fire dying in her eyes. I realized then, and have known ever since, that there was something new to me in those eyes—something known only to her and to the mountain. I was young then, and full of trigger-itch; I thought …. that no wolves would mean hunters' paradise. But after seeing the green fire die, I sensed that neither the wolf nor the mountain agreed with such a view.

> (Leopold, 1948, p. 129)

He then describes how he watched the gradual eradication of wolves and the multiplying of deer until "every edible bush and seedling (was) browsed, first to anaemic desuetude, and then to death". In the end the deer herd starved, "dead of its own too-much" (Leopold, 1948, p. 129).

After this experience Leopold developed a land ethic which "changes the role of Homo sapiens from conqueror of the land-community to plain member and citizen of it. It implies respect for his fellow-members, and also respect for the community as such." (Leopold, 1948, pp. 243–244) and "A thing is right when it tends to preserve the integrity, stability, and beauty of the *biotic community*. It is wrong when it tends otherwise" (Leopold, 1948, p. 262). Stephan Harding comments: "The attitude that saw nature as a dead machine, as there solely for human use, vanished. [Leopold] had recognised the existence of an active agency far greater than himself in the great wild world around him" (Harding, 2009, p. 43. With thanks to Stephan Harding from whom I first heard this story.) This is a major transformation from human-centric to eco-centric perspective.

Feelings of both tenderness and sadness are stirred in me as I listen to how Leopold became open to the presence of the wolf as she lies dying. In that moment there is an intimate meeting between the fierce green fire of souls, changing the relationship between hunter and hunted. The wolf has ceased to be a threatening object for Leopold to erase. Her death triggers a "sense" that his actions are not right, implying that now he is embodied and connected in a feeling way to world around him. He listens to the views of the wolf and the mountain as equal participants within the earth community. How this startles the western mindset. How poignant that it takes her death for him to awaken.

This story is a metaphor for our time. Leopold stands for humans as hunter, intent on dominating, controlling and taming wild nature for our own ends. Having virtually wiped out our predators, we are also like the deer—multiplying, consuming and denuding the earth of her bounty. Will we, too, die of food shortages? As climate change quickens, the ecological crisis faces us with the potential of our own species death, along with so many other species in this sixth mass extinction.

What if, like Leopold, we dare to stare into the eyes of nature, to be present to what and who is dying? Can we awaken to the fierce green fire of wild nature, to know that the world is inhabited by aware, living subjects, each with their own view? Can we also awaken to that fierce green fire inside, our own wild nature, often buried beneath centuries of human domestication? This is the Great Joy of Joys.

Yet in the same moment comes a tsunami of grief for what is dying and what has been lost, for the tragic abuse of the other-than-human world, for the loss of connection with our own nature, the resulting self and body hatred, and a fear that it is now too late to reverse climate change. What have we done to our *home*? What will become of our children's future? This is the Great Grief.

Many writers, especially in the field of ecopsychology describe this process as reconnecting with nature (e.g., Roszak, Gomes & Kanner, 1995). However, this can give the rather simplistic impression of going *back* to nature, returning to a state of blissful harmony, a nostalgia for Eden often projected onto indigenous peoples. It also reinforces that old paradigm dualism that we are not part of nature. Perhaps a more accurate description of what is needed is to return, in the present, to realize our *intimate relationship* with nature. What we know from human relationships is that intimacy—sustaining a close relationship with the other—is beautiful, complex and difficult. It involves all the fears, hurts, losses, grief and trauma that may accompany love in any reciprocal relationship. Embodiment, and recovering an intimacy with the other than human world, is therefore a mix of joy and pain. Crucially, it is about finding a way of being with our vulnerability as creat ures.

The process of change

Leopold's story describes a significant moment of change that was instant and spontaneous. These kinds of transformative experiences are not uncommon among people who spend time in the wilds (Key, 2003; Key & Kerr, Kerr & Key, this volume). Indigenous cultures have always recognized that spending time alone in wilderness can return humans to original nature. However, their ritual practices, which have been developed over thousands of years, recognize the need to prepare for, digest, and integrate such powerful experiences into the wisdom of the community. This is a reminder that we have lost many of the rituals and vital safe containers for collective change, as well as a knowledge about the process of change itself.

The shift to an ecocentric view can be triggered in many other ways. People who have spent time in other, non-western cultures may come into contact with sophisticated cosmologies and lifestyles which embody a more earth centred way of living. Artists, philosophers or anyone who inhabits the borderland (Bernstein, 2005 and this volume), may be more in touch with what has been pushed out of mainstream view, or experiences which do not fit into modernity. Those who have the courage to speak out are often the people who are initially seen as fools, but who may become the visionaries of our time, acting as conduits for new ways of seeing.

Crisis can also trigger a major change in perspective. While this may begin with a startling new insight, the ripples of this may take years to become integrated into the minutiae of everyday life. In psychological language, this involves facing the shadow (aspects of self and other that are difficult to own), untangling projections and inviting back what has been pushed into the margins, as well as grieving for what has been lost and making amends. This is a painful process for the ego to endure, but the rewards are many.

What does this process of change look like in ecological terms? How do we recover an ecological intimacy in our everyday lives? I will give some examples below.

Ecological loss and grief

For several decades Buddhist scholar and eco-philosopher Joanna Macy has pioneered "the work that reconnects", offering carefully facilitated workshops for people to express and explore their feelings in relation to global crisis. This reconnects us to ourselves and to each other, and empowers us in working for change (Macy & Brown, 1998). In 1992 she offered a series of workshops to people living in areas contaminated by the nuclear disaster of Chernobyl, Russia (what follows summarizes Macy, 2009). They describe themselves as "people of the forest" and yet because of contamination, the only contact they had with trees was the forest wallpaper inside their homes. The effects of the disaster included a range of physical illnesses, as well as explosive anger and grief. Yet when Joanna invited them to talk about this she was met with reluctance; they said they'd had enough pain and wanted to get on. "Why have you done this to us?" one woman cried out. "I would be willing to feel the sorrow, all the sorrow in the world, if it could save my daughters from cancer. Can my tears protect them? What good are my tears if they can't?"

Joanna responded with "I have no wisdom to meet your grief. But I can share this with you: after the war which almost destroyed their country, the German people determined that they would do anything to spare their children the suffering they had known. They worked hard to give them a rich and safe life. They created an economic miracle. They gave their children everything—except for one thing. They did not give them their broken hearts". The following morning everyone returned to the workshop. The first to speak was the above mentioned woman who said: "It feels like my heart is breaking open. Maybe it will keep breaking again and again every day, I don't know. But somehow, I can't explain, it feels right. This breaking connects me to everything and everyone, as if we were all branches of the same tree." One by one they said that it had been very hard, but now they were beginning to feel cleansed, uncontaminated, for the first time.

It is an understandable wish to protect ourselves, each other and our children from the pain of the world. But the desire to "get on" and "be positive" in the face of overwhelming grief and anger, keeping a stiff upper lip, is part of the old "onwards and upwards" story. It is a drive not only to conquer land and peoples, but to conquer the emotional world as well. Vulnerability is so hard to stay with; but when grief (or any strong emotion) is blocked then a series of problems may follow such as feelings of disconnection, eating problems or other addictions, or physical illness.

Part of the new story is a more therapeutic approach, learning to go with the flow of emotions and how to ride the waves of grief which come and go. This is a move away from linear progress for it completes the circle by including backwards and downwards, honouring the need to go *back* over things and *down* into the body and the unconscious. Wise action depends on reflection.

A loving relationship with the rest of nature inevitably includes the pain of losing loved ones, or trauma when places or creatures are damaged. Often our first experience of death in childhood is losing a pet. A favourite tree which has become a familiar companion in play or solace, may be chopped down with no warning, nor any recognition of the feelings of loss involved. Moving home involves loss in relation to place. There is also the trauma of revisiting a special place only to discover it has been desecrated by development or pollution. The larger traumas such as earthquakes, floods, famine, and the many different kinds of ecocide may take generations to recover from. In all of these ways and more, our bonds with the whole earth community run deep, and call for recognition.

A memorial to lost species—possibly the first—is in the making, in Portland, Dorset, UK (www.memoproject.org). This will be a stone monument bearing the images of all the species of plants and animals known to have gone extinct in modern times. A bell will be tolled when a species becomes extinct. Marking the loss of what is happening in our world is an important step towards making amends and rebuilding ecological community. This is an expression of love.

Unlearning consumerism

Cutting down on carbon emissions also brings loss, but a loss that is complex. Most people are now aware we must give up having so much stuff, so many exotic travel experiences, or the excitement of constantly updated technology. Affluent countries are obese with stuff while millions of people in other parts of the world starve. We are caught in a giant eating problem. But facing our ravenous consumption of the earth can arouse strong feelings of guilt for what has been branded as greed— a quality that humans would prefer to project onto animals, especially pigs.

The danger is that sustainability becomes a new form of diet: The Carbon Diet. Diets use old paradigm methods of using the mind to discipline the body. Bodily appetites are not to be trusted and must be kept under strict control for fear, perhaps, of insatiable hunger; body hatred is one of the by-products. This is a top down approach which is all about being "good". The inevitable then follows: breaking the rules to binge on "naughty" food, a sensual orgy not unlike the sexual excitement of having an affair. The carbon diet urges people to live the good green life, while rampant consumerism and life in the fast lane can easily become part of the naughty, exciting, sensual orgy of modernity.

A therapeutic approach goes beyond these "good" and "bad" labels to explore the longings and fears that propel us into consuming too much. Exposing this hunger is difficult in a culture obese with privilege. The assumption is that it is simply human nature to want unlimited access to everything all the time, as if this easy comfort and sensual stimulation brings happiness. In fact it is about avoidance of frustration and as a result this dream of consumer happiness is carefully guarded, and any attempts to set limits (e.g., for sustainable living) are seen as an infringement on our freedom of choice. The irony is that most people are well aware that such a dream does not bring lasting satisfaction, but the easier the access to the quick fix solutions, the harder it becomes to live through the frustrations to find experiences which satisfy in the long-term.

This is further complicated in a culture where our status symbols, rites of passage and indicators of success, are tied up with material wealth. For example, learning to drive and acquiring a car has become one of the rites of passage into adulthood; it is a symbol of power in our society. Advertisers compare cars to jaguars and other powerful animals. Exchanging a car for a bike can feel like going backwards in life, losing power and status. Power *over* nature has become a mark of success: conquering mountains, killing wild beasts, taming the wild, developing "empty" spaces. Manufacturing and having more stuff is part of a colonizing agenda. What does it mean to leave space unfilled, to leave parts of the garden unmanaged, to have only what is needed?

When stuff becomes a symbol for status or safety, feelings emerge in the process of downshifting. It may trigger fears of not having enough, of losing status, of feeling powerless or of not being seen. At a deeper level it may stir primal fears of hunger and deprivation. So hanging onto stuff is a way of warding off those fears, keeping the dividing line very firm between the fantasy of some dark and primitive past, and our apparently civilized present.

Recovery involves asking, what is it we are really hungry for? Spending time in the garden, listening to the birds in the local park, lying on the beach and feeling the rhythm of the waves, are all experiences which nourish our sensual selves in a more satisfying way than consumer goods. Such experiences open portals into the timelessness of simply being—as opposed to the frantic doing, compartmentalized into hours, so prized by our cultural norms.

Over the past few years I have co-facilitated one week courses in Scotland which offer time in wild nature to deepen an exploration of sustainable living. At the heart of the week is a one day solo experience, where participants leave at dawn to find a spot to stay in for the rest of the day in silence, returning at dusk. There is nothing to do. This is about simply being, listening, watching outside and watching inside, all day. And it is not all bliss, of course! There are fears of bad weather, being cold, or getting lost—not just in the mountains, but in the openness of time. Yet the immensity of the day allows for ample contemplation in which anxieties and frustrations have the space to surface, to be met and lived through. It never ceases to amaze me how profoundly nourishing this simple experience can be. How hungry people are for the adventure of meeting nature in the raw, yet how seldom do we allow ourselves uninterrupted solitude in the presence of the wild. The ego fears what the soul yearns for: to stare into the eyes of the wolf, to meet and be humbled by the mysterious and powerful universe we inhabit, to feel the excitement of meeting Eros in raw, wild nature, to surrender to boundlessness, to recover original nature. (For stories of solo experiences see Kerr & Key, this volume.)

Untangling projections

It is through these meetings with the other-than-human world that we begin to untangle projections and find what belongs to whom. In one of the most well-known David Attenborough documentaries, he inches his way into a gorilla family, demonstrating their gentle, placid nature. He ad libs on camera: "The male is an enormously powerful creature but he only uses his strength when he is protecting his family and it is very rare that there is violence within the group. So it seems really very unfair that man should have chosen the gorilla to symbolize everything that is aggressive and violent, when that is the one thing that the gorilla is not—and that we are" (Attenborough, 1979).

Few humans are ever killed from attacks by wild animals. However, millions of animals are killed by humans each year (e.g., for food, sport, clothes, and medical research) and thousands of humans are murdered by other humans. So it would seem that the most dangerous wild animal on earth is the human being! Yet many wild animals are still killed for sport and this is justified by the need to protect humans. This is, in part, in order to maintain a myth in which hunters can remain heroes and animals can continue to carry our projections of wildness and uncontained aggression (Russell, 2006).

This does not make wild animals or wilderness safe. The problem is about attitudes to risk and danger. The hero in the Myth of Progress tries to make his world safe by making increasingly elaborate defence systems, (as demonstrated by today's health and safety measures) or worse still, killing off "the other". Yet understanding the rest of nature, being able to read the language of the other, knowing wild as our own condition, is a far more skilful route to safety.

Canadian naturalist Charlie Russell, known as "the bear man of Kamchatka", has been co-existing peacefully with grizzly bears in Russia for forty years. He started out as a rancher and discovered that getting to know the habits of the local bears was an effective way of protecting his cattle. Russell writes, "For eons the only acceptable way to think about bears has been in terms of them being totally unpredictable and ferocious" and "I understood that disharmony between bears and humans was not the 'bears' fault. It was a human inadequacy brought about by our fear and distrust of them" (Russell, 2006).

Biologist Dr. Lynn Rogers has been studying black bears in Minnesota for several decades. He runs courses to educate people in a place where bears are regularly shot for sport. *Bearwalker of the Northwoods* is a moving documentary about his work which shows what is possible when humans are willing to have the patience to understand bear language. For example, a clip shows Rogers standing outside a bears' den with cubs. The bear is snarling at them and banging her paw ferociously against the side of the den. Rogers remains calm, and says "She's not a mean bear, she's just a nervous bear … Juliette trusts me—she's just worried about the extra camera. She'll do that ritualised display and then settle down". Rogers then feeds her from the palm of his hand; in the space of thirty seconds she is calm and friendly, and he is able to stroke her (Rogers, 2010).

Wild nature is often feared as being aggressive, dangerous, and out of control. Stories of werewolves, Count Dracula and other human-animal characters embody the worst fears of our own animal nature (cf the wild/human relationship explored in Totton, 2011, pp. 138–157). At the other end of the spectrum are fears of apathy, becoming a couch potato, or stuck in a comatose vegetative state; or sprawling out with no boundaries, in an amoeba-like state. Human nature includes the entire spectrum of animal, vegetable, and mineral. Yet the story of evolution— our current Creation Myth—would have us believe that we left all those qualities behind in others "lower down" the evolutionary scale, while we at the top have the gift of consciousness, analytic thinking, and the capacity to resist instinct. But increasingly scientific research is erasing the thick line between humans and animals and our identity as humans is unclear.

We project onto aspects of the world all the time; this is a helpful way of learning about self and other. The problem comes when what has been projected out cannot be re-owned. It is clear from the history of apartheid, women's rights and slavery that untangling cultural projections is very complex. For those in positions of "power over" this involves unbearable guilt for the damage inflicted, as well as humiliation. This psychological work takes generations, and it sheds some light on the difficulties involved in recovering ecological intimacy, for humans are in a position of "power over" the nonhuman world. The implications of this are radical, including recognizing the rights of nature in law. (Ecuador was the first country to recognize Rights of Nature in its constitution: http://therightsofnature.org.) This is a radical re-thinking of so many of our habits, such as experiments on animals, factory farming, zoos, and the thousands of ways in which we make use of the nonhuman world.

What is often missed in this process of recovery is that the process of projection means losing vital parts of ourselves.

When the white man projects his wild animal instinctual self onto black people, all the colour is taken out of the white man; he is left like a monochrome print, cut off from his colour and creativity, inhabiting monoculture.

When a man projects his vulnerability and intuition onto women he is left in a cut-off, disconnected world of his analytic mind, unable to relate.

When a woman projects out her wild animal self, she becomes afraid of the fur on her face, the hair on her body, her flesh, her instincts, her body.

When we idealise wilderness, we go off in search of our own divinity, beauty, and wild mind, flying to unspoilt places in hordes, in search of peace and tranquillity, inevitably spoiling the places we visit.

Some final thoughts

Coming back into relationship with inner and outer nature means inviting back in aspects of self and other that have been pushed into the margins. While there may be loss on this journey, in fact this is healing—a process of becoming more whole. The new story is not created by erasing the old story, but emerges out of its retelling. The young male hero who battles against nature is, like all of us, a vulnerable creature who is trying his best to defend himself against the terrors of nature. He deals with this by trying to rise above everyone and everything, but in doing so he loses touch with his earthy nature, his bodily instincts and intuition, lost in a cloud of intellectual abstraction. His ego needs the teachings of intimate immensity. Then he can reweave himself back into the web of life and recover his animal, vegetable, and mineral natures. This is a move from being a solar hero to a lunar hero, one who is able to die and be reborn, who knows of "power with" rather than "power over" and that progress returns to zero. He is brought back into relationship. This new story is in fact an ancient story, known by indigenous cultures, and it will take time for us to piece this together in our modern world.

Here is a final story of transformation from astronaut Edgar Mitchell who is on his way home from space in Apollo 14 in 1971, contemplating his carbon origins. It shows what is possible when a modern hero becomes present to his mineral nature. He is returned to his original nature, and surely this speaks to our deepest longings. He calls this experience the "Big Picture Effect":

> We were rotating, and every two minutes a picture of the earth, the moon and the sun, and a 360 panorama of the heavens, appeared in the window as I looked. From my training in astronomy ...

I realised that matter in our universe was created in star systems and thus the molecules in my body, in the spacecraft, in my partners body, were manufactured in some ancient generation of stars ... we are all part of the same stuff and in modern physics you'd call this interconnectedness. It triggered this experience of saying, "Wow, those are my stars, my body is connected to those stars" and this was accompanied by a deep ecstatic experience which continued all the way home. This was a whole body experience. When I got home I wanted to find out what this meant. I asked scientists, but they couldn't help me, so I appealed to anthropologists who pointed out to me that in the Sanskrit is what's called Samadhi which is an experience of seeing things as a unity accompanied by ecstasy. I realised that in virtually in every culture in the world there is a similar experience—you see things in a larger context than before. I do believe that is beginning of all religions, when some mystic had that kind of experience and tried to make sense of it and put a story around it .... Thereafter I became a peacenik.

(An abbreviated version of Mitchell, 2011)

Will we die out as Homo Industrialis Destructivensis (Henriques, 2011) or can we make the leap to really become Homo Sapiens?

CHAPTER TWELVE

The politics of transformation in the global crisis

Mick Collins, William Hughes, and Andrew Samuels

Introduction

The current ecological crisis confronts us with an opportunity for a radical revision of what it means to be a politically active human being. It poses serious challenges for our collective ability to respond to change. Any serious notion of transformation in the current global crisis will have political implications; however, the reductionist mind-sets and political ideologies that have contributed to the crisis may not be fit to lead the changes required. The question is, where will the impetus for change come from? It is becoming evident that a radical vision for living sustainably in the twenty-first century will require a much deeper relationship between human consciousness and nature. We propose that the scale of collective change within the current global context represents an archetypal level of transformation.

In this chapter, we depart from conventional discourses which attempt to find professionally crafted solutions to the current crisis, and investigate how consciousness may already be attempting to redress the balance of modern humanity's one-sided materialism. We contend that archetypal patterns of change arising from people's encounters with spiritual emergencies should be viewed as "solution bearers" for a state of emergent transformation. Spiritual emergencies could be a catalyst helping to inform a deeper relationship to learning, citizenship, democracy, culture, ecology, and human occupation as part of a re-sacralized political vision for the twenty-first century.

Modern politics and the task of collective transformation

It is hard to ignore the effects of consumerism and the dissociation between humans and nature, which is a contributing factor towards an escalating sense of disenchantment in the world (Reason, 2002). Other factors such as global economics and political ideologies have also made a profound contribution to the current crisis, which has been steadily gathering pace since the middle of the twentieth century. In the early 1960s Herbert Marcuse (1964/1991) observed how people in modern technological societies were increasingly passive and bound to overly administered structures. He described modern individuals and societies as "one-dimensional", asserting that although human agency and productivity are presented as freedoms, the reality of people's daily activities within industrialized countries are mostly centred on affluence, material gain, and consumption.

The extent of humanity's alienation from the wider ecology is illustrated in a report published by the United Nations. The World Federation of UN Associations *State of the Future Report* (Glenn, Gordon & Florescu, 2008) outlines how much of the world's population is vulnerable to social instability due to the scarcity of food and water, increasing energy prices, and climate change, as well as worsening economic conditions. The report also cites other threats to the future such as corruption, violence, and an escalation of terrorism (Lean & Owen, 2008). Humanity is facing global crisis on an unprecedented scale, highlighting a need for radical change and transformation. The WFUNA report suggests that modern communications, especially the internet, could provide greater access to the world's knowledge and act as a force for democratization, education, and sharing information (Lean & Owen, 2008). Some believe that if humanity acts quickly and cooperatively disaster could be averted (Lean & Owen, 2008). From a psychotherapeutic/psychological perspective, we need to determine how we could facilitate such a major transformational process, which could also bring about deeper and more meaningful connections to life.

Research psychologist Mihalyi Csikszentmihalyi (1993) has asserted that if the future is to be an improvement on the past, more people will have to transform themselves and their goals in life. He posits that people will need to integrate individual goals with those of larger entities, including families, communities, humanity, and the planet. He envisions that we will need to cultivate transcendent selves and goals in life, going beyond competitiveness and personal advantage for the "collective well-being of all life" (Csikszentmihalyi, 1993, p. 249). However, equal attention needs to be paid to the underlying bind that modern consciousness is in. "Albert Einstein once observed that we cannot fix the problems of the present with the mindsets that created the problems" (Bussey, 2006, p. 41). We need to find solutions outside of our everyday habitual ways of knowing, being, and doing.

Returning to Marcuse's incisive analysis, it is evident that a one-dimensional, overly conforming, and bureaucratic mindset is unlikely to help engage the transformative potential of human beings: "How is it even thinkable that the vicious circle be broken?" (Marcuse, 1964/1991, pp. 250–251). The one-dimensional mode of modern consciousness recognizes the need for change and transformation, yet cannot free itself from the self perpetuating binds of its own creation. The political one-dimensionality which underpins our administered lives is a reflection of our compromised relationship to a greater multi-dimensional representation of reality.

Jung (1964, p. 94) was also troubled by modern people's "one sided consciousness", favouring everything rational, which has cut humanity off from a deeper engagement with myth and mystery in life. He believed that modern attitudes had begun to widen the gap between conscious life and a productive relationship to the unconscious, and said that if a modern person had a mystical experience they would be sure to misunderstand its true character. Jung argued that modern people run the risk of pathologizing their experiences or developing symptoms through one-sided attitudes. He maintained that the development of consciousness is the way out of "imprisonment in unconsciousness" (Jung, 1959, p. 272). An aspect of this transformation of consciousness is the recognition that everything in nature eventually flows to its opposite, which he referred to as *enantiodromia* (Jacobi, 1980); a term that reflects the potential for a natural shift in consciousness. However *enantiodromia* as a transformative process is not without its own perils, as it involves encountering the shadow, which

Jung was adamant, is always involved in deep processes of change (Jung, 1959, p. 272).

At a collective level, Arnold Mindell's work (1988) is useful for tracking processes that become split off in societies, which in turn become "city shadows". This concept illustrates how transformational crises associated with spiritual emergencies confront the limitations of collective norms, particularly as these profound psycho-spiritual experiences radically challenge the one-sided (split-off) materialistic consciousness that underpins much of the modern socio-political consensus (Collins, 2007a, 2008a). Rather than being problematic, spiritual emergencies may reflect a tipping point in the collective psyche that heralds a radical shift in consciousness through a naturally occurring *enantiodromia*. This highlights the need for a deeper exploration of the meaning found within the experiences of spiritual emergencies, which have been described as carrying the potential for developing "transcendent action in the service of collective transformation" (Collins, 2008b, p. 19).

The enantiodromia of spiritual emergencies as an archetypal transformation

It is evident that our very existence has become unbalanced and unsustainable. If humanity were stripped of its consumer based addictions and distractions what would modern consciousness fall back on? This question probes the current foundations of our collective consciousness, highlighting the need for a deeper recognition of the relevance of the personal and collective dimensions of the unconscious. A dialogue between Ervin Laszlo, Stanislav Grof, and Peter Russell (2003, pp. 5–9) asserts that modern cultures are in the midst of a collective spiritual emergency. This is not only a profoundly important declaration about the vulnerable state of modern consciousness in the face of an ever growing global problem; it also illustrates the potential for an encounter with the split-off processes that reside in the collective shadow, which can act as antecedents for an emergent *enantiodromia*.

Laszlo, Grof, and Russell (2003, pp. 5–9) suggest that a substantial group of people currently treated for psychosis within mental health systems are actually experiencing transformational crises, or spiritual emergencies. In their conversation, Stanislav Grof speaks about his work as a transpersonal psychiatrist, describing how people's orientation shifts when they discover the numinous dimension of their psyches.

This revelation leads people to "a whole new orientation toward themselves, toward other people, nature, and life in general" (Laszlo, Grof & Russell, 2003, pp. 98–99). Spiritual emergencies are organic manifestations of ripening psycho-spiritual propensities that can lead to transformations in consciousness. However, the process of collective change—as a transition to another way of living—may be challenging for many. The important point is that journeys of psycho-spiritual development will unfold naturally (Collins, 2006).

Laszlo, Grof, and Russell (2003) call for a consciousness revolution within the modern world, based on a need to transform ways of living, from the surface to the depth. This coheres with the observation of Richard Tarnas (2000, p. 10) who asks if the modern psyche is undergoing a rite of passage. If so, the transition will need to address those collective processes that have been split-off; for example, how will humanity redress the damage done to the world and to each other? Tarnas (2002, p. 10) suggests that: "It will take a fundamental *metanoia*, a self-overcoming, a radical sacrifice to make this transition". This sacrifice—linked to the word "sacred"—within modern consciousness will confront humanity with the materialistic appetites, the hedonistic lifestyles, and nihilistic attitudes that have numbed possibilities for establishing any real, deep, and lasting relationship to life as a whole. Even the simple act of weeping—for what the world has become, and what human beings have done to one another as well as to other species—could initiate powerful processes of reflection and potential transformation (Barbalet, 2005). Such a transition, according to Tarnas (1996, p. 37), is like a spiritual birth that heralds a "world-view shift", reflecting a deep archetypal pattern of transformation.

The presence of an archetypal level of change reveals how deep patterns of human potential are crystallized, able to create myths; influence religions; shape philosophical ideas; as well as influencing whole nations and eras (Jung, 1998). Indeed, it is during times of great transition that Jung recognized the occurrence of an "archetype of transformation". "These are not personalities, but rather typical situations, places, ways, animals, plants, and so forth that symbolise the kind of change, whatever it is" (Jung, 1940, p. 89). Not only have modern humans dissociated collectively from a deeper relationship with the psyche and nature, there is also no precedent for how collective transformation could happen on such a grand scale. This makes the current *zeitgeist* a potent encounter which people will find it increasingly difficult to defend against, distract from, or deny. However, at a collective level, transformations in consciousness are based on a willingness to engage in new ways of learning and engaging a gradual process of change, which happens over a period of time (Blatner, 2004).

Modern consciousness is confronted with the need to connect to "the inner reaches of our psyche and the outer realms of nature" (Yunt, 2001, p. 117). An important first step would be to treat any natural manifestations reflecting transformations in consciousness, such as spiritual emergencies, as productive potentials that could support the process of growth and ongoing spiritual emergence (*enantiodromia*). Recognizing the healing and transformative potential of spiritual emergencies could begin to transform the political consensus that shapes modern ideas of human consciousness and development.

Spiritual emergencies: transforming consciousness and changing politics

Any vision of human transformation has to include the possibility that human beings have a "pull towards self-transcendence" (Walsh & Vaughan, 1983, p. 412). Such a development involves consciousness, as indicated by Walsh and Shapiro (1983, p. 3) who have asked: "Are we all that we can be? Or are there greater heights and depths of psychological capacity within us?" These questions challenge the one-sided consciousness (Jung, 1964) and one-dimensional nature (Marcuse, 1964/1991) of modern humanity's orientation in the world, including the collective neglect of our human potential (Walsh & Shapiro, 1983) as well as our separation from a wider ecology of life.

There is a pressing need for us to recognize our deep connection to life as a whole. Elam's research into mystical experiences shows how spiritual encounters can open people to a wider spectrum of consciousness and a greater sense of universal and ecological belonging. For example, a participant recounted: "My senses were heightened … I had an acute sense of being a part of everything. It was an instant that didn't last long, but it was beyond time, it was endless" (Elam, 2005, p. 55). This example reflects a process of spiritual emergence, which also has the potential to overwhelm people's ego/identity boundaries and lead to a transformational crisis (Grof & Grof, 1989, 1991, 1993; Lucas, 2006; Watson, 1994). The antecedents for these types of spiritual emergencies are varied and can include surgery, sexual relations, childbirth, near-death, transitional stages of life and spiritual practices (Guiley, 2001, p. 567). The current global crisis could be acting as a trigger for increasing numbers of people to experience spiritual emergencies (Collins, 2008b).

What would Jung have made of the connection between the current global crisis, as a "state of emergency" (Manuel-Navarrete, Kay & Dolderman, 2004, p. 226), and the occurrence of spiritual emergencies? When he built his tower at Bollingen it enabled him to commune deeply with nature as part of his individuation process, which he felt was a process of birth from the "maternal unconscious". This natural process of psycho-spiritual renewal enabled him to be intimately connected to all nature, as if he were inside all living things (Jung, 1983, p. 252). The connection between nature and individuation can lead to an expanded view of consciousness that in turn can lead to occasional experiences of unity, or *unio mystica* (Jung, 1954/1993). However, in the modern world these types of connective experiences are not discussed in mainstream discourses on human development. Indeed, people experiencing spiritual emergencies may be treated by the psychiatric services (Laszlo, Grof & Russell, 2003), which has political implications for understanding the power of mainstream responses to altered/extreme states of consciousness (Collins & Wells, 2006).

Human beings have the capacity to experience a wider sense of universal belonging (Maslow, 1999) in stark contrast to the modern sociopolitical mind-set that has bound people to a one-dimensional existence (Marcuse, 1964/1991). It is hardly surprising then, that the psyche is beginning to stir and is attempting to reassert a deeper connection to consciousness through spiritual emergencies. Perhaps spiritual emergencies are the very heart and soul of a collective process for a renewal that could begin to re-affirm humanity's relationship to the psyche. Rust has identified the need to keep an open mind: "We need to dig deep, to retread our own myths as well as find inspiration from the stories of others who are outside the box of western culture, and inside the web of life" (Rust, 2008a, p. 160).

Spiritual emergencies need to be taken seriously as transformational phenomena, with the potential to connect human beings to the psyche and to experiences of universal connectedness. However, the spiritual vacuum within the modern world shows the prevalent depth of dissociation, where humanity no longer views the world as being sacred, but rather sees it as a commodity that can be exploited.

The transformational potential that exists between psycho-spiritual and socio-political realities is tempered by the sobering realization offered by Samuels (1998) who has cautioned against seeking cheap forms of holism in relation to the complex problems of our modern world. The challenge for humanity is to dig deep and find sustainable solutions to the problems we face collectively. The field of psychotherapy could make a valuable contribution to the transformation of political thought, through engaging with people's deep experiences. Samuels has suggested that "what an individual citizen experiences, in his or her heart, body or dreams, about the political and social world in which he or she is living tells us a great deal about that world" (Samuels, 1998, p. 361).

People's deep experiences can reflect contact with the numinous (Samuels, 1993a), and this is certainly evident in the case of spiritual emergencies (Collins, 2008a, 2008b). If we acknowledge that the personal is also political, as summarized by Samuels (1998), we cannot ignore the collective implications of the transformative narratives of people who have transited the growth experiences of spiritual emergencies (Collins, 2008a), which parallel the process of sacred renewal and the transformation of a political vision that informs our collective actions and interactions. Spiritual emergencies are diametrically opposed to the superficial reality of a consumer-based consensus, and unless they are processed individually and collectively they will remain split-off within the collective shadow, which will continue to perpetuate the collective disavowal of sacred encounters within modern consciousness. However, Samuels (1993b, p. 211) has reminded us that "only things of real substance and value cast a shadow". The process of transforming the shadow happens through allowing what has been ignored or repressed back into consciousness. The question remains: how can transformation—from a superficial existence, to a greater depth of living—be considered at a collective level? This is probably the most compelling question that confronts humanity today.

Political transformation through multi-levelled engagement

If Laszlo, Grof, and Russell (2003) are correct that the modern world is going through a collective spiritual emergency, we have to consider how the flow of such an *enantiodromia* could be used productively to help facilitate a wider collective transformation. This radical perspective requires an appreciation that our collective awareness will be challenged in the current global crisis to explore new ways of living, and a deeper engagement with reality. Slaughter (1999, p. 152) has asked what possibilities could be reconsidered to reflect greater depths within such transformational processes in the Western world "such as myth, ritual, connectedness, spirituality and the numinous".

Deep processes of transformation can involve a period of de-structuring, leading to new potentials, directions, and renewed purposes for living; however, deep transformative processes can often be frightening and anxiety provoking (Canda, 1988). Transformation that attempts to deal with change at a collective level will need to establish safe parameters, which, we suggest, can be developed through *deep transitions* (see below) that enable transformation to be meaningfully engaged (Canda, 1988). This further identifies the need to manage the tension between conscious and unconscious processes, through the transcendent function, as conceptualized by Jung (Miller, 2004). Spiritual emergencies are connected to an archetypal level of transformation (Collins, 2008b), which requires a deep understanding and respect for how such transitions in consciousness operate.

The key issue for acknowledging the archetype of transformation *in potentia* is through the development of awareness (Avens, 1976). However, at a collective level we contend that there can only be frameworks that help to guide such transitions towards greater collaborative understanding, without prescribing how transformation should be cultivated. A vital first step for collective transformation would be to go beyond competitiveness and personal gain to the "collective well-being of all life" (Csikszentmihalyi, 1993, p. 249). The need for such a collective process of transformation is twofold. First, all humanity is facing an unprecedented global crisis, requiring collaborative reflection and action for sustainable living and future survival. Second, each individual will need to consider their personal relationship to the process of transformation, and how they are capable of engaging it. The process of collective transformation is unlikely to be a linear process of change, and may even appear paradoxical at times; however, the notion of a paradox of transformation may itself be useful. Jung (1989, p. 259) states that the acceptance of paradox can be meaningful; thereby providing a more faithful picture of the real state of affairs, rather than grasping for "uniformity of meaning".

The journey of transformation can be witnessed in people who have successfully encountered spiritual emergencies (Collins, 2008a). These transformative narratives can encourage others to trust the development of a productive relationship to a wider spectrum of consciousness through cultivating levels of attention, awareness, reflexivity, and trans-reflexivity (Collins, 2008b). Spiritual emergencies are natural and profound encounters with consciousness and life; if they can teach us anything, it is to trust that human beings are capable of deep levels of transformation within daily life. The six propositions for *deep transition* outlined below (Collins, Hughes & Samuels, 2010) are based on the understanding that if humanity relates to the depth now, we stand more chance of integrating spiritual emergence and emergencies later.

Deep learning: reflects human beings' great potential for living creatively, through engaging their imaginations and innovations in daily life (May, 1976). Deep learning involves being interested and motivated in life (Jarvis, 2005). And it is the depth of the learning process that connects people's potential for meaningful engagement (Moon, 2000) and transformative experiences (Kolb, 1984). It is instructive to note that the Latin word *ēducāre* means to "bring out" (Wyld, 1961, p. 351), which identifies that deep learning is not only transformative; it is a lifelong process (Knapper & Cropley, 1985).

Deep citizenship: identifies what it means to be engaged in life as a citizen, which naturally cultivates a deep political outlook. Deep citizenship reflects a process of discovery about what it is to be human, as well as having concern for self, others, and the world (Clarke, 1996). Citizenship from this perspective is allied to the politics of everyday life, between the inner life of people's private world, and the outer life of public engagement (Samuels, 2001). Deep citizenship is not a one-dimensional association to a given society (Marcuse, 1964/1991), it is a multi-levelled perspective for ways of living and being-in-the-world.

Deep democracy: Jung (1994, p. 236) believed that true democracy is a psychological process. However, the spiritual attitude of deep democracy has been developed by Mindell (2002) and his colleagues, with a strong socio-political emphasis. Deep democracy encourages dialogues and interactions between diverse viewpoints, including consensus and non-consensus experiences (Mindell, 2000), and is based on facilitation skills that lead to the cultivation of awareness (Mindell, 2008).

Deep democracy is essential if humanity is serious about creating a just and fair world, based on diversity and respect for all ways of being.

Deep culture: Global living provides many challenges and opportunities for understanding the diverse world views that we share with others through cultural dialogues and exchanges. The concept of deep culture is based on the need to encourage greater intercultural communication and awareness. Deep culture reflects a desire to explore and understand the variety of meanings contained within human behaviours, with an emphasis on cross cultural learning (Shaules, 2007). This viewpoint provides opportunities for developing self-other awareness, based on the appreciation of how processes of enculturation are internalized (Ho, 1995).

Deep ecology: as discussed by Naess (1986) reflects a deeper, wider, and more expansive relationship to the world that exists both within and around us (Fox, 1990b). Deep ecology goes beyond the surface concerns of environmental problems and represents a much more comprehensive philosophical standpoint (Reser, 1995). It is a perspective that provides opportunities for human beings to reflect on the ways that they are participating in the world, whilst acknowledging the interconnectedness of all life (Reason, 2002). Thus, human beings are embedded within a deep ecology of life, not separate from it.

Deep occupations: refer to how people's active participation in daily life contains the possibilities for evolving their consciousness and awareness, linked to their abilities for engaging creative and fluid adaptations (Collins, 2001, 2007b). Psycho-spiritual developments within daily-life (Collins, 1998) can occur through intelligent engagement of occupations (Collins, 2007c, 2010a, 2010b, 2010c). The depth of human occupations can be revealed through their connection to unconscious processes (Collins, 2001, 2004; Nicholls, 2007) as well as reflecting transpersonal ways of knowing, being, and doing (Collins, 2008c, 2010a; do Rozario, 1997; Kang, 2003).

Our collective need for a more ecological outlook coheres with the need for spiritual emergence that is allied to political transformation. We cannot overlook the psyche's potential for healing (Collins, 2007d) and the impact of politics upon the psyche (Samuels, 1993a). A vital first step is to orientate ourselves to the shadow side of collective change, which could start by acknowledging the deep transformations already happening to many people in the modern world who are encountering spiritual emergencies. A key reflection at the heart of collective transformation is; how will humanity embrace deeper ways of *doing* and *being* to co-create a sustainable future? The political implications of engaging deeper connections to a wider ecology of life are that humanity could begin to take more responsibility for the quality of its reflections and actions in the world; thereby enabling spiritual emergence, as well as integrating the transformative effects of spiritual emergencies.

Conclusion

Spiritual emergencies appear to be a tipping point in modern consciousness, which link to an *enantiodromia* within collective consciousness. The politics of transformation in this global era will need to reevaluate humanity's dissociated relationship to a wider ecology of life, in which all life is embedded. We have argued that spiritual emergencies are confronting humanity with the neglected collective shadow, which if recognized, could inspire a tipping point for transformation. The six propositions for deep transition outlined in this article are a rallying point for political action and transformation, which address the deep ecological issues of this age towards more sustainable ways of living.

CHAPTER THIRTEEN

"Heart and soul": inner and outer within the transition movement

Hilary Prentice

Looking into the mirror: what are we like?

Perhaps one of the most exciting aspects of this time of planetary turmoil, breakdown, potential, despair and hope, is that it confronts us so strongly with profound questions about what we are like, as human beings. Is it "human nature' to be greedy, and not to change until we are forced to? Are we a technologically brilliant, dominant species who will easily solve our current problems with our rational minds? Or are we, actually, rather a bad lot, and the planet will recover and be better off without us, if we shortly create our own demise? These are very common first-off responses, ones I have heard many times as people are confronted with some piece of challenging information about our environmental situation. What they have in common, I feel, is precisely that immediate beginning to face up to ourselves just a bit as a species.

As someone passionate about ecopsychology for nearly twenty years, I have been present at many events where there is, essentially, some space and safety for people to explore their responses to the developing environmental crisis at a somewhat deeper level. As well as painful emotions or numbness (fear, anger, despair, disbelief, grief, cynicism), there often arises this deeper wondering about humanity: What is our nature? How did we get into this situation? How do we need to change? Can we change? What is in the way of that? And, ultimately, what is being called forth from each one of us, as we endeavour to really respond to what we are seeing?

I work as a psychotherapist, and these questions immediately came alive for me as I began, in the early 1990s, to meet with other therapists to explore the relationship between psychotherapy and current human presence on this earth. We soon discovered that they are profoundly interesting questions, with no easy answers.

Ecos and Psyche, outer and inner (five faces I saw in the mirror)

For me, one of the most telling insights was contained in the word "eco-psychology"; the bringing back together of Ecos and Psyche, *because they have been split apart*. I came to understand that, where indigenous societies have lived sustainably, in balance and harmony with the earth and other beings around them, beliefs, practices, and cosmology are all rich in the understanding that we are in no way separate from the earth from which we spring. After spending time with shamans in Bali and Nepal, David Abrams expressed this particularly beautifully;

> Humans are tuned for relationship .... This landscape of shadowed voices, these feathered bodies and antlers and tumbling streams—these breathing shapes are our family, the beings with whom we suffer and struggle and celebrate. For the largest part of our species existence, humans have negotiated relationships with every aspect of our sensuous surroundings ... from all of these relationships our collective sensibilities were nourished ... The simple premise ... is that we are human only in contact, and conviviality, with what is not human.
>
> (Abrams, 1996, p. ix)

Conversely, it seemed clear that collective denial about our current unsustainable and destructive consumption of the earth co-exists with a mindset that constantly reinforces our separation from, and superiority over, the rest of life on this earth. John Seed amongst others has termed this attitude of separation and superiority to the earth "anthropocentrism" (Seed, Macy, Fleming & Naess, 1988), and it seems to function in a way which is remarkably parallel to other human-to-human oppressions and exploitations. Interestingly, those on the under-side of major inequalities are often seen as "earthier", as well as "less than" (for example women, people of colour, peasants, working class people in general: Prentice, 2002).

It struck me, in fact, that this "split" or disconnection between our inner worlds and the earth has many faces, and much significance. One face is the separation of science and technology (outer focused) from religion and the humanities (inner focused) in the western cultural tra-dition that is currently dominating our planet. This separation is cred-ited with having enabled science to suddenly leap ahead, freed from the constraints of rigidly held beliefs about how the universe works and is intended to work. Humans appeared as separate beings, defined by our apparently superior minds, able to investigate and manipulate the world of "inanimate" matter—taken to mean all other substances and life forms—with impunity. Our emotional responses, our dreaming, intuitive or indeed mystical selves, our concerns with relationship, with our impact on the other, with community, with the growth of compas-sion or wisdom or love or social justice—all of these could and should be kept separate.

The clear consequence of this, it seems to me, is the runaway machine of the "industrial growth society", which is chewing up and spitting out the life of this planet with little regard for morality, consequence, sustainability, or wisdom. The growth of our capacity to manipulate an "outer" world which cannot be wounded because we have taken it to be inanimate, has massively outstripped our inner growth—all that might allow us to use what we have discovered judiciously, with wis-dom, and in balance. The theoretical physicist, psychologist, and writer about spiritual change, Peter Russell puts it like this:

> Any intelligent tool using species enters what is, in effect, a win-dow in time. The window opens with the emergence of self con-sciousness. The species then embarks on a dash through history. Can its inner evolution keep pace with its material development? Can it make it through to a full awakening of consciousness before the side effects of misguided creativity force the window closed?

> (Russell, 2009, p. 186)

It seems furthermore that not only have we (firstly) separated the outer "material" world (earth) from our inner life, and (secondly) collectively focused on outer development massively at the expense of inner growth, but that to some degree we have also (thirdly) confused the two, tending to look on the outside of ourselves for that which is only to be found on the inside.

In the past I worked for many years in the field of addictions, witnessing countless people as they increasingly discovered what had been going on as they ingested substances (alcohol, food …) or through addictive behaviour (overwork, material acquisition, compulsive caregiving …). Usually this involved on the one hand attempting not to feel (pain, sadness, fear, inadequacy, meaninglessness, rage) and on the other attempting to feel (alive, sexy, powerful, spontaneous, "high", in control, free, confident, connected, present). However, to put a profound point simply, our growth as people usually involves feeling and learning from our feelings rather than running from them, and results from the integrity and courage with which we live our lives, face up to our inner demons, and meet the challenges life brings us. It was apparent to me that looking for something in a place it cannot be found tends to be profoundly weakening. In fact I have never seen an addictive process not end up creating precisely the opposite state to that which was initially sought. Mary Jayne Rust (2005, 2008b) and Chellis Glendenning (1995) are amongst those who have explored the parallels between individual addictive journeys, and collective addictions to material and consumer products, including perhaps fossil fuels themselves.

In effect, it is as though we are constantly projecting our inner issues onto the outside world, and seeking to solve them by manipulating that world. Sometimes this involves seeking to acquire that which seems to hold the inner state we seek. Other times we attempt to destroy or change that onto which we have projected the aspects of ourselves we judge negatively. When one enemy becomes our friend, miraculously, another country appears as the new threat.

Perhaps this very deep habit of looking on the outside for that which is ultimately to be found on the inside, is what was pointed to in the famous tale about Nasruddin, in which the Sufi sage is found looking for the keys to his house under a street light. When asked if this is where he lost them, he replies no, he lost them indoors, but that he is looking here, because it is lighter! He is not looking inside his house (self) or looking into the darkness (shadow), and whilst short term this apparently appears easier, ultimately it is destined to be absolutely frustrating, to keep him endlessly searching, and thus to keep him in suffering.

As Peter Russell points out, the amplification of this error by modern technology makes it particularly disastrous:

> Unconsciously assuming that these needs can also be satisfied by changing the world around us, we have applied our creative energies and our technologies to the search for more powerful ways of getting what we think we want. ... It is the demands we make on the world in our relentless search for inner fulfilment that lead us to consume far more than we physically need. No other species consumes more than it needs. This is because no other species has our inner needs, or the means to amplify the demands they create. It is this combination that is causing us to suck the earth dry.
>
> (Russell, 2009, p. 62)

Again, the "us" about whom he is writing refers to those of us who are in the position of consumers within this global system; larger numbers of people find themselves in the position of relatively extreme material poverty, often working appalling hours to support this system, and more likely to find themselves in a state of envy and resentment than of unaware complacency and arrogance.

I saw a fourth face of this inner/outer split in its impact on movements for change. I spent half my adult life around people who saw that human and planetary well-being were primarily shaped by economic and social forces and structures, which currently create inequality and oppressions of many forms. The solution would involve political and social change, and relative happiness would naturally follow. Later, in the worlds of psychotherapy and inner/spiritual growth, I met the opposite belief; that change begins not on the outside, but on the inside ("peace begins with me"), and that only if we transform the structures of aggression or domination, greed or restlessness within each one of us, will we begin to be able to create the society we dream of. I have encountered considerable separation and mutual wariness between people committed to these apparently opposing views. This is perhaps because of an urgency to make things better and so to get it right, and the passionate energy released by the insight held by each "camp", but also perhaps because this split is so profound, and so painful, that we find ourselves living it out, again and again.

Lastly, a fifth face; the relationship between individual work, such as psychotherapy, and the big political picture. In the 1990s, I joined Psychotherapists and Counsellors for Social Responsibility (PCSR, www.pcsr.org.uk), an organization wishing to find ways to bring the insights gained in the therapy room out into the bigger political and social process, and somehow to balance the apparently intense focus in our work on the individual with an awareness of the larger context within which this work takes place. Whilst it is often easy to see the parallels between individual therapeutic journeys and collective issues (addiction, denial, narcissism) it can be much harder to know what to do with this insight. How does our quiet, private individual work, as clients or meditators or therapists, feed into the wider society, and our collective state of consciousness? How has more than a hundred years of psychotherapy (Hillman & Ventura, 1992), the humanistic psychology movement, a plethora of self-help movements and much more, impacted on our society? I have sometimes struggled with the feeling that what I feel called to do—psychotherapy—is a ridiculously small drop in the ocean. At many other times I am filled with awe at the privilege to be present with another human's courage as they turn inside, speak what is true for them, face old wounds and emotional pain, feel, digest, learn and grow. At such moments this work seems truly precious, and I can but trust it serves the bigger picture as well as the individuals concerned. Nonetheless, the question remained alive for me, as to whether inner and outer transformation could come more closely back together.

Inner and outer in the transition movement

In 2006 I found myself living just ten miles from Totnes, the small country town in South Devon in which Rob Hopkins and others were initiating what was called Transition Town Totnes (TTT), a simple, positive, and very appealing plan to begin the transition from an oil-dependent way of life, to a sustainable, human- and life-centred local economy and culture (www.transitiontowntotnes, www.transition-culture.org). The underlying premise was that change is inevitable, the key choice being whether we start now to create the most positive future, or head unawarely towards an ecological, economic, and social catastrophe (Hopkins, 2008). Rather than leaving this to governments, the idea was to start local, and within a few months of its launch TTT had groups looking at such issues as food, energy, housing, transport, local government, and the arts. The idea quickly went viral, and within a year the first national conference of Transition projects around the UK was to take place. At the time of writing nearly 800 transition initiatives have registered with the Network, in more than thirty countries (www. transitionnetwork), and it is thought that there are in fact many more. Whilst the initial impetus came primarily from Rob's awareness of the significance of Peak Oil, two other key drivers are now acknowledged; climate change, and economic contraction.

For me as an ecopsychologist this was of course very exciting, and the possibility immediately arose of starting a working group. As Rob often spoke of the "Head, Heart and Hands" of Transition, our group was dubbed "Heart and Soul", dealing with the "Psychological, Spiritual and Consciousness Aspects of Transition". Recently the group has renamed itself "Inner Transition", and there are now groups with both names, and others, as part of Transition Initiatives all over the world.

Here was an extraordinary opportunity. People drawn to the practical "outer" aspects of transition to a sustainable wise human presence on the planet, and those initially drawn to the inner dimensions of that same change, could and did, literally, sit round the same table and work together. We took the position that there is no inherent contradiction here; the outer creates the inner, and the inner creates the outer. For me, having explored over time something of the significance of our inner/ outer disconnection, imbalance, and confusion, this was particularly exciting; how would this work in practice, might it prove remarkably potent, or rather difficult and challenging as resistance was inevitably encountered?

The inner is implicit? Where we began

Or, in fact, could it be the case that a shift in consciousness and values, an emotional literacy, and some spiritual inspiration were already implicit in the very arising of the transition movement? To me, that was clearly the case.

There was, for example, a moving beyond our collective denial that fossil fuels will peak and decline, that climate change results from our use of them and must urgently be addressed, and that economic growth can be infinite on a finite planet. Facing difficult truths and rising to meet them with a positive vision is perhaps one hallmark of inner work. There was a strong emphasis on the positive, on coming together as a community, and on dreaming out a vision for the future that would support human and other than human life, based not on greed, inequality, power-over or increasing material wealth, but on practicality, sharing, creativity, and celebration. The implicit values, in short, were not other than those embraced by spiritual teachings throughout the world.

Furthermore, much of how business was conducted had clearly been influenced by various ways "inner work" has come into culture. Meetings were often begun with sharing "go-rounds", for example, or silence. Creative, open formats for events such as "world cafe" (www.theworldcafe.com) or "open space technology" (http://www.openspaceworld.org/) were often used. So the question became, what if anything could the Heart and Soul group add to what would in any case be taking place? Who would be interested, what ground would we spring from, and what would we do?

A world-wide movement of consciousness: three strands

If it is the case, as I have suggested above, that our external material development appears to have dangerously outstripped our inner growth as wise or awake human beings, is the remedy for this imbalance also appearing alongside the problem? There are many who would argue that this is so, that from different parts of the globe come teachings and wisdom that support our growth, our coming back into balance, and that together these could be seen as a world-wide movement of consciousness. I am particularly aware of three strands here. Potentially, an inner transition focus would draw from all three, and would need a strong presence both to bring the inner forward in relation to the habit of outer dominance, and then to work towards the re-integration of the two sides which have been split apart.

One strand in this movement of consciousness comes from the many peoples who still remember, and practice, earth-centred wisdom, who have not forgotten how to live sustainably on the earth, and for whom ecos and psyche have not been split apart. Not to acknowledge, honour, and learn from them, would be, it seems to me, to be yet again disrespectful to our true elders. All over the world indigenous peoples are coming together as they find the lands on which they live under environmental assault—from oil spills in Nigeria, Louisiana, and Ecuador, to climate change, deforestation, and other forms of pollution. As well as campaigning for their rights and lands, (www.cwis.org) frequently there is a clear call to the rest of the world to "wake up".

One example comes from the Achuar, from deep inside Ecuador. They sought alliance with the industrialized world, and from this the Pachamama Alliance was born:

> From the beginning of our partnership, the indigenous people urged us to focus on "changing the dream of the modern world", since it is our "dream"—over-consumption without regard for social and environmental consequences—that is driving the destruction of the rainforests around the world. Out of our work with these ancient cultures, we have come to understand that we in the so called "modern" world truly are in a kind of trance, living a dream that is threatening not just the rainforests, but the health and wellbeing of the entire planet .... In response their request, we launched the Awakening the Dreamer Initiative.
>
> (www.awakeningthedreamer.org)

The Pachamama Alliance now works with peoples spanning five different South American countries.

Secondly, many have been drawn to teachings and writings about the transformation of consciousness, drawn very often from eastern spiritual traditions. Peter Russell refers to a "centuries old Hopi prophecy that ... at the height of the white man's foolishness great wisdom returns, coming from the East. If he listens to this wisdom there will come a conscious transformation and re-birth of humanity" (Russell, 2009, p. 141). Similarly Joanna Macy tells of an ancient Tibetan prophecy, that at a time when life on earth hangs in the balance, the Kingdom of Shambhala will appear. "Shambhala Warriors" (you and me) will come to help bring this about. Their weapons are Insight and Compassion; they understand that the problem, being "Manomaya", made by the human mind, can and must be dismantled by the human mind (Macy & Brown, 1998, p. 60).

There are now countless teachers and practitioners of meditation, presence, mindfulness, yoga, and Tai Chi, in various flavours, and new teachers, such as Tolle (e.g., 2005), with huge followings in many countries. Women teachers have increasingly appeared (Batchelor, 1996; Robinson, 2007). There is a new Center for World Spirituality (www.centerforworldspirituality.com), bringing together large numbers of cutting edge spiritual teachers with larger numbers of followers worldwide. "The emergence of a World Spirituality based on integral principles is one of the great and urgent invitations for the evolution of consciousness in our time" (Wilber, quoted at www.centerforworldspirituality.com).

And thirdly: the last century has seen an extraordinary mushrooming of schools and practitioners of psychology, psychotherapy, and counselling, particularly in the west (Norcross & Goldfried, 1992). These have in common a quest to understand the roots of human destructiveness and dysfunction, the role of trauma, abuse and neglect in childhood— and to become skilled in the healing of the wounded, and wounding, human psyche. Understanding of psychological "defences" such as denial and displacement, which seem so relevant to our times, has also come out of this movement. Practitioners could potentially bring to Transition skill and experience in supporting people through times of difficulty and change, in processing and making sense of difficult emotions, in helping us emerge from collectively addictive lifestyles, and much more.

Finally: Heart and Soul in practice

Beginnings

Firstly, people were drawn to Transition who might not otherwise have thought it was for them. Early on, we were able to organize some big "speaker meetings" with famous speakers from the consciousness movement, such as Peter Russell and Marianne Williamson. These were sell-out meetings, with many people at their first transition event. Some of these people then got involved in the practical dimensions of the task, beginning to reduce their carbon footprint, participate in garden share schemes, and much more, thus finding new ways to ground their vision in how we live our lives. Inner work which is not lived and embodied in our outer lives is also arguably hopelessly weakened. Flying off unquestioningly to visit a spiritual teacher the other side of the world, with no awareness of the contradictions involved in the impact of that flight, became for many a thing of the past.

Who is interested?

In Totnes, people who have taken part in our Heart and Soul group once we had our own launch and "put out the call" have included: counsellors, Buddhists, ecopsychologists, dance and movement teachers, people who have dealt with trauma and difficulty in their lives and in one way or another found resource in inner work and inner growth, Christians, atheists, psychotherapists, pagans, meditators and teachers of meditation, addictions workers, Quakers, coaches, psychoanalysts, social workers, teachers, poets, facilitators, mediators, people learning about nonviolent communication, a teacher of native American spirituality, teachers and practitioners of "mindfulness", practitioners of T'ai Chi, Chi Gong, and Yoga, women who've been part of consciousness raising groups in the womens movement, people who run workshops on healing difficulties between men and women, interfaith ministers, someone from an alternative to violence project working in prisons—and even our very own Professor of Consciousness! But of course this is not really about what job you may do, and everyone who is interested is welcome.

It is perhaps extraordinary that such people are coming together with each other, to discover how to be part of, be changed by, and contribute to a grassroots environmental movement.

Enquiry

As people came together in open meetings, workshops and other sharing spaces, they found themselves enquiring for themselves into the psychology and spirituality of what we are in, what it means, where we are going. Perhaps, again, because the split and denial have been so deep, this seems to be an inevitable part of the process; however often it seemed to some of us that the basic territory had been sketched out, again and again someone would say "I don't really understand what we are doing here, how are these things connected? and a new discussion would open up. We would share in circles, in small groups, in smaller working groups on themes, in constellation formats, in brainstorms, in an open space day with many inner transition themes, in big ceremonies, and insights and "aha!" moments would abound. Yet still that question kept coming, perhaps testimony to just how much needs to be processed and digested here, just how powerful the dominant mindset we are attempting to go against.

In the way of paradox, the opposite was also true, the insight contained in such words as "in the end this is about a change of heart/a complete change of values/a deep spiritual shift/an evolution of consciousness; if that does not take place alongside the windmills, I'm not sure there is any point" arriving fully formed and simply and beautifully put, over and over again, from countless different people at all kinds of events.

Parallel process

This was a reminder for me of something learned in my early days in ecopsychology; that ecological parallel process exists, whereby as we come together to process these issues, the very psychological or spiritual issues themselves will tend to constellate in the field of the group. "What are we doing here and why, I can't remember, how is everything connected?" is perhaps just such a question. Similarly, I remember parallels such as the tension between overfeeding (too much in an event) and the need to digest what is already an abundance; feelings of overwhelm; a tendency to urgency and doing too much whilst speaking of the need to slow down and become present to what is; issues of belonging, inclusion, and exclusion—do I really belong here?; issues of power and control versus trusting the process, occasional very painful attacks on the love and hard work that had gone into what had already happened; oscillations between feeling small and powerless and moments of grandiosity in which the heart and soul group could sort out anything, including the rest of the movement! The capacity to name parallel process as it occurs is one piece of emotional literacy that hopefully helps somewhat.

Offerings

As people grappled with the questions of inner and outer transition and found ways of making sense of this, different offerings to the wider movement began to take shape. These included workshops, such as those based on the work of Joanna Macy (Macy & Brown, 1998), or developing family constellations workshops into eco-constellations, such that other-than-human participants took part and questions brought could be about the wider process. Links were made with mindfulness teachers, and meditation and enquiries from that tradition were offered, as were earth-based ceremonies and celebrations, and teaching of a Native American way. We offered process input to other transition events, such as big meetings and conferences, helping to facilitate, and to establish a highly participatory style at such events. It became unlikely that a film or speaker offering painful and difficult environmental information would be followed by a dry intellectual discussion, or everyone going straight home (or to the pub!)—there would be space to share the feelings generated, and to come together with others in this, so community would replace the fear and isolation potentially generated.

We facilitated the setting up of small "home groups", a bit like the consciousness raising groups of the early women's movement, in which people could meet and share thoughts, feelings and experiences, and support each other to take practical steps. This was largely replaced by, but fed into, the larger and very successful "Transition Streets" project, in which people came together with their neighbours, initially about funding for solar panels, but through which a great deal of community has been built. Another successful project was the setting up of a "mentoring scheme", through which skilled and experienced people such as counsellors and coaches donated ongoing support to some of the most active people, offering place for reflection, emotional support, and thus combating the likelihood of burnout. Very importantly, "inner transition" has also been woven into the Transition Trainings, which have now taken place all over the world.

Effectiveness: a resilient field of consciousness?

The world is changing and moving around us very fast, as we release our offerings into the big stream, knowing little of who they touch and where they end up. It may be particularly difficult to see from within, as resistance comes and goes and the inner/outer dance continues, how far "Heart and Soul" has contributed to the excitement, positive energy, rapid growth and effectiveness of the Transition movement. My sense is that we have helped the task of Transition to make sense to many at a deeper level than might otherwise have been possible, in a richer, more diverse and more supportive and transformative way.

My hope is that overall we have contributed, in this movement towards community resilience, to the creation of a more *resilient field of consciousness.* Naomi Klein has said in a public meeting that what happens at a time of crisis has much to do with what ideas have been left lying around; perhaps it equally has to do with what community has been built, and how resilient (loving, generous, compassionate, insightful, openhearted, forgiving) the field of consciousness has become— how far it has moved from being fear and separation based, towards being love and connection based.

Looking again into the mirror: the earth is still our spiritual teacher

I began with the observation that as soon as we begin to confront difficult environmental information, it is as though we are looking into a mirror, seeing something about what we humans seem to be like.

I went on to talk about what most impressed me as I looked into the mirror—the perception that for indigenous peoples the earth and our psyche are not split violently apart, but are appropriately interwoven. We knew or know self-evidently that we are part of the web of life, and that what we do to the web we do to ourselves, because all things are connected. In that way of being, everyone knows not to take more than is needed, and learns to share as a child. The earth is not in-animate, it is full of spirit, which we are also, so to wound it is immediately as painful as wounding ourselves. Our life is about the integrity and growth of our spirit—we do not project this onto the world around us, but rather see the world clearly, in all its beauty, and it is this which nourishes our soul. It is an extraordinary gift to be here on the earth, and there is gratitude, and presence, and reverence.

> *Oh Great Spirit,*
> *Whose voice I hear in the winds,*
> *And whose breath gives life to all the world,*
> *hear me!*
> *Let me walk in beauty, and make my eyes*
> *ever behold the red and purple sunset. Make*
> *my hands respect the things you have made*
> *and my ears sharp to hear your voice.*
> *Let me learn the lessons you have hidden in*
> *every leaf and rock ... .*
> *Make me always ready to come to you with*
> *clean hands and straight eyes.*

So when life fades, as the fading sunset, my
spirit may come to you without shame.

(Native American, in Exley, 1997, n.p.)

I explored some of the faces of the inner/outer split in cultures that have moved away from indigenous wisdom, a split in which we have been outer-focused, have confused inner with outer, and have lost awareness of the sacredness of what surrounds us, just as we lost focus on our own inner growth. Western psychology and Eastern spiritual teachings can help us to heal, and to turn again within. However, both have in various degrees been subject to an anthropocentric disconnection from, or a rising above, the earth. Ecopsychologists of course endeavour to correct this, as do earth based and embodied spirituality (www.Greenspirit. com), and indigenous teachings. If we do inner work but fail to address what is also happening on the outer, to the earth, we will also be reproducing the split, the wound, rather than healing it.

I have described the attempt in practice to bring inner and outer change, and the earth, together in the Transition Movement, one no doubt of many places in which this is happening.

Ultimately, what I see in the mirror, as we look at ourselves as we are on the earth, is a spiritual teacher, telling us everything we need to know about where we are in our spiritual journeys, and how we need to go forward. This insight excited me several years ago, but it was only recently I saw more deeply the significance of this; to indigenous peoples the earth is our teacher, *and this has not changed at all*. Now we are being shown how out of balance we have become, how unwise, what "spiritual" qualities need to come forward for us to transform this situation, to come back into balance.

Grandfather,
Look at our brokenness.
We know that in all creation
only the human family
has strayed from the sacred way.
We know that we are the ones
who are divided
and we are the ones
Who must come back together

To walk in the sacred way.
Grandfather,
Sacred One,
teach us love, compassion, honour
that we may heal the earth
and heal each other.

(Ojibway Prayer, in Exley, 1997, n.p.)

CHAPTER FOURTEEN

"What if it were true …"

Jerome Bernstein

W̱e see and hear what we are open to noticing.
Several years ago I was in session with a woman I call
Hannah (You can read more about her in Bernstein, 2005,
Chapter Two). We had been working together for a year and a half.
During this session Hannah became so angry at me that she took her
shoe and began slamming it on the floor—in large measure to avoid
hitting me with it. She was angry because she was sharing a deeply
moving experience she had had involving two cows being hauled in
a truck to market. I was interpreting her experience as more symbolic
than real.

Two years ago, the father of a ten-year-old boy reported that his son
recently had said to him, "I'd rather be an animal than a boy. I like animals better." When I pursued it, he said that his son was not upset when
he shared this intimacy with him and that he seemed well-adjusted and
happy with life, including with his friends. But given the choice, he
would choose to be with animals, particularly in the wild, more than
with people. The father wanted to know if I felt he should *do* something
about this.

Sitting with a patient who had never looked me in the eye in one and
a half years of therapy, suddenly she bent down towards the floor and

in a near whisper shared with me a deep and personal communication she had had with her horse. Then she fell silent. After a moment she looked up at me sideways and said, "Do you think that's crazy?" I said no, I did not think she nor the story that she shared was crazy. After a couple of long minutes she sat upright, looked me fully in the eye and said, "OK, I think I can trust you." What followed was three years of amazing work with a Borderland woman who had had ten years of previous therapy never once mentioning to her therapist any of her transrational experiences.

Another person wrote to me that since she was little, when she touched doors, the wood would tell her about the trees from which the wood came.

In an initial session, a man said, "The woods and nature are my second church." He then went on to describe how nature, and particularly his connection with dogs, are his deepest spiritual communion and the only context in which he feels safe and happy. Being in Nature obviously was his church of choice.

I have found over a number of years that such stories are not as unusual as they may seem. Indeed, it is a matter of what we as clinicians are open to hearing. None of these people were crazy. Their experiences were not pathological. They were presenting a different clinical profile than any I had been trained to recognize and one which ultimately raised questions in my own mind about what we identify as normal and as pathological behavior. These people were exhibiting what I came to call Borderland consciousness.

Borderland consciousness is being shaped from forces outside of the ego, to open itself up more to the fact that all living systems are inter-related and inter-dependent—especially as it concerns our psyche's separation of the human race from what is referred to as the "natural world." More than reflecting pathology, Borderland consciousness appears to represent a new and emergent form of consciousness that is changing our collective cultural experience and the very nature of our conscious awareness—and, quite rapidly I would say. Its primary characteristic is its apprehending right brain phenomena, what I call "transrational experiences," along with the more familiar rational left brain phenomena that we are used to. The experience of Borderland consciousness is expressed more through the imaginal, metaphoric, mytho-poetic and somatic dimensions than in the more left brain rational cause and effect linear and verbal mode that has been a defining characteristic of western culture.

Borderland personalities perceive and receive communications coming from the unconscious psyche in dreams and in visions and in direct "intuitive" messages between themselves and the "natural world." And this relationship between Borderlanders and the natural world is an intimate one wherein there is two-way communication between the individual and plants, animals, rocks, the earth and the ancestors. They experience more of a "oneness" with the natural world, than a separateness, and not just when they are *in* nature. What I am describing is their psychic reality all of the time. In this sense their psychic experience resembles the indigenous psyche which has never experienced a separation from Nature. These experiences are neither delusional, dissociative, nor hallucinatory. They are transrational *experiences*. They carry a new kind of consciousness that we need to recognize and honour.

This idea poses quite a challenge to our rational dualistic mind-set. It is much easier and less scary for us to brand the Borderland personality with a pathological label than it is to honour their reality and the messages they bring of the sacredness of all of life.

An article in the NY Times Magazine by Charles Siebert (Siebert, 2009) described Gray Whales off the coast of Baja California, as appearing to be seeking out connection with humans—even after having been driven to the edge of extinction by our species. The article speculated that perhaps there is some element of "knowing forgiveness" on the part of the whales towards us humans. Perhaps.

I would say that more than forgiving us they are endeavouring to sacralize us because they know that we have lost our connection to the soul of our species and its place in God's world. We have forgotten our own sacredness in the midst of our species' materialism and addictive greed. It is as if they—the whales—remember it and are trying to give it back to us. This is a dimension of truth that Borderlanders know and experience. This idea bears reflection because, well, what if it were so?

The Borderland Personality exhibits the following characteristics:

- Borderland personalities have a deep and primary connection to nature. Most are more comfortable in relationship with animals and/ or the land than with people.
- All have transrational experiences such as communicating with plants and animals and somatic identification with earth's suffering.
- Many have experienced trauma as children or adults. Many have not.

- Unlike the Border*line* personality, the Border*land* personality has a stable identity.
- Most hide their Border*land* nature—often including from their therapist—for fear of being branded "crazy" or weird. This leads to living parallel and camouflaged lives—their hidden life in the Borderland (which is their primary identification), and their life in the mundane world.
- Most feel isolated and lack a sense of community and belonging because they are unaware that there are many others like them.
- All experience their Borderland reality as sacred.
- Most tend to be hypersensitive on the somatic level. Many experience Environmental Illness. But, many do not.
- 100% of all Borderland personalities with whom I have had contact say they would not give up that connection if they could—even if it were to diminish their suffering.
- Although many would identify with being Nature's "canaries," most are at a loss as to the imperative for transformation that they have been given.

In Part I of my book (Bernstein, 2005), I present my theory of how what we have come to know as the highly developed and technologically dazzling western ego was born at the expense of our psyche's cleavage from its roots in nature. The Garden of Eden story sums it up well: When Man ate of the fruit of the Tree of Knowledge he was cast out of the Garden of Eden never to return. We got the Knowledge and our science and technology; and in the bargain we lost our living connection with the earth and thence forth saw it as an object, a commodity to be used and plundered.

I do not see Borderland consciousness as the return to a psychic state that once was—not to a Rousseauesque bliss, the world of Thoreau or a New Age nature worship. Rather I see it as an emergent form of consciousness resulting from evolutionary process.

When we use the word "evolution," our minds automatically tend to go to biological evolution. Certainly that was Darwin's focus. But psyche evolves as well as biology and in my view psyche is the most rapid dimension of evolutionary process as it directly affects species *Homo sapiens*. Thus, Borderland consciousness is not a regressive process going back to a state that once was. Rather it is developmentally progressed.

WHAT IF IT WERE TRUE ..."

I see Borderland consciousness as a compensatory response from the collective unconscious that appears to provide an alternative path in our headlong fling towards species suicide. By this I mean our addiction to materialism and acquisition fed by a technology that herds us along at ever increasing speed and results in uncontrollable global warming leading us towards ultimate extinction as a species.

Actually it is *our* species in particular, along with thousands of others, that is threatened with extinction. Just what is it about us, about species *Homo sapiens*—what is it about our form of consciousness—that can look self-extinction in the eye and continue on as if the Emperor were clothed?

Which brings me to "dominion." It seems increasingly clear that dominion by Man as mandated in the Bible, is how we arrived at the point of looming self-annihilation. Dominion and its insistence on human hierarchy is psychologically inherent in the monotheistic religions and the cultures that derive from them. Benevolent dominion is little improvement over arrogant dominion. It is still dominion, whatever its stripes.

Some environmentalists are coming to learn that *at most* our science and technology can teach us how to stop our own futherance of global warming and destruction of the ecology. The conviction that *we* know how to heal the earth seems hubristic to me and another characteristic of our cultural addiction to dominion. We do not have the wisdom to heal the earth. Rather, the earth has its own wisdom about healing itself. But if we can learn to control our addictive destruction, get out of the way, and let the earth regenerate of itself, perhaps *our* species can heal.

In a recent article (Mahall & Bormann, 2010), B. E. Mahall, a biologist at UC Santa Barbara, and F. H. Bormann, Emeritus Professor of Forest Ecology at Yale, wrote:

> The Earth has its own set of rules ... solidly grounded in laws of physics and chemistry. ... Our anthropocentric economic model for interacting with the world ignores and is proving to be incompatible with Earth's rules, and is therefore on a direct collision course with them.
>
> ... We need to see ourselves as *part of nature*, governed by nature (*not economics*), beholden to nature ... We need to view our existence in nature as dependent on numerous functions we are unable

to perform ourselves, and without which we couldn't survive ...
[Shortsighted anthropocentrism disrupts] these functions to the
degree that Earth will become uninhabitable for us.

This is a viewpoint expressed by two scientists. Their way of listening is
through science—through biology, physics and chemistry. And that
is crucial. But science and technology leave out psyche. At the same
time, when these authors say that "we need to see ourselves as part of
nature, even, *beholden* to nature," knowingly or not, they have taken a
step towards the inclusion of psyche in their science. I would say that,
whether they realize it or not, they are also suggesting that collectively we
must learn to *Listen to Psyche/Listen to the Earth*.

Which takes me back to the Borderland personality ...

One of the things—perhaps the single most important thing—that
I have learned in the nearly forty years of being invited into Navajo culture and its traditional medicine practices and what I have gained from
years of friendship and learning with Navaho medicine man Johnson
Dennison, is to listen differently. Johnson Dennison frequently reminds
me that western culture suffers greatly from the "Hurry-Up Sickness"
and that non-indigenous people, "Biligaanas" as they are referred to in
Navajo, don't know how to listen. It is those two things, in all of their
levels and dimensions of meaning, that western culture needs to learn
from indigenous cultures and traditional medicine.

Last December Johnson Dennison performed a healing ceremony
for one of the two Borderland groups that I lead. The first part of the
ceremony took place on a Saturday night and the second part took
place early Sunday morning with the rising of the sun. In the group's
discussions over the three months since the ceremony two of the most
prevalent themes which group members return to are "the Hurry Up
Sickness" and "listening." Two other themes, among several, that keep
surfacing are "awakening the body; having one's feet planted on and
in touch with the earth," and attachment and oneness with Nature.
In the words of one participant, "Who I am is attached to animals and
Nature—finding my way home is through my body and in being in
touch with the earth."

Borderlanders reflect the emergent reconnection of the western psyche to a living relationship with Nature. In the safety of their
group they often refer to themselves as the "canaries" who pick up the
symptoms and suffering of a beleaguered and assaulted earth. Many

experience somatically in their own bodies the symptoms of a poisoned and traumatized earth. Many suffer from the various manifestations of what is referred to in western medicine as Environmental Illness, or as it is otherwise known Multiple Chemical Sensitivities, Chronic Fatigue Syndrome, Fibromyalgia and puzzling auto-immune disorders. Their identification with the earth's suffering is very costly and most feel mired in the conundrum of feeling earth's pain in the midst of its blessings.

My focus as a clinician in my work with Borderlanders, individually and in the two groups I lead, is to assist in a psychic shift from being caught in the pathology of our species' relationship of dominance of the earth to one of reciprocity with Nature. I would say that all Border-landers *know* this truth, but making the psychological and emotional transition from feeling caught in the conflict between dominion and reciprocity is where most are captive and is the core of our work. This entails learning that one can support the earth's healing by giving back to it, not only through the path of one's life and through their respect, prayers and intentions—as they naturally do—but to be able to do so without having to have a *symbiotic* relationship wherein they psychi-cally and somatically take on earth's symptoms and the guilt of our culture for its disrespect and reckless destruction of the earth. I think it is this collective guilt that we understandably carry as a species that ultimately compromises our own sense of sacredness. It is that sense of guilt that I think Borderlanders unconsciously carry on behalf of our culture and our species as a whole that is their sacrifice and their offering in the interest of healing our collective deep wound. And that is where my work with Johnson Dennison has proved important: the Navajo ceremonies which he has performed for individuals in my prac-tice and for the Borderland group helps reconnect Borderlanders to their entitlement to a reciprocal and healing relationship with the earth. The ceremonies mitigate the burden of the collective guilt that they carry for all of us and brings them blessings from the Holy People.

There is no word for "guilt" in the Navajo language. Whatever that word represents in the Western psyche for me seems to be healed by the Navajo words for Blessing, Beauty and Harmony—most particularly when experienced from the feet up, rather than from the head down. That is the gift of these ceremonies.

Johnson Dennison has said that: "Healing the individual heals the world." Certainly I agree. In my work with Borderlanders I have learned that an essential part of what heals them is learning to put their wisdom about the earth, what they hear from listening to the earth, back into the world through story and through their deep connection with the meaning of reciprocity. This is their struggle—and their gift.

Our world—western civilization and the seeds of our culture we have sown around the world—operates on the principle of disembodied power and seeming economic expedience. Specifically it has become dissociated from its spiritual roots in the natural world.

"Reciprocity" is a different kind of power. It is guided by a spirit of kinship between all of life, animate and inanimate. I would say the binding essence of reciprocity is respect.

Rather than discuss "reciprocity" further, I will share with you a dream of a Borderlander with whom I worked. Here is her dream:

> I was standing in the foyer of a rich lady's house. Ann, Barbara and Joyce and I are chatting. The house was opulent.
>
> Suddenly George [the dreamer's husband] comes bursting through the door and breathlessly says to me, "We're playing a game of Jeopardy. I need to know the answer to this question." Joyce, the rich lady, says to George, "The answer is, 'What is The Eye of Africa?'"

The Borderlander who dreamed this dream had never heard of "The Eye of Africa." When she brought the dream to our session she said, "Have you heard of 'The Eye of Africa?'" I said that I hadn't. She said, "Apparently there is one." She had Googled it.

The Eye of Africa is a natural formation in what is now Mauritania. It is 31 miles in diameter. Only with the advent of sub-orbital space flight in June of 1965 was it perceptible as "earth's eye" peering back at Man. To the dreamer, the Eye both demanded reciprocity and sparked it within the observer. It was as if the Eye posed the question: "What is it about your species that you think you can ravage me as if I were lifeless, as if I had no spirit, as if it didn't matter?" And then, she, my patient, said, "Now we know. And now we know that the earth knows we know. It does matter—it matters so deeply. I will never be the same. We will never be the same."

PART V

WHAT TO DO—INFLUENCING ATTITUDES

CHAPTER FIFTEEN

Back to nature, then back to the office

Tom Crompton

Proportional responses to environmental challenges like climate change are unlikely to emerge without far stronger expressions of public concern about these issues—and commensurate public pressure on governments for more ambitious action. Regardless of whether such public concern and pressure is expressed—for example— through ambitious life-style changes or through participation in direct action campaigns, there is extensive evidence that it will be underpinned by particular goals and values that people hold to be important.

Values, environmental identity, and environmental concern

A set of goals referred to by social psychologists as "intrinsic", and a set of values referred to as "self-transcendent" are of particular significance here. Intrinsic goals include a concern for personal growth, affiliation to others, and community feeling. Self-transcendence values include concern for the welfare of all people and for nature (Grouzet et al., 2005; Schwartz, 1992, 2006).

Using a range of different investigative approaches, social psychologists have found that the more individuals endorse intrinsic goals and self-transcendence values, the more they also express positive attitudes and behaviours towards other-than-human nature (e.g., caring more about environmental damage or the value of other species; engaging in more behaviours like recycling and using public transport; and using less resources to support their lifestyles). This basic finding has been corroborated through studies on self-reported attitudes and behaviours, with game simulations of natural resource management dilemmas, and using nation-level archival data (see Crompton, 2010 for review).

Across many different nations, self-transcendence values are found to be strong predictors of ecocentric concern (which centres on the intrinsic value of animals and plants), and of the tendency to view humans as part of nature (as opposed to either custodians, or consumers, of nature) (Schultz & Zelezny, 1999). In reflecting on these results, researchers have suggested that "self-transcendence reflects a broader cognitive representation of self, and measures the degree to which a person includes other people and other living things in their notion of self" (Schultz & Zelezny, 1999, p. 263).

Consistent with this, it has been found that self-transcendence values are associated with a tendency to "perceive the world in terms of a special connection"—whether with others, with nature, place or the universe (Hyland, Wheeler, Kamble & Masters, 2010, pp. 313–314). Such a tendency can be assessed through responses to questionnaire items such as: "I sometimes experience joy just from being in a beautiful place", or "I never feel any special connection with a part of nature such as a flower, tree or mountain" (Hyland, Wheeler, Kamble & Masters, 2010).

As might be expected, therefore, studies on connectedness with nature have established that such connectedness is strongly correlated with environmental attitudes and behaviours (Frantz, Mayer, Norton & Rock, 2005; Mayer & Frantz, 2004; Schultz, 2001). For example, in a large cross-cultural study of residents in 14 countries, connectedness with nature emerged as one of the strongest and most consistent motivational predictors of pro-environmental behaviour (Schultz, 2001).

Drawing on work studying values and pro-environmental behaviour, social and behavioural scientists have introduced the concept of *environmental identity*. Clayton (2003) defines environmental identity as:

> A sense of connection to some part of the non-human natural environment, based on history, emotional attachment, and/or similarity,

that affects the ways in which we perceive and act toward the world ... An environmental identity can be similar to another collective identity (such as a national or ethnic identity) in providing us with a sense of connection ... and with a recognition of similarity between ourselves and others.

(Clayton, 2003, pp. 45–46)

Further elaborating on an understanding of environmental identity, Wes Schultz writes:

Environmental concern is tied to a person's notion of self and the degree to which people define themselves as independent, interdependent with other people, or interdependent with all living things. From this perspective, concern for environmental issues is an extension of the interconnectedness between two people.

(Schultz, 2000, p. 394)

In recent years, a number of studies have begun to examine pro-environmental behaviour and environmental attitudes from an identity framework (Bragg, 1996; Clayton, 2003; Hirsh & Dolderman, 2007; Kals, Schumacher & Montada, 1999; Light, 2000; Neisser, 1995; Reist, 2004; Schultz, 2002; Zavestoski, 2003).

It seems that intrinsic goals, self-transcendence values, connection to nature, and environmental identity are related and interconnected concepts. It is also clear that these things have important implications for addressing environmental problems. There is good evidence that intrinsic goals, self-transcendence values and connectedness to nature—including a feeling of "special connectedness"—are associated with greater concern about environmental problems and higher levels of motivation to help address these problems.

There is no doubt, of course, that particular pro-environmental attitudes and behaviours can be promoted through appeal to other values or aspects of our identity. It is clearly the case, for example, that economic imperatives can be an important motivation for householders to embark upon measures to improve energy efficiency—such as insulating loft-space. But there are many problems with such approaches. Firstly, appeals for people to adopt pro-environmental measures in pursuit of financial savings are likely to strengthen people's perception of the importance of financial concerns. And yet in many other cases, pro-environmental choices may entail *greater* financial costs. Secondly, adopting pro-environmental measures solely in line with financial concerns is unlikely to address the problem of rebound. If I insulate my loft simply to save money, rather than as part of a collective response to the challenge presented by climate change, I may simply spend the money I've saved on a cheap weekend flight to Barcelona—undoing any environmental benefit. Thirdly, an extensive range of studies reveals that individual's values are held in a universal and dynamic system, such that activating some values tends to reduce the importance a person attaches to opposing values—and to diminish the motivation they experience to act in line with these values. So, for example, appeals to self-enhancement values—such as financial concerns—serve to undermine motivation to adopt other pro-environmental and pro-social behaviour. This is because self-enhancement values oppose the self-transcendence values that underpin social and environmental concerns. Fourthly, motivations to pursue behaviour in line with extrinsic goals are found to be less persistent over time. It has been found that people are more persistent in engaging in a wide range of behaviours (including pro-environmental behaviours) when these are pursued in line with intrinsic goals (for example, a sense of "community feeling"). There is not space here to elaborate on these points, which are explored fully elsewhere (Crompton, 2008; Crompton, 2010; Crompton & Kasser, 2009; Thøgersen & Crompton, 2009).

Taken together, these findings suggest that promoting intrinsic goals and self-transcendence values, and a greater sense of connection to nature, is likely to promote environmental concern—and behaviour consistent with this concern. On the other hand, promoting extrinsic goals and self-enhancement values, while sometimes effective in piece-meal fashion, is likely to undermine comprehensive and durable commitment to addressing environmental problems.

It is very important to recognize that the implications of these findings extend well beyond concerns about environmental problems. It seems that strengthening intrinsic goals and self-transcendence values as these are instantiated in relation to other issues (global poverty or child neglect, for example) is also likely to increase concern about environmental issues. Reciprocally, strengthening these goals and values as they relate to environmental problems is also likely to increase concern about social or development issues. This is crucially important, because it opens the possibility of a wide range of groups, expressing a diversity of social or environmental concerns, finding common cause in working to activate and strengthen intrinsic goals and self-transcendence values. This case is outlined in full elsewhere (Crompton, 2010). In the remainder of this article, however, focus is maintained on approaches to building a stronger connection with nature. All those working on issues of environmental concern are well placed to contribute to building such connection. But in doing so, they can derive satisfaction from the conviction that they are not merely helping to build durable concern about environmental problems: they are also helping to strengthen concern about a range of other social and development issues.

Personal experience and environmental identity

One of the most obvious approaches to nurturing connection to nature is to promote new forms of outdoor learning. There is good evidence that educational activities can promote pro-environmental behaviour (Rickinson, 2001; Zelezny, 1999). It seems, however, that attempts to foster a sense of connection between a person—often a child—and the natural environment require a specific type of educational approach. Educational activities that promote separation, objectification, or distancing seem unlikely to instil such a sense of connection. Rather, hands-on, nondirective, explorative, personal experiences are needed.

Appreciative experiences (e.g., bird-watching, hiking, star-gazing) tend to be particularly positively related to environmental concern (Ewert, Place & Sibthorp, 2005; Kahn, 2006; Nabhan & Trimble, 1994). Other researchers suggest that simply spending time in natural areas is unlikely to be sufficient; there also needs to be "planned opportunity for self-reflection or environmental awareness" (Rickinson et al., 2004, p. 29).

As the social psychologist Wesley Schultz writes:

> "[A] hike in the woods, a class trip to a natural park, a family camping trip (in a tent, not a recreational vehicle), an animal presentation in which students can see and touch the animal, or creating birdhouses or gardens should all lead to greater interconnectedness and inclusion. By contrast, a trip to a zoo to see animals in cages, watching animals perform skits or trained shows, hearing information about animals or nature taught abstractly in the classroom, or

environmentally destructive recreational behaviours (like off-road motorcycles, jet skis, and snowmobiles) will likely lead to less perceived interconnection ..."

(Schultz, 2000, p. 403)

Childhood experience of nature should become a core element of children's education—such that adolescents leave formal education equipped with a conceptual framework that enables them to relate to their own experiences of nature, a vocabulary with which they feel comfortable in discussing their relationship with nature, and educational experiences that lead them to identify nature as something in which they are immersed even in an urban environment (for example, through the air they breathe and the water they drink).

Early childhood outdoor experiences are often reported as being important in forming later-life attitudes and values (Chawla, 1999; Louv, 2006). Indeed, a sizeable number of environmentalists often highlight childhood as the foundation of their relationship with the natural environment (Degenhardt, 2002; Tanner, 1980). But the research here is sparse and the data are usually collected using a retrospective methodology. It appears, though, that spending more time in natural environments as a child tends to correlate positively with a number of environmental outcomes, including attitudes, behaviours, and adult career choices (Bixler, Floyd & Hammitt, 2002; Wells & Lekies, 2006).

Outdoor learning among adults invites different approaches. For example, the conservation organization WWF has taken groups of leaders from the public, private and third sectors into wilderness areas of Scotland for several days at a stretch on "ecopsychology" retreats, as part of its Natural Change Project (WWF, 2009; Key & Kerr, this volume). This project engaged participants in a range of experiential activities designed using transpersonal and ecopsychological approaches, and facilitated using psychotherapeutic techniques. At its heart lay a dawn till dusk solo experience in a wildness setting. Such solitary encounters with nature have a very long and culturally diverse history—often popularized and oversimplified through Native American associations. Participants in these programmes report, almost unanimously, significant changes in their sense of priority, and in some instances this has led them to make major changes in their lives—for instance, a change in career.

There is no doubt that such experiences—whether organized for children or adults—can be formative, and the effects durable. In some instances they can apparently influence decisions made many years afterwards. But for many others, the impact of the experience fades quickly once a person has returned to his or her daily routine. The Natural Change Project attempted to mitigate this effect by engaging participants over the course of several months. Nonetheless, programmes such as this inevitably confront the problem of a dominant cultural context which serves, in many ways, to erode those values which direct experience of nature may help to strengthen.

Back to the classroom or office

The social psychologist Tim Kasser has worked extensively on the factors that influence peoples' values, and the relationship between values and behaviour. He suggests that taking someone away from their school or work to participate in outdoor learning sessions or a wilderness retreat is analogous to taking a child out of an abusive home environment for a counselling session. Throughout the session, the child's counsellor is acutely aware that, once the session is finished, the little girl will be picked up and returned to her home—perhaps to abusive and alcoholic parents. It may be that a great deal can be done to help the little girl during the counselling session: but what can be achieved in that short time that is going to be durable enough to be of help even a few days later, after she is re-submerged in her day-to-day environment? By analogy, participants in wilderness retreats may well report personally significant experiences. But if these experiences are to lead to durable changes in attitudes and behaviour, they must withstand re-immersion into a person's home, work, or school environment (Kasser, *personal communication*).

Like a thumb-print on glass, the influence of such experience may fade. But it is likely to fade more quickly in a cultural context that fails to validate these experiences—a culture that suppresses conversation about them, that dismisses them as unimportant, or that works to strengthen values and other aspects of identity that are antagonistic to a sense of connection to nature.

Most obviously, there is a need for individuals to be more open in talking about such experience and the influence that this may have had upon them. In a social context which is often dismissive of such experience, simply speaking in this way may itself entail a degree of courage.

But there is a need to go further—to begin to tackle those cultural influences that tend to oppose values and aspects of identity that support a sense of connection to nature. As we have seen, factors that lead individuals to attach greater importance to the self-enhancement values of social status, prestige, or dominance over others, are also likely to diminish the importance that an individual attaches to self-transcendence values, and to erode motivation to adopt pro-environmental behaviour (Maio, Pakizeh, Cheung & Rees, 2009; Sheldon, Nichols & Kasser, 2011).

An understanding of the structure of individuals' values points to a difficult challenge. Valuable as educational experience or wilderness retreats are, it seems that we cannot anticipate that such approaches will necessarily catalyse widespread and durable concern about environmental problems. At least, such widespread concern is unlikely to emerge while these approaches are pursued in a cultural context that serves to reinforce extrinsic goals and self-enhancement values. Such goals and values are opposed to the intrinsic goals and self-transcendence values that are associated with a stronger sense of connection to nature.

Self-enhancement values are modelled by many aspects of contemporary society: for example, competitive educational environments, the culture of many workplaces, pay structures and incentive schemes, and a range of public policy priorities that our governments pursue. But among these, the role of the media is likely to be critically important. In the remaining part of this chapter, I will examine just one facet of the influence that the media exerts: that of television.

A large number of studies have found a positive relationship between television viewing and self-enhancement values (see Good, 2007 for review). Other work has looked at the impacts of television viewing on attitudes to the environment. There is good evidence for a correlation between television viewing and a sense of apathy regarding environmental issues, including less concern about environmental problems, lower levels of environmental "activism", and a lower sense of agency in addressing environmental issues. (Shanahan, 1993; Shanahan, Morgan & Stenbjerre, 1997). Of course, this is to be predicted if heavier television viewing is correlated with increased prevalence of self-enhancement values, and self-enhancement values are negatively correlated with environmental concern. Following this line of inquiry, Good (2007) investigated whether materialism mediates the relationship between television viewing and apathy about environmental problems. ("Materialism", as defined and measured by social psychologists is closely associated with self-enhancement values.) Good found a positive relationship between television viewing and materialism—something which is to be expected on the basis of earlier work. And she also, as expected, found a negative relationship between materialism and environmental concern. Finally, she found that "materialism does mediate the relationship between television and attitudes about the natural environment" (Good, 2007, p. 376).

Studies which reveal such associations do not, however, examine the nature of the relationship between television viewing and materialism: it's possible that people who are, for other reasons, more materialistically oriented, may simply choose to watch more television. Other studies have focussed on the effects of watching a great deal of television, and present evidence that this itself leads people to become more materialistically oriented (Shrum, Burroughs & Rindfleisch, 2005). This is perhaps to be expected—many television commercials and popular television programmes (such as *The Apprentice* or *The X-Factor*) model values of financial success, social status, and prestige.

It seems, then, that television is one example of a cultural influence that tends to promote self-enhancement values and to undermine the importance that people place on self-transcendence values. Heavy exposure to commercial television is likely, therefore, to contribute to undermining a viewer's environmental identity.

Examination of the ways in which self-enhancement values are modelled and promoted in society leads to a set of possible policy interventions that might be advocated by those concerned to build wider public concern about social and environmental issues. So, for example, pursuing the example of television, one possible response may be to launch campaigns to encourage responsible television companies and the agencies that advertise on commercial television to avoid modelling extrinsic goals and self-enhancement values.

Crucial as it is to increase people's contact with nature—particularly where this encourages self-reflection—it seems that the benefit of this is likely to be eroded by a range of cultural influences: of which commercial television is just one example. Whatever the success of approaches to building people's sense of connection with nature, it seems that this alone is unlikely to generate public pressure for policy interventions proportional to the scale of environmental challenges we confront.

Those concerned about environmental problems must also be engaging in sustained campaigning to support business practices and government policies that will tend to promote intrinsic goals and self-transcendence values—and to oppose those practices and policies that will promote extrinsic goals and self-enhancement values.

The author is grateful to Tim Kasser, Dave Key and Wes Schultz for conversations that contributed importantly to the perspectives outlined in this paper.

CHAPTER SIXTEEN

Denial, sacrifice, and the ecological self

Sandra White

During 2009, studies revealed that the proportion of people in the UK who accept that climate change is both real and to a crucial extent human-made is declining, despite increasing evidence that this is the case. (Norgaard, 2009; Crompton & Kasser, 2009.) This is known as "climate change denial" and subsequent opinion polls have revealed that this phenomenon continues to increase. (*BBC*, 2010). With the onset of financial crisis, government resources for and media attention to climate change have decreased, even though there is a general acceptance that rapid climate change is happening. In some quarters, this combination has produced more efforts to inform the general public with clearer scientific information. Yet we are discovering that better data are not reducing the prevalence of denial.

In this chapter, in order to help us think about how to address more effectively denial in the context of climate change and ecological sustainability, I will first look more deeply into the psychology of denial, what purpose it serves and how it functions. The ideas offered here sit alongside understandings that denial is rooted in neurobiology, where climate change is not yet close enough in space or time to trigger fight or flight responses, and also, conversely, that the size of the problem is so overwhelming that many people are closing down, in a freeze response.

Given that the proposition from the environmental movement to the population at large is "to make sacrifices for the greater good" by reducing their carbon footprints, I will go on to examine "sacrifice", drawing upon Jung's (1969) definition of it as an archetype. Doing so will involve looking at ancient ritual practices and comparing their context with today's. Recognising that today's context is a reflection of the path that western civilization has taken over millennia prompts me then to consider our creation story of the Garden of Eden, in order to pose some psychological questions about how difficult it is for modern people to engage with climate change and ecological sustainability. Finally, I will bring in ecopsychology which can make a powerful contribution towards easing those difficulties.

Applying a psychological and ecopsychological lens to the problem of how to engage all sectors of UK society with climate change and ecological sustainability is not intended to imply that I locate the problem at the level of individual behaviour, for I do not. It is systemic, with many interlocking factors ranging from human characteristics and cultural norms to the demands of technology, law, economics and politics. Understanding denial, however, provides an additional underpinning for thinking about how to influence change.

Denial

In any context, "denial" is psychological jargon for the mind's defence mechanism which protects us from what we cannot cope with knowing, because the right internal and sometimes external resources are not in place. Its onset is not a matter of conscious choice. This innate and necessary psychological defence corresponds to involuntary bodily systems that activate when needed without our knowledge or consent.

One of the most powerful triggers of denial is fear of loss. For Western civilization the pursuit of an ecologically sustainable world heralds the prospect of fundamentally changing much of what has been believed in and achieved over centuries, implying a change in the very foundation of our collective identity. For most people, ecological sustainability threatens the loss of what is precious to them, for example the car which often in our society carries status as well as utility.

I have developed a metaphor for conceptualizing in closer detail the mechanisms involved in denial. When denial is triggered, a shutter slams down in the mind, separating it into two. In front, huge emotional, cognitive and motivational energy remains available to fuel two activities: first, holding on to and increasing what is precious but threatened, and second, negating and thereby trying to destroy what is providing the threat. Behind the shutter, locked away and unavailable, an equal amount of energy is unconsciously applied to warding off unbearable and conflicting feelings. There is fear not only of loss, but also of facing the scale of destruction caused by modern human activity and experiencing the enormous anguish this produces. Further, not reducing our destructive impacts produces unbearable guilt and shame, rooted in core desires to be intrinsically good and valuable to society. Without access to these feelings, there is no driver for change and denial continues to hold sway.

Another element of this metaphor is that, as the shutter slams down a genuinely believed story is created. This story may be irrational or rational; it does not matter. Its sole purpose is to restore and uphold the person's core sense of validity when confronted with a major threat to their identity. Such stories include "climate change is due to sunspot activity" and "we can only act when we are certain of all the facts and sure of the outcomes." The latter sounds rational, but it contrasts starkly with how political and economic decisions are really made. Challenging the story is usually futile, because its purpose is not to understand external reality: it is instead to uphold the person's internal sense of being legitimate.

The importance of all this is that the psychological protection of denial is essential—and here lies the crux of our difficulty. Right now, we are in a clash of two opposing but equally valid and vitally compelling needs: the physical need to protect the earth's systems from further deterioration, and the psychological need for people to protect their sense of legitimacy. Although it is clear that there is no ultimate conflict between looking after the earth and looking after ourselves, a substantial risk to a person's identity blocks out that perception. In essence, the defence of denial is triggered because people need to preserve their sense of innate goodness against the mounting evidence of human destructiveness.

Thus the impact of denial is to multiply the behaviours which increase emissions and disable an ordinary but vital element of the human mind, namely conscience. As social creatures, when human beings are functioning ordinarily, anguish, guilt and shame activate conscience and ensure a quality of self-regulation which maintains the glue of social cohesion, mutual respect, and consideration. In view of this, perhaps the primary task is no longer to present better information about climate change but to address the question "how can we enable the mechanisms of denial to relax?" Denial mechanisms relax when the threat has passed, or a new desire emerges which renders the perceived threat irrelevant, or there is an expansion of psychological resources which enable the threat to be faced, connected with and addressed. If we treat the "threat" as being to a person's identity and sense of validity, rather than climate change itself, then thinking about how to awaken new desires or enabling psychological resources to be expanded both offer possibilities for enabling denial to relax.

Sacrifice

It seems that exhortations to "make sacrifices for the greater good" cannot take hold while denial is prevalent. While I will enter into a much fuller discussion of Eden later, it is worth mentioning here that there has been a collective, needed and psychologically valid retreat to what I think of as an "ersatz Eden", an unconsciously constructed artificial state of blissful ignorance in which people unconsciously hold themselves in order to defend their sense of innocence and goodness, until conditions change and something else becomes possible.

Exploring sacrifice as an archetype adds to our understanding of what is needed to bring about change. Jung's construct of an archetype is as an innate pattern of human behaviour embedded as a potential in the deeper layers of the collective psyche:

> The archetype is a tendency to form such representations of a motif—representations that can vary a great deal in detail without losing their basic pattern ... They are indeed an instinctive *trend*.
>
> (Jung, 1978, p. 58)

For example, experience of her own mother will feed and shape how a woman relates to the archetype of the mother already within her. When her baby is conceived and needs a mother, all will go well if the woman feels able to be a mother. If not, she might abort the foetus or abandon her newborn. So, an archetype is an innate pattern of behaviour embedded as a potential in the deep layers of the mind which can become active when the circumstances demand it and the conditions are right. To apply this to global warming, the circumstance requires sacrifice, but are the right conditions in place?

The Oxford English Dictionary defines sacrifice as a verb: "To surrender or give up (something) for the attainment of some higher advantage or dearer object"; and as a noun: "The destruction or surrender of something valued or desired for the sake of something having, or regarded as having, a higher or a more pressing claim; the loss entailed by devotion to some other interest; also, the thing so devoted or surrendered."

If what we are making sacrifices for is "dearer" or commands our "devotion", for sacrifice to be possible there needs to be the presence of love. An example of this in everyday terms is the ongoing sacrifices parents make for the sake of their children. Yet the prospect of worsened living conditions for their children due to global warming is not producing the required behaviour change on the part of most parents. I wonder if this is because, despite the millions of people like bird watchers and gardeners who do love aspects of nature, the kind of loving relationship with nature in which significant lifestyle changes could be volunteered is not prevalent.

I also think that the notion of a "higher or a more pressing claim" is relevant and to explore this more I look to ancient rituals, where humans and animals were sacrificed to the Gods. With respect to human sacrifices, it is impossible to imagine the feelings of terror and anguish alongside loyalty and devotion experienced by those offered up and their families. Although there are many different interpretations of these rituals made by anthropologists, some themes can be suggested. Sacrifice rituals occurred at significant times, like when making a long journey or at the start of a new season, and were largely propitiatory requests for benevolence and loyalty from divine entities who were tempestuous and fickle. Only the best was offered up for this most important task, in recognition of divinity's claim to what was superior. The rituals took place in the presence of the whole community and what the sacrifice represented was understood and upheld by that community. Ritual sacrifice served to express a unified view of their world and also to reinforce unity, to prevent the sacrifice being made in vain. Everyone participated through witnessing each ritual and then sharing in the associated feast so that the ritual's specific purpose was integrated by all. These events signal a dynamic, powerful, and reverential relationship between ordinary human lives and something larger and mysterious.

In our civilized times, it is easy to look back and disregard this phenomenon as superstitious and barbaric. In a predominantly secular culture, there is no universally shared experience of something larger than ourselves with which we are all consciously participating in a comparable relationship. We can interpret some of the ancient Gods as personifications of nature, weather and climate. Today's collective attitude towards these aspects of earth was aptly described by Freud some fifty years ago:

> The principle task of civilisation, its actual raison d'etre, is to defend us against nature. We all know that in many ways civilisation does this fairly well already, and clearly as time goes on it will do it much better. But no one is under the illusion that nature has already been vanquished; and few dare hope that she will ever be entirely subjected to man. There are the elements which seem to mock at all human control; the earth which quakes and is torn apart and buries all human life and its works; water, which deluges and drowns everything in turmoil; storms, which blow everything before them .... With these forces nature rises up against us, majestic, cruel and inexorable; she brings to our mind once more our weakness and helplessness, which we thought to escape through the work of civilisation.
>
> (Freud, 1961, pp. 15–16)

In the aftermath of the 2011 earthquake and tsunami on the north east coast of Japan and tornado at Joplin, Missouri, USA, these descriptions are particularly poignant.

It is inconceivable that ancient cultures would set out to "vanquish" their Gods. Perhaps as an unconscious compensation for unbearable feelings of "weakness and helplessness" in the face of nature's vastness and real ravages, Western culture's pursuit of civilisation over centuries has forged a path founded on a construct of humanity as "separate from" and "superior to" the very influences which early people revered. This has taken most of us out of relationship with the larger world of which we unknowingly remain a part. (By "we" I am referring to the dominant cultural norm and do not intend to deny people who live in reverent and participatory ways with the earth.) To turn now and enter into a more reverential relationship with nature feels alien and regressive to modernity's expectations. Under these conditions, for most people there is not a unified, strongly bonded context of a shared frame of reference in which sacrifices can be lovingly or fearfully made and their purpose commonly understood, compassionately witnessed and universally upheld. So, at a collective level, the archetype remains dormant.

Could it be that, rather than sacrifice not being possible when denial is prevalent, the opposite is true: namely, if the conditions for sacrifice are not in place, then denial becomes the needed psychological recourse? At the heart of ancient attitudes lay a complex relationship with the larger whole, acknowledged and culturally expressed in prescribed collective forms which provided a container for shared hopes and terrors. Without this complex relationship being explicitly and collectively honoured in ways which activate communal solidarity, today's lone individual is deprived of necessary psychological resources which enable both love and fear to be consciously known and articulated. This absence of containment fosters a greater propensity for denial's shutter to slam down and the corresponding need for a story which upholds the sense of self. Today's lone individual also experiences a state of separation from nature in which the benefits of living in conscious, respectful relationship with other species and the larger systems around us have long passed largely unrecognised.

Revisiting Eden in search of the ecological self

Creation stories, early mythical accounts of how the world came into being, depict humanity's place within it and often describe critical psychological tasks which enable life to be lived well. They can contain complex ideas difficult for us to fathom now. Interestingly, the fourth centenary of the King James Bible has provoked considerable interest in how it provided the cultural foundation for much of the West's way of pursuing civilization. Our creation story originated in the Middle east with its particular landscapes and cultural norms and yet it has taken root in the Western psyche, revealing that it holds deep psychological resonance and meaning. In the light of Jung's "suppos[ition] that every religion is a spontaneous expression of a certain predominant psychological condition" (1969, para. 160), revisiting the Garden of Eden is timely. Jung was also careful, however, to make clear that he was not defining religious symbolism or experience as purely psychological, nor was he commenting on the religious significance of observed phenomena (Jung, 1969, para. 2). It is in that spirit that I am bringing a psychological lens to the Garden of Eden as one line of enquiry among possible others.

I have looked at many paintings of Eden and sat with the story as if it were a dream. This has helped me to think about its events in a different way, drawing upon association rather than linear causality. By treating the paintings as expressions of archetypal images arising from the collective unconscious I have found new ways of thinking about our creation story which might hold relevance to our predicament.

In the story (Genesis 2, 4–3, 24), Adam and Eve are the first humans in the world created by God and they live in the Garden. The one thing forbidden to them is eating the fruit of the Tree of the Knowledge of Good and Evil. The Serpent entices Eve to go against God's edict and she then persuades Adam to do likewise which calls out God's wrath and punishment against all three. Their eating what has come to be thought of as the apple propels them into self-consciousness, with the capacity to feel shame for the first time, and out of his fear that they will go on to eat of the fruit of the Tree of Life and live forever, God expels them from the Garden, prohibiting their return. To prevent their re-entry, He guards the east gate nearest the Tree of Life with two cherubs and a flaming sword. Images of Adam and Eve in exile show them utterly desolate.

My attention has been caught by the "apple moment" and the transition it brings from one state of consciousness into another, by God's association to the Tree of Life once they have eaten of the Tree of Knowledge of Good and Evil, and by the devastation of being expelled from Eden. I will explore these themes in the context of humanity's relationship with larger nature.

It is culturally well understood that the Eden story is a mythical way of describing the development of the human mind from the earliest baby-state of oneness with the world into a consciousness of one's separate individuality, agency, and responsibility. Separation brings with it awareness of linear time and, terrifyingly, of one's own mortality. Simply put, linear functioning makes available the faculties of logic, reasoning and understanding cause and effect, closely related to the Tree of Knowledge of Good and Evil.

The various schools of depth psychology have taught us much about the baby's experience of living without a sense of boundaries in which everything is seamlessly connected with everything else. The tenor of the caring environment is therefore critical, for without boundaries the baby receives and resonates with everything that happens, every change in feeling quality around it, good or ill. This first state provides a foundation for the later development of empathy, the capacity to imagine and feel what another experiences because there is a residual echo within oneself.

If I imagine Adam and Eve as embedded in the Garden of Eden in a similar state of seamless interconnection, unaware of their separate individuality, then the resonance and attunement they experience is not with the human realm but with all of life. Over time, Eden has culturally become associated with "paradise", a blissful, timeless place of harmony, and visual representations are of beautiful lush landscapes teeming with many species and full of colour. The first couple are depicted in a state of peace amidst this abundance of life, which goes some way to explain their extreme distress at having to leave it behind.

In recent years, I have been struck by the TV series *Tribe* in which anthropologist Bruce Parry visited many different indigenous communities throughout the world, living much closer to the vicissitudes of nature than industrialized people. He consistently commented on the quality of contentment and happiness he met among people often on the edge of survival and I wonder if this is due to their being more directly embedded in the larger natural world. It seems possible that their intimate contact with the interplay between life and death yields a wider perspective on any individual life and death within the larger life cycle, including their own. Perhaps this is a source of their contentment.

When Jung described the ritual performed every morning by the Pueblo Indians he visited in New Mexico, in which they helped the sun to rise (Jung, 1993, pp. 274–282), he was showcasing what becomes available in a shared mindset that knows that it is integral to and participating in a larger cycle of nature. The desire of those people to play their part in maintaining the sun's ability to keep rising and bringing life to the planet through its warmth and light reveals their sense of interconnectedness with the whole world beyond their horizons. An understanding that they are tiny in the overall scheme of things is balanced by a sense that nevertheless they have a vital role in the continuation of life. This kind of consciousness is sophisticated. The tribe's commitment to the daily ritual provided a container to both give form to the expression of love and reverence for life itself and counteract the terror of living one finite life separated from the whole.

Modern Western culture has no equivalent conceptual framework that upholds an individual life as part of and contributing to the life of a larger whole which includes all of nature. Instead, its emphasis is on the separation. For me now, the roots of this attitude lie in the Eden story. The word "paradise" in its oldest Iranian form refers to a walled enclosure and many of the paintings I looked at show Eden as a walled garden within or next to another landscape. Sometimes the walls were impenetrable, a quality reinforced by God placing the cherubs and fiery sword at the east gate to protect the Tree of Life.

It seems to me extremely important, however, that God so quickly associated with the Tree of Life once he learned that Adam and Eve had eaten the apple. He created a connection between separated consciousness and life itself, knowing that there was a new quality of threat present. This threat was named as the danger that if Adam and Eve also ate the fruit of the Tree of Life, they would "live for ever" (Genesis 3.2). He aimed to prevent this by banishing them. Today, as we know, the combined effects of human industrialization and population growth are threatening the earth's systems upon which our species depends, so in a literal reading of the Bible story we could consider that his strategy worked.

We could equally but less literally consider that he intended to protect the Tree of Life from Adam and Eve in their newly separated state. With seemingly God-like power, we industrialised humans are now holding in our hands the future of the whole of life at its current stage of evolved complexity. Here, just as in Greek tragedy where the feared prophesy comes to pass directly due to the steps taken to try to avoid it, God failed.

Because I think it is worth taking our creation story seriously, I want to suggest a different interpretation, drawing upon images of Adam and Eve's devastation outside the Garden and in particular Thomas Cole's 1828 painting *Expulsion from the Garden of Eden* (http://www.mfa.org/collections/object/expulsion-from-the-garden-of-eden-33060), where there is a stone bridge leading out from a rock archway through which Adam and Eve have just left. The radiance of Eden shines through, lighting some of the bridge and beckoning. The world outside is dark, barren, and threatening—testament in itself as to why leaving Eden is so terrible. Cole's painting communicates that living without access to a quality of seamless interconnection and resonance with all life is a degraded condition. In the belief that we cannot go back, our culture has cut itself off from knowing what we yearn for, which creates the conditions for addictions like power, wealth, alcohol—unsatisfying substitutes for the nourishment of connecting with the beautiful and abundant whole. We may be just like the apple which when halved— severed from itself—quickly deteriorates.

I wonder if the barrier of cherubs and fire was not so much a prohibition but rather a description of the reality that once separated consciousness arrives, there is no possibility of living only in seamless interconnection with the whole. Yet boundaries are paradoxical by nature, they both separate and connect. Through God's instant linking of separated consciousness and the Tree of Life, we could infer that the psychological task described by our creation story is to find a way to stay connected with all of life, through the supreme difficulty of living as one separated finite person with our valid individual needs, desires, and fears. The cherubs and sword of fire depict too the immensity of this challenge. Having forged its civilization without this perspective, the West's economic, scientific and technological methods are rooted in the sense of being separated from larger nature and so their destructive aspects have been disregarded. For me, Cole's archway and the beckoning light of Eden convey that our psychological task is rather to access and live with both kinds of consciousness and allow their interplay to shape how we define "civilization" and "progress".

That is why, as singer/songwriter Joni Mitchell suggested, we need to get back to the Garden. If we can discover anew a sensibility that we are part of a valuable living entity, we will gain a context in which sacrifice makes sense. When indigenous people ritually thank a creature they have hunted and killed for "sacrificing itself" for their needs, they acknowledge and make sacred the dance between the one and the whole. As they acknowledge this dance for the creature, they do so also for themselves and locate their own finite lives in the larger natural cycles of life and death. Morgan (1995) and Alexander (2005) take the Western reader into this cosmology through their evocations of indigenous practices. Without this essential perception, without a capacity to identify with the earth and to know that our individual deaths feed the evolution of life in the same way as do the deaths of every other species, I think the Western tendency towards ego-inflation and identification with our own creations become inevitable. Once identified with only ourselves, the "downsizing" required by climate change and ecological sustainability feels like amputation and triggers denial.

Jung expressed being back in the Garden in this way:

> At Bollingen, I am in the midst of my true life, I am most deeply myself …. At times I feel as if I am spread out over the landscape and inside things, and am myself living in every tree, in the splashing of the waves, in the clouds and the animals that come and go, in the procession of the seasons.
>
> (Jung, 1993, p. 252).

Mary-Jayne Rust included this description and Freud's passage about civilization and nature which I quoted earlier in her ecopsychology lecture to the Guild of Psychotherapists (Rust, 2008a) and contrasting them reveals something of the psychological journey to be made in changing the way our industrialized society conducts its affairs.

Ecopsychology offers practices which support that journey and strengthen our experience of ourselves as fully human when we are woven into the larger natural world which has evolved over eons. Within this field, Norwegian ecophilosopher Arne Naess' proposition of the Ecological Self (Naess, 1988, p. 20) highlights the importance of the empathy that can become available in an expanded sense of self when we identify with others, not human as well as human. In my experience, such heightened sensitivities shape us differently and awaken new desires to discover how to change the course of our civilization, away from destroying the foundation and fabric of life, rooted in empathy with the other species which inhabit our world alongside us.

With such expanded psychological resources, denial's shutter can relax and allow conscience to enter into dynamic relationship with fear, need, desire, pride, passion, and aspiration. Rather than prizing and enhancing only the psychological talents afforded by separated consciousness, I can imagine the West's project becoming to foster equally our attributes which enable access to seamless interconnection, in order to put all of our psychological powers in service to the bigger project of the evolution of life itself, secure in our knowledge that we are part of its magnificence. What is required is the sacrifice of our collective illusion of separated superiority. The morning ritual of the Pueblo Indians is a beautiful example of a dignified and creative participation in upholding life beyond the individual that can arise from a large sense of oneself whilst still knowing one's small place in a vast system. For me, this is the real light of Eden, awaiting and beckoning those who will include ecopsychology in their journey of change.

Fragile identities and consumption: the use of "Carbon Conversations" in changing people's relationship to "stuff"

Rosemary Randall

Introduction

A number of writers (for example Hamilton, 2004; Layard, 2005; O. James, 2007) have explored the proposition that high levels of material consumption do not lead to a contented population. It is also clear that the economic growth that feeds these levels of consumption is unsustainable. (See for example Daly, 1977; Jackson, 2009; Victor, 2008). Changing this state of affairs is likely to be difficult however. Insights from psychoanalysis and psychotherapy suggest that, even without the demand for economic growth and the pressure of advertising, the relationship between identity and "stuff" may be too complex to allow a simple rejection of the "affluenza" lifestyle.

In this chapter I link ideas on the patterns of consumption in late modernity with trends in psychotherapy, ideas from psychoanalysis about the relationship of people to their objects and the challenges of climate change. I suggest that trying to persuade the public to live more sustainable lives may touch deep levels of crisis around personal identity. Finally I describe the Carbon Conversations project as one strategy that may help—but not solve—some of these difficulties.

Prelude: the extra-terrestrial hedgehog

Christmas: time for gifts. My niece fizzes with excitement as I unwrap the present she has chosen for me. It buzzes beneath the wrapper and jumps in my hands. I uncover a half sphere of knobbly, soft, green plastic, a kind of extra-terrestrial hedgehog. "Try it!" she encourages. I stare at it in astonishment. It is a battery powered foot massager. All I can think of is the waste of talent and the destruction of resources that went into the creation of this pointless object. But my niece is dancing with excitement. She has chosen this for me. It is a triumph of empathy and identification. She has trailed the shopping malls in search of something that will fit what she knows of my moods and desires and the market has provided the perfect answer—a DIY foot massage, available at any time, with no risk of the unfortunate masseur getting their head bitten off by a grumpy aunt. I recover, smile and play with the strange object. An uncle sends it skidding across the kitchen floor like a football. Offended, my niece retrieves it and places it solicitously beneath my foot where it makes the floorboards vibrate. Periodically, throughout Christmas day, she remarks with satisfaction on the appropriateness of her present. Who would not be touched and delighted by such a gift? Outwardly I smile. Inwardly I am disappointed and ungracious.

In this juxtaposition of my niece's excitement and my grumpy response we find one of the dilemmas of the twenty-first century: the extreme of difference between exuberant, delighted wonder at what the world can produce and curmudgeonly weariness about what the true cost may be.

There is something however that my niece and I share. We both believe that the gift should fit and that it is likely to be a work of some skill to make it do so. We both live in a world of rapidly changing expectations, where the person you thought you knew is likely to have changed their aspirations, shifted their allegiance and moved on from last year's fantasy to one you have not yet heard of. The gift must fit neatly with the recipient's shifting identity and desires. Getting this right is likely to be difficult.

Late modernity

Contemporary culture is sometimes described as narcissistic (Lasch, 1979) and the current period as one of "late modernity", "high modernity" (Giddens, 1991), or "liquid modernity" (Bauman, 2000) where questions of anxiety, choice and identity dominate personal life. The situation described by both Bauman and Giddens is one where the strong and solid reference points of the modern period, defining role, place, rights and responsibilities have been replaced by a myriad of competing and confusing choices. Identity has become a personal project of the self, where "Who am I?" and "Who do I want to be?" are legitimate and urgent questions.

Parallel to this analysis from the social sciences, psychotherapy, and psychoanalysis have shifted their focus from Freud's concerns with the inhibition and repression of desire to a preoccupation with questions of selfhood and identity. Bauman's anxious consumers, shopping for self-determination and fulfilment and adrift in the constant responsibility of choice, arrive in the consulting room with feelings of disintegration, shame, and uncertainty. Their sense of self is no longer a stable and certain background but is fragile and pulled to centre-stage where it preoccupies and disturbs. The bedrock of basic attachment seems uncertain.

Psychotherapists remark on the increase in the levels of disturbance they encounter. Working in a university counselling service between the mid 1980s and 2005 I noticed this shift from problems that were primarily concerned with the vicissitudes of a relatively stable "I" to problems that called the very nature of "I" into question—instabilities of the physical self in eating disorders, self-harm, and sexual uncertainty, instabilities of the psychological self in an increase in borderline states and personality disorders.

In a world that requires flexibility, an identity that is fixed and solidly structured is a disadvantage. In the twenty-first century, adaptability is everything. To choose, to be flexible, to decide for oneself is the ideal. The downside is anxiety, confusion, and uncertainty. Is my choice right? Will I fit in? What will truly fulfil me? This uncertain, unconfident self is a marketer's dream. Such people can be easily persuaded that each new object is necessary for social acceptance or personal fulfilment. Identity becomes something that is shopped for, supported by lifestyle choices and purchases, morphing with each new fashion.

Interlude: a soul adrift

Martina is about to get married. This is her third marriage and she wants it be right this time. I am one in a succession of experts she has consulted. Engaged in the arrangement of the wedding are not just the expected dressmaker, hairdresser, flower-arranger, caterer and photographer, but a life-planner, wedding-arranger, nutritionist, personal trainer and masseur. Martina has no confidence that either the wedding or the marriage will succeed. Her self-esteem is low and she is eaten up with doubt. Whether this is the cause or the result of the proliferation of expert opinion she has marshalled is unclear. She wonders whether I can help, or whether hypnotherapy might be more useful. She is a soul adrift in a sea of choice.

Fragile selves

A useful framework for looking at these problems is provided by Phil Mollon in his book *The Fragile Self* (Mollon, 1993). Mollon lists the following features of narcissism:

1. an incompletely differentiated sense of self,
2. a weak sense of personal agency
3. a poor self image, perhaps coupled with a grandiose self-image,
4. a tendency to mental disorganization,
5. a preoccupation with the other's view of the self at the expense of his or her own experience,
6. a tendency to retreat to illusions of self-sufficiency
7. an uncertain sense of origins and lineage. (Mollon, 1993, p. 178)

People who are in these fragile states require a continued empathic responsiveness from their immediate environment. There is a need to feel perfectly recognized and understood that persists into adult life. Such people lack the robustness to shrug off personal slights. The fragile self cannot deal with limits, boundaries or disappointments.

In their milder forms, these problems are the stuff of modern self-help books. Titles like *The Little Book of Confidence* (Jeffers, 1999), *Learning to Love Yourself* (Wegscheider-Cruse, 1991) and *Overcoming Low Self-esteem* (Fennell, 2009) suggest that there is a ready market of people seeking help for such difficulties.

It is my contention that one of the ways that people supply that missing empathic responsiveness is through their relationship to the market. They seek services, lifestyle, or objects that will support the fragile ego, will reflect back and confirm a sense of reality or embody qualities that the person feels uncertain of. Consumer goods lure and then

they grapple with the implications of home energy, travel, food, and the stuff they buy. People share stories of favourite journeys, much loved purchases and memorable meals. One person talks of the shame he would feel if people saw him in a smaller car—"They'd think I'd lost my job." Another stumbles on the insight that keeping her home at 22°C is connected to her sexual confidence—jumpers are frumpy. A third speaks movingly of his compulsion to compete with his siblings over who will have the biggest, finest, swankiest house.

When stories like these are listened to, shared and explored, people can work through the conflicts and feel supported in the changes they make. Loss can be acknowledged. New social norms can be strengthened.

The groups walk a tricky line. They are not therapy (the facilitators for the most part are not therapists) and the participants have not signed up to have their lives and psyches interpreted. Neither are they education. The facilitators are not teachers and although the participants often express gratitude for what they have learned through the group, they are rarely referring to the facts they have acquired. Each meeting has a particular emotional valency. Themes of loss and identity recur again and again but in the opening meeting feelings of apprehension, anxiety, and guilt often dominate. In the "Energy in the home" meeting, issues about comfort, autonomy, and security emerge. In the travel meeting anger, frustration and impotence are common alongside special pleading and the desire to be an exception. The food meeting is often a more joyous affair while the meeting on consumption is tough, as issues of identity, shame, and greed become unavoidable.

Interlude: loss

Jane speaks openly about loss. She had been planning a major trip to Thailand but as a result of joining the group she has decided not to go. The anticipated trip of a lifetime is on hold. There is something self-punishing in her tone. She accepts too easily that she should not have what she desires. She shifts ground and appeals to the idea of a greater good. Surely travel broadens the mind and makes us tolerant? She is searching for a good reason still to go—this feels like Kubler-Ross's (1970) description of one of the stages of grief where the person seems to be bargaining with a greater power for a postponement of the inevitable—just one more trip, just one more chance, just one more birthday.

Stephen responds by speaking of how enriched he has felt by trips abroad. I remark that it's hard for Jane, who until now has not had the money to travel, to hear this. Jake talks of only having flown twice in his life and of his amazement the first time he did so. They are sliding away from the earlier connection with loss. I tell the story of my grandmother's grief at the separation from her favourite son who emigrated to the US in 1950. It took her six years to save the boat fare to go and see him. There's a quieter moment in which the group share some thoughts about the sadness they are feeling and we acknowledge how difficult a subject this is.

The consumption meeting

Of the six fortnightly meetings, the fifth meeting on consumption and waste is often the most difficult but also the most rewarding. Part of the challenge is practical. Carbon is embedded in everything purchased— services as well as goods—through the use of energy in manufacture and delivery. Although shifting one's purchases from high-intensity to low-intensity ones may be useful, reducing one's impact can only really be done by reducing the total amount of money spent. (See Berners-Lee (2010) for some examples of the varying carbon intensity of different goods and services. In general there is a strong correlation between income and carbon emissions—higher earners are responsible for higher carbon emissions. See Baiocchi, Minx, and Hubacek (2010) for an interesting discussion of the factors that have impact.) The bigger part of the challenge however is psychological, for the reasons suggested earlier in this chapter. Identity, shame, fulfilment, regret, and obligation are the common themes in this meeting. By this point however, trust has developed and discussions have become more open. It is possible to begin to explore the issues.

The meeting starts by asking people to share memories of a purchase they have been pleased with and a purchase they have regretted. The regrets are often for ephemera—items that were bought on impulse that disappointed or were frivolous or poorly made. The associated feelings are not just regretful but guilty. There is sometimes an element of indignation, sometimes one of confession in people's tone. Often laughter lightens the mood as people speak ruefully of soda streams, bread makers, and sandwich toasters lurking unused at the back of cupboards. The purchases that are valued have arrived through all kinds of routes—luck, serendipity, careful planning. With these stories there is often a sense of an object that is used in complex ways—a bicycle that expresses the personality of its owner, a garden that speaks to someone's values, a dress that carries memories of a special occasion every time it is worn. In his book *Stuff*, the anthropologist Daniel Miller (2010) emphasizes how people are both made by and make the material objects of their lives. We are neither impotent slaves nor free agents but personalize, adapt, subvert, and create relationships with the stuff we purchase. People both create and are subject to the culture in which "stuff" is such an important factor.

The conversation deepens with the next activity. People talk in pairs about their reasons for buying. A prompt list helps to remind and unravel the complexity—need, safety, anxiety, curiosity, approval, self-esteem, status, enrichment, depression, illusions, bargains ... The group continues with discussion of their grandparents and times when people had fewer possessions. Lacking the power to buy what others have is associated with social isolation and shame, but people's relationships to their material objects and the services they buy are very varied. People whose personal relationships are straightforward also seem able to enjoy the material objects they surround themselves with. Their attachments to favourite items are significant but it is a relationship with differentiation and separation. The self is involved but boundaried and intact. Those whose relationships are most troubled also seem to have the most troubled relationships to stuff.

Interlude: shame or delight?

Twenty- year-old Glenda speaks hesitantly of her teenage years when she hated her physical appearance. Embarrassed by puppy fat and acne she spent each Saturday searching for the t-shirt, shoes or make-up that would lift her depression or restore her self-esteem. I ask if this resonates for anyone and one of the other women nods and offers a similar story. Glenda is relieved and her smile returns. The group stay with stories of low self-esteem and shopping for a few minutes. There is relief in sharing this common experience. The word "shame" is spoken and the conversation shifts a gear. Gordon talks of his daughter's accusation that he is ruining her life by forcing the family to live in a shabby house. "Sometimes I don't like myself" he says, "I've become obsessed with where stuff comes from and what its real cost might be." Marcus challenges: "What's wrong with wanting nice stuff and having pride in it?". Manju responds by recalling her grandmother's pleasure at being the first of her neighbours to own a twin-tub washing machine. The conversation shifts around themes of shame, pride, delight and guilt at the materiality of life. There is a sense of relief at being able to talk about the feelings attached to consumerism.

The facilitators then turn people's attention to what is known about the carbon emissions embodied in stuff. The facts are not pretty. Clothes and pointless gadgets are just the tip of the iceberg. Home improvements and building work, kitchen makeovers, holidays and hotels, the gym, cinema trips, football, new cars, services as well as objects—all have a carbon impact. The rebound effect means that money saved in one place has an impact in another. Living sustainably means living with less. The rebound effect is an economic concept that describes how increased energy efficiency leads to greater use—for example more efficient car engines make longer journeys more feasible, better insulated homes lead to the heating being turned up higher or kept on for longer. The indirect rebound effect describes the phenomenon where the decreased cost of one item leads to increased consumption of others—for example, buying second-hand clothes may release income for a equivalent to or greater than the carbon cost of the new clothes that have been relinquished. See Alcott (2005) for an explanation and discussion.

The mood in the group often shifts at this point. The realisation that income is a strong predictor of carbon emissions is a tough one for those on good salaries. People can feel defensive. The compensation of becoming time-rich and less stressed doesn't always appeal. Some who thought they didn't care about status discover that perhaps they do. And if there is someone in the group inclined to be pious about their minimal lifestyle this can be a difficult moment. Holding the group through the expression of these conflicts can be a delicate task.

Interlude: greed and normality

Rob is indignant. "All my salary goes on the mortgage and paying the bills," he says. He sees himself as poor although he earns well above the average. Arnie agrees. He doesn't do anything extravagant either: just the usual. "Are we greedy?" asks Manju. "It's like we've been invited to a great party" says Glenda "and we're so pleased to have been asked we don't notice what's going on outside." Pam tells a childhood story of being offered the last biscuit by an aunt at a family gathering, accepting it and then being told by her mother that the correct behaviour was to offer it to a guest. I remark that it's horrible to feel accused of greed when you've just been behaving normally. Rob becomes more reflective. It's not extravagance that is the problem he says—it's all the things we think of as usual.

The group ends with a guided fantasy that asks people to return in imagination to the home they lived in fifteen or twenty years ago and trace what has happened to all the objects there—the carpets, the furniture, the gadgets, the clothes and decoration. Are some of them still in their possession? What remains and is treasured? What has been passed on? Re-used? Recycled? Rejected? Sent to landfill? People open their eyes and share stories of objects loved, preserved, lost and discarded. The mood usually lifts with this activity and becomes more relaxed again. The group closes by talking about plans for change and plans for their reunion meeting.

Impact

Clearly individual action on carbon reduction is limited by the short-comings in infrastructure, energy supply and policy. Halving an individual footprint is probably the best that can be achieved without action at national and global level and without significant cultural shifts of the kind described by Tom Crompton in his report *Common Cause* (Crompton, 2010) where he calls for a realignment of the dominant values in UK society, away from materialism and towards a genuine concern for issues "bigger than the self". Nonetheless the achievements of many Carbon Conversations participants are impressive. Recent research by Pam McLean found people making immediate savings of up to 3 tonnes as a result of participation (McLean, 2011).

A more interesting limitation, however, is the psychological one described earlier in this chapter—the relationship between individual identity and consumption. Where the basic relationship to the material object world is healthy it seems possible for people to change, to let go and mourn objects that are unsustainable and to consider a down-sized life where "less" might feel "more". For many people however, their relationship to the cornucopia of market possibilities is more difficult, characterized more deeply by the narcissistic features Phil Mollon describes (Mollon, 1993). In contemporary culture this is normality for many people. The discussions in a Carbon Conversations group can help some people reflect and detach from an unsustainable relationship to "stuff", but can only be one element in a programme of deeper cultural change.

Conclude: the dinosaur

"It's got to go," said Ivan. He had pictures of the beast, a Range Rover Sport, lovingly cared for, polished and presented: carbon emissions off the scale. "It's who I was," he explained, "I used to go off-road. It was a man-thing. Pride. Then I realised I was mostly using it to drop the kids at school, and get to work. I feel sad because it's the first really flash set of wheels I've had. But it's going. It's not me any more. It's a dinosaur."

CHAPTER EIGHTEEN

The Natural Change Project

David Key and Margaret Kerr

Introduction

In 1903 the Scottish-born conservationist John Muir took President Theodore Roosevelt on a camping trip to California's Yosemite valley.

As a result of his experience, Roosevelt created five national parks … along with 150 national forests, 51 bird refuges, four game preserves, 18 national monuments, 24 reclamation projects, and the US Forest Service. The President's experience also led him to argue that it was undemocratic to exploit the nation's resources for present profit. "The greatest good for the greatest number", he wrote, "applies to the number within the womb of time" (Roosevelt, 1916, p. 300). It's hard to imagine more powerful social and environmental outcomes … from spending three days in the mountains!

This chapter describes WWF's Natural Change Project, which develops the principle of outdoor experience as a route to personal and social change—so beautifully illustrated by the example of John Muir and Theodore Roosevelt. Following this principle, Natural Change works with people who hold positions of influence in society, offering them potentially life-changing experiences of wild places.

After establishing the Project's background, we will describe its purpose, the people who created it and some of the theoretical perspectives that have informed it. We will then explore the content of the Project's programmes and how it is facilitated, and describe the kind of outcomes it can produce.

Background

In 2006, Jules Weston, Communications Manager for WWF-Scotland, attended an ecotherapy training course led by David Key and Mary-Jayne Rust. Jules' own transformative experience during this course gave her the idea of organizing a similar programme as a communications project for WWF. Her hope was that if a group of influential people from Scotland could have similar experiences and communicate about them publicly, this would inspire others to realize their own potential for change towards a more sustainable future.

Jules asked David Key if he could design a programme for WWF-Scotland. This became known as the Natural Change Project.

The birth of the Natural Change Project came at an interesting time in the history of environmental activism. It had been suggested that "traditional" approaches to campaigning—using challenging statements and shocking imagery—were not necessarily a good way to motivate people to take action (Crompton & Kasser, 2009). It was becoming evident that such campaign tactics tended to overwhelm people with fear and guilt, and trigger coping strategies based on denial and escapism (Freud, 1936; Lazarus, 1991; Zeidner & Endler, 1996). Ironically these ways of coping could often involve environmentally destructive behaviours—for example consuming more resources as a way of seeking security (Homburg et al., 2007).

In an attempt to find a more "positive" way of motivating change, some organizations had started to use social marketing techniques—which harnessed the mechanisms of consumer society to promote pro-environmental behaviour. Researchers were finding that social marketing successfully encouraged small, peripheral changes in some areas of personal behaviour (Crompton, 2008). However, because these mechanisms capitalized on the psychology of consumerism, it was also suggested that they could actually embed consumer psychology more deeply into society (Lakoff, 2006).

The assumptions and attitudes of our consumerist culture are at the root of many of our unsustainable lifestyles and behaviours (Cushman, 1990; Kanner & Gomes, 1995). It seemed that established methods of environmental campaigning which attempted to challenge consumerism were at risk of inadvertently reinforcing its root cause.

From the early 1990's the emerging discipline of ecopsychology began to offer a way out of this impasse, by exposing the assumptions and psychological processes of consumerism. At the heart of consumer psychology is a perception of the self which sees humans as separate from, and usually superior to, the rest of nature … as if the rest of nature were there exclusively for human benefit. This view of a separate superior self is so all-pervasive in industrial culture that we often take it for granted (Naess, 1986; Washburn, 1995). Ecopsychology suggests that it is vital to challenge this notion of a separate self, if we are to address the extent, scale and speed of the social change required to live sustainably.

Grounded in ecopsychology, the Natural Change Project works to heal—or make whole—the separate self. In this process of healing, we start to experience ourselves as an interconnected part of nature. This creates a relationship of gratitude, love and solidarity with the rest of nature, and motivates us to work for ecological balance.

By working with the sense of self to motivate activism, the Project provides a unique perspective on change and leadership for sustainability.

Purpose

The Natural Change Project's purpose is to catalyse and support personal, cultural and structural change that will lead to greater ecological sustainability.

The project works at the personal level by catalyzing and supporting personal change, at the cultural level, by creating stories of transformation, and at the structural level by developing new approaches to leadership and action for social change. These three levels are in some ways distinct from each other, but in other ways they cannot be separated.

Catalyzing and supporting personal change is the first purpose of the project, but we have been careful not to anticipate, expect, or demand this. Participants are simply invited to explore their own experiences of the process as it unfolds. Paradoxically this creates excellent conditions for change to happen, as Gestalt Therapist Albert Beisser notes:

> Change does not take place through a coercive attempt by the individual or by another person to change him … By rejecting the role of change agent, we make meaningful and orderly change possible.
>
> (Beisser, 1970, p. 77)

Participants are encouraged to create their own stories of personal transformation. The practice of writing helps each person reflect on and deepen their understanding of the changes they are experiencing. The stories created in this process also work at a cultural level to develop a language of social change for sustainability within participants' communities of practice and in the wider world.

Throughout the project, participants have communicated their experiences in ongoing blogs on the Natural Change website (www. naturalchange.org.uk). As their experience has deepened, each person has represented the subtle and complex psychological changes they were going through—not only in conventional prose but also in visual and poetic form. Through photography, film, sculpture, land art, drawing, painting and performance, rich and vibrant narratives have developed.

At a structural level, the Natural Change Project works with people who hold leadership positions in their own organizations. As illustrated by the example of John Muir and Theodore Roosevelt, policies can be shaped by the personal experiences of those who hold power. Natural Change is not only about motivating individuals to live more sustainably. It is about supporting individuals to translate personal transformation into social action and leadership for a more sustainable future.

There is compelling anecdotal evidence that the personal transformation represented in participants' narratives has led to social action. The movement from personal transformation to leadership for sustainability has also been found to happen in professional practice beyond Natural Change (Key, 2003) and is predicated by the psychological theories explored later in this chapter. To formally investigate this, there are plans for a longitudinal study of participants' involvement in action and leadership for sustainability after they have completed the Natural Change Project.

People

The Natural Change Project was originally developed by Jules Weston and David Key in 2008. Psychotherapist Margaret Kerr joined the

Project team almost immediately after it was established. On the first programme Amie Fulton, and on the second Rob McKenna, provided physical and emotional nutrition in their crucial roles managing the kitchen. Once each Project is operational, Jules works as Project Manager while we work together as co-facilitators.

The first programme consisted of seven people selected from the health, education, private, youth, arts, and NGO sectors in Scotland. When they were recruited to the Project, none of these participants was active in the field of sustainability. One of the participants was also a researcher, responsible for representing the group's experience in the first Natural Change report (WWF, 2009). In the second programme, eleven people were all selected from the education sector in Scotland— all have influence in shaping the school curriculum, professional development of teachers and educational policy.

Each programme of the Project runs for six months. The first started in 2008 and the second in 2010. A total of 18 people have participated at the time of writing and their stories have spread globally via the Natural Change website (www.naturalchange.org.uk).

Theory

Reflecting on the ecopsychology literature, and on our own professional practice over the years, we have found that the deepest experiences of psyche and nature make more sense if a wider interconnected self—rather than the everyday skin-bound sense of self—is used as the datum (Kerr & Key, 2012).

One of the central philosophical influences on our work, which reflects this interconnectedness is Arne Naess's (1989) "gestalt ontology". Naess's perspective finds resonances with many indigenous descriptions of self as an integral part of an ever-changing ecological context (e.g., Armstrong, 1995; Bernstein, 2005; Kailo, 1998; Williams, 1997), and with the Buddhist concept of "dependent arising" (HH The Dalai Lama, 1997).

From this philosophical base, Natural Change challenges "egoic" psychological approaches to sustainability which represent humans as rational decision-makers, who exert influence on a separate "non-human" world. Egoic approaches appeal to the parts of the psyche which build and enact an "identity project" in the world (Washburn, 1995). The parts of ego involved in this identity project may be at different stages of maturity. Here, the Transactional Analysis framework

Table 1. Transactional analysis ego states and environmentalism.

Transactional analysis ego state	Transactional analysis description	Manifestations in environmentalism	Natural change participants' perspectives
Critical parent	Critical, punitive, persecuting, moralistic. Dictates what "should" be done.	Blaming and shaming. Warnings of "doom and gloom".	"I despise some of the hairshirt frugality of the eco-movement (it doesn't feel very nurturing to me) and resent being made to feel guilty over my informed choices."
Nurturing parent	(Over) protective, rescuing, potentially smothering. Care-taking from a stance of greater power.	Stewardship and conservation— "looking after" the world.	"Guilty because it's my husband who has been remembering to fill the birdfeeder the past few days, not me."
Adult	Rational, balanced conscious expression of thoughts, feelings and behaviours. Compassionate and appropriate to the here-and-now.	Political and scientific action based on reason and research.	"There has been a fundamental shift. Previously, I think I did my recycling duties and environmental worrying more out of a sense of intellectualism rather than anything else …. Now, I'm doing it because I WANT to, because it's important, because it matters—it matters very much indeed.

(Continued)

Carbon Conversations groups aim to help people face the reality of climate change and reduce their personal impact on the problem. They aim to face rather than avoid the complex emotional issues that arise as people begin to understand the depths of their personal connection to the problem.

There is a long history of using groups to provide support and facilitate change. Kurt Lewin, originator of the term "group dynamics", wrote in the 1940s of his experiments using group discussion to encourage mothers to give fresh milk and orange juice to their babies (Lewin, 1947). Dorothy Stock Whitaker's *Using Groups to Help People* (1985) details their use in supporting a wide variety of people who share a problem—from burn victims to prisoners' wives to children making the transition to secondary school. More recently the term "psychoeducation" has been used to describe this type of work (Brown, 2011). These approaches vary in the extent to which they use therapeutic techniques but all make use of the basic building blocks of understanding group process and providing space and support for people to talk and work out their own solutions to the problems they face.

Carbon Conversations is usually run by volunteers in community groups. Many of those who use it have little prior experience of group facilitation and only rudimentary knowledge about climate change and carbon reduction. The twin needs for Carbon Conversations facilitators are for well-researched, reliable information and the support and training that can transform a self-help group into something closer to a professionally run experience.

The first need was solved by creating the materials for which Carbon Conversations is well-known—the Carbon Conversations handbook, facilitator's guide and pack of three games. The handbook is attractive, professionally edited, designed and illustrated and is given to each group member. It presents basic information about climate change, home energy, transport, food and consumption but its starting point is the complex way in which carbon emissions are embedded in the structures of society and in personal life and aspiration. Although it has instructions on how to measure and monitor the key areas of a carbon footprint and lists many sources of further information its emphasis is on the process of achieving a more sustainable lifestyle and the psychological and family conflicts that may arise.

More important than the materials however is the package of training and support that helps the facilitators deliver the groups and deal effectively with some of the emotional issues and defensive reactions that arise. All the groups are co-facilitated by people who have already taken part in a group themselves. Prospective facilitators receive a day's experiential training in group work and facilitation. While running their first group, they attend three mentoring sessions which focus on group process and participants' responses. Throughout the training and mentoring they are encouraged to observe the group process and reflect on their own responses. Their goal is to hold a space where people are free to express how these difficult issues make them feel. Their own experience as participants, the emphasis on reflective practice and the support provided help them develop the skills to cope with negative as well as positive reactions and support people in working through them. Backup is also provided by the Facilitators' guide, which contains plans for each meeting and information on the psychology of climate change, group process and commonly encountered group problems.

What happens in a group?

Each group has six–eight members who meet six times over a period of three–four months. Five fortnightly meetings are followed by a break and a reunion six weeks later.

Before the group starts the facilitators measure each participant's carbon footprint. This gives each person a rough picture of where they sit in relation to the UK 12 tonne average footprint and introduces the uncomfortable fact that a sustainable footprint is somewhere between 1 and 2 tonnes. The personal information is not shared with the group at this stage. It is common for people to feel anxious about the result. Most wish to be good citizens. They may be fearful of being found wanting or anxious that the constraints on their lives may not be understood.

The first meeting uses a mix of pair and group activities to help people get to know each other and explore their connection to the rest of the natural world, the changes required by climate change and people's visions of a low-carbon future. At the end of the meeting the facilitators introduce the idea that a realistic practical goal would be for people to aim to halve their personal carbon footprint over a period of about five years. Someone with an average footprint would aim to reach 6 tonnes. Someone with a 24 tonne footprint would try for 12 tonnes.

Subsequent meetings weave together discussions of practicalities with discussions of how people feel and what change means to them as

Fragile identities and consumption: the use of "Carbon Conversations" in changing people's relationship to "stuff"

Rosemary Randall

Introduction

A number of writers (for example Hamilton, 2004; Layard, 2005; O. James, 2007) have explored the proposition that high levels of material consumption do not lead to a contented population. It is also clear that the economic growth that feeds these levels of consumption is unsustainable. (See for example Daly, 1977; Jackson, 2009; Victor, 2008). Changing this state of affairs is likely to be difficult however. Insights from psychoanalysis and psychotherapy suggest that, even without the demand for economic growth and the pressure of advertising, the relationship between identity and "stuff" may be too complex to allow a simple rejection of the "affluenza" lifestyle.

In this chapter I link ideas on the patterns of consumption in late modernity with trends in psychotherapy, ideas from psychoanalysis about the relationship of people to their objects and the challenges of climate change. I suggest that trying to persuade the public to live more sustainable lives may touch deep levels of crisis around personal identity. Finally I describe the Carbon Conversations project as one strategy that may help—but not solve—some of these difficulties.

Prelude: the extra-terrestrial hedgehog

Christmas: time for gifts. My niece fizzes with excitement as I unwrap the present she has chosen for me. It buzzes beneath the wrapper and jumps in my hands. I uncover a half sphere of knobbly, soft, green plastic, a kind of extra-terrestrial hedgehog. "Try it!" she encourages. I stare at it in astonishment. It is a battery powered foot massager. All I can think of is the waste of talent and the destruction of resources that went into the creation of this pointless object. But my niece is dancing with excitement. She has chosen this for me. It is a triumph of empathy and identification. She has trailed the shopping malls in search of something that will fit what she knows of my moods and desires and the market has provided the perfect answer—a DIY foot massage, available at any time, with no risk of the unfortunate masseur getting their head bitten off by a grumpy aunt. I recover, smile and play with the strange object. An uncle sends it skidding across the kitchen floor like a football. Offended, my niece retrieves it and places it solicitously beneath my foot where it makes the floorboards vibrate. Periodically, throughout Christmas day, she remarks with satisfaction on the appropriateness of her present. Who would not be touched and delighted by such a gift? Outwardly I smile. Inwardly I am disappointed and ungracious.

In this juxtaposition of my niece's excitement and my grumpy response we find one of the dilemmas of the twenty-first century: the extreme of difference between exuberant, delighted wonder at what the world can produce and curmudgeonly weariness about what the true cost may be.

There is something however that my niece and I share. We both believe that the gift should fit and that it is likely to be a work of some skill to make it do so. We both live in a world of rapidly changing expectations, where the person you thought you knew is likely to have changed their aspirations, shifted their allegiance and moved on from last year's fantasy to one you have not yet heard of. The gift must fit neatly with the recipient's shifting identity and desires. Getting this right is likely to be difficult.

Late modernity

Contemporary culture is sometimes described as narcissistic (Lasch, 1979) and the current period as one of "late modernity", "high modernity" (Giddens, 1991), or "liquid modernity" (Bauman, 2000) where questions

Table 1. (*Continued*).

Transactional analysis ego state	Transactional analysis description	Manifestations in environmentalism	Natural change participants' perspectives
Free child	Experimental, playful, absorbed in exploration and expression of self. Typically does not involve responsibility to others.	Outdoor recreation, gardening, arts and crafts and other "escape" activities, often where we feel close to nature.	"Normally I'd feel the need to rush in to the countryside and consume the environment at this time of year. But each day I get more excited as I watch the few trees I can see from my attic flat change ever so slightly each day as the green shoots fill the gaps between their branches."
Adapted child	Defensiveness, compliance and submission motivated by fear. Passive resistance motivated by anger.	Doing whatever we can get away with. Guilty compliance. Denial— "hiding" from the problems; "What's the point". Belligerent resistance.	"I was being told I had to worry about it, and that I was a good citizen if I did my bit, so I did."

of "ego states" is helpful in illustrating common egoic responses to our ecological predicament (Fox, 1990a; Stewart & Joines, 1987) (Table 1).

As we have described earlier, recent evidence has emerged that traditional methods of environmental campaigning—which appeal to the preoccupations of the ego—have limited capacity to motivate people to make pro-environmental changes to their lives, and may even be counter-productive. For example, in Transactional Analysis terms,

Critical Parent strategies of blaming and shaming may lead to Adapted Child responses of denial, token compliance, and angry resistance; Nurturing Parent inducements of social marketing may also induce competitive responses from the Adapted Child ego state. On the other hand, rational-scientific Adult approaches, while motivating for some, seem to lack the emotional energy to catalyse deep change.

Supporters of the Deep Ecology movement, in particular, Fox (1990a), have suggested that a move from egoic to transpersonal approaches, based on interconnectedness, is needed to catalyse a profound and enduring motivation for pro-environmental behaviour. Fox sees deep "identification" or relationship with our ecological context as the basis of such a "transpersonal ecology" (see also Sessions, 1995).

The journey through the Natural Change process leads from an egoic sense of self, to one that is transpersonal and interconnected. In this way, it parallels many accounts of individuation and spiritual insight (Firman and Gila, 1997; Jung, 1963; Preece, 2006; Underhill, 1993/1910; Washburn, 1995). For this alone, going through the Natural Change process would be worthwhile as a personally healing and transformative path. However, that is only a part of the outcome. If our sense of self is widened to include the rest of nature through transpersonal experiences, a powerful new understanding of the world can emerge. We come to live as part of the earth's whole system of life, rather than as if we are separate from it. And from this knowledge of our interconnectedness, comes a desire to take action in service of the rest of nature.

Facilitation

Because of their power, it is essential that the transpersonal experiences which happen on Natural Change, are held in a compassionate ethical framework. As with the core conditions for person-centred therapy (Rogers, 1980), certain qualities are essential to the process of Natural Change. These qualities include compassion, fairness, respect, trust and community—and they become norms (Yalom, 1970) in the relationships between facilitators and group, within the group, between the members of the Project team and critically, between everyone and the body of the earth.

In keeping with the philosophical basis of the Project, there is a strong focus on "being", rather than "doing". This means that, although there are key activities which constitute the Project, our attention is as much on how these activities are facilitated as it is on what activities are offered.

Shared practices such as co-counselling, focusing (Gendlin, 1978), mindfulness meditation, contemplative practice in the land, solo time, shamanic journeying and work with imagery help us, as facilitators, listen closely to the group's needs, and to subtle shifts in group process. We engage in these parallel practices in the time between sessions during the workshops, and before and after each workshop. This enables a constant cycle of reflective practice and peer supervision. It also allows us to open our sensitivity not only to participants, but also to each other and to the places in which we are working.

Content

The Natural Change process comprises two, one-week-long, residential workshops. These are held four months apart in wilderness areas. A series of one-day meetings in urban settings are also held before and after these residential workshops.

Before the first residential workshop the group meets for a day to introduce themselves to each other and prepare for their first wilderness adventure.

From the beginning, we use a reflective way of working with the group. At the start of the first week, we offer a co-counselling activity, where participants can listen carefully and openly to the expressions of each others' needs. This is followed by a walk, in which the group progressively slows down, becomes quiet, and starts to experience the land around. During this walk there is time to sit quietly—in a guided mindfulness meditation, and alone.

This experience acts as preparation for the next day's solo—a day spent alone in the land from dawn to dusk, in silence, in one spot. From the group's return at dusk, until the next morning, silence is held. The next day, the participants share their stories. The structure and containment of the storytelling process creates a sacred and respectful space, where everyone can listen at depth to what is being told. The focus in the first workshop is on personal healing—and personal relationship with the land and sea.

The intermediate day between workshops tends to act like a bridge, where the focus of the work shifts out from personal, to social,

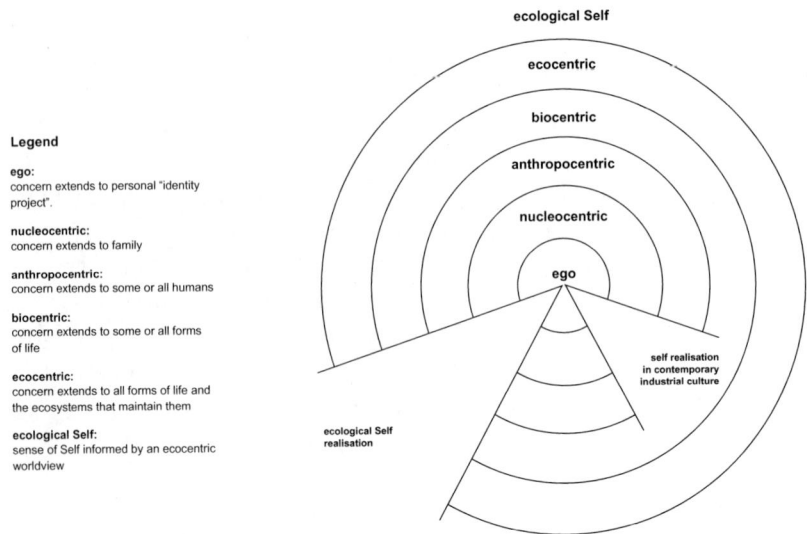

Legend

ego:
concern extends to personal "identity project".

nucleocentric:
concern extends to family

anthropocentric:
concern extends to some or all humans

biocentric:
concern extends to some or all forms of life

ecocentric:
concern extends to all forms of life and the ecosystems that maintain them

ecological Self:
sense of Self informed by an ecocentric worldview

Figure 1. The ecological self.

to ecological self (Figure 1). This work involves creative, experiential and theoretical exploration of models of self, and an investigation of consumerism and identity. Although this widening of perspective from the personal world is a vital part of Natural Change, we have found from experience that it is wise not to rush or prescribe this transition. If the shift is premature, any unacknowledged personal trauma will act as a brake on the engagement with activism.

In the time between workshops, we ask participants to spend a short time "on solo" in an urban environment, and to research stories of social change movements in preparation for the next workshop.

At the second workshop, participants share their stories and discoveries from the urban solo. Early in this week, the group explore utopian and dystopian scenarios in the face of ecological challenge. This is done first as a guided visualization, then making images on paper, and listening reflectively to each other's responses. There is further time alone in the land to contemplate this, and to share stories on return.

The participants then share the findings from their research into social change movements. These stories are told during a journey on foot in the local area.

There is then further time alone in the land, to reflect on personal motivation to act—as framed by the question where is "… the place where your deep gladness and the world's deep hunger meet"? (Buechner, 1993, p. 119).

Towards the end of the week, participants engage in a deep exploration of the processes of change, first individually, by making representations in a land art session. Then, collectively, producing a group model of social change. The week concludes with a discussion of potential routes for personal and collective action, and this move to activism is strengthened in the ensuing weeks, and in the final one-day workshop.

Changes

The changes that flow from the Natural Change Project are not easy to specify using conventional "tick-box" outcome measures. Participants have initiated new projects and experienced lifestyle changes, for sure. However, the nature of change is more complex than these behavioural outcomes. It is a radical systemic and personal transformation. The process of change is ongoing and acausal—part of an internal reorganization of self; part of an external reorganization in which participants generate an evolving community of peers who work to deepen their experience, understanding and activism.

One of the Natural Change participants put it like this:

> So … has it worked then? It's the question everyone has been asking …
>
> The simple, "surface" answer is yes. Yes, I tell people, it's made me more aware. Yes, it's made me think more about the whole range of interconnected themes around nature and our relationship with it as human beings. Yes, it's made me act different—from changing my shopping habits, to introducing new sustainable procurement policies at work to feeding the birds.
>
> But whilst it's a true answer, it is an answer of convenience. The more complex answer is also yes, it has worked, but …
>
> … in ways it is so hard to articulate, because the impact has affected me inside and out, at every level.
>
> … in ways that have made my life much harder, not easier—deep questioning of your values in relation to the world will do that to a girl you know.

… in ways that have led to huge frustration—particularly around the issues of engaging the public in tackling environmental issues. There is an element of what I would be tempted to term delusion around how a lot of the key "green" groups are tackling this.

… in ways that have led me to uncomfortable truths around choices I have made in the past, but equally having given me the tools to be kind to myself, to understand and forgive, and appreciate what it really is to be human …

A key issue throughout NC has been the journey between being a participant in the project, and then where it would take us as activists—the next steps we, the "chosen leaders in our sector", would take to cascade what we had learned, the action we would take to put our "personal change" into practical action authentically. It's been a heavier responsibility than any of us anticipated at the start—well, for me anyway. That word "authentic" is a killer by the way … makes you stop and think …

That step has been an interesting one—there's been a sense of wanting to "hold the circle" of what we have been through and experienced together, but then the responsibility to step out into the wider world has been so strong, so necessary—the world needs more from us.

… First—NC gave me back my heart. And for that I will always, always be profoundly thankful.

Second—I'm ready. Ready to act. Ready to step out into the world.

And so more change is afoot—deeper change. The stone has been cast into the water, and the powerful ripples are spreading. It's just that sometimes, those ripples take longer to reach out than you—or others—expect.

(Macdonald, 2010)

PART VI

WHAT TO DO—CLINICAL PRACTICE

CHAPTER NINETEEN

"Nothing's out of order": towards an ecological therapy

Nick Totton

Introduction

Until quite recently, there hasn't really been a great deal of close thinking about the relationship between ecologically inflected ways of thinking and feeling ("ecopsychology") on the one hand, and the practice of psychotherapy and counselling ("therapy") on the other. With some exceptions, the tendency has been to bolt therapeutic ideas onto ecopsychology, or ecopsychological ideas onto therapy, without really letting the two meld together into a new whole. As a simple example, practitioners want to do therapy with clients out of doors, and realize that conventional notions of the therapeutic frame and boundaries will no longer work; but mostly they think in terms of *adjusting* the frame, rather than radically *reconceiving* it—indeed reconceiving the whole "frame" metaphor. Working towards an ecological reconception of therapy is one purpose of my book, *Wild Therapy* (Totton, 2011). This chapter is something between an afterword to the book, a companion piece, and a reconsideration; it focuses on just one strand of *Wild Therapy*, the development of a truly ecological practice.

In writing the book, I realized that in order for therapy to think and feel ecologically it has to change some of its core attitudes. But I also found that the elements of an ecological therapy were already present in the field, often without being perceived as such. What I therefore try to do in the book is to identify these implicit elements and assemble them in a coherent way, so as to describe a way of doing therapy which is both new and also always-already present—an ecosystemic therapy, which recognizes that humans don't stand alone in the universe, but are profoundly connected with and interdependent with the other species and entities who share this earth; and recognizes also that skilful living flows from a capacity for spontaneity and yielding to what is, rather than from a struggle to exert control over self and others.

These recognitions and others stem from positions which I think are held in common by ecologists and many therapists. The list which follows is different from, but in dialogue with, the one I offer in *Wild Therapy* (Totton, 2011, p. 184), which was more a set of descriptions of a possible practice, and included elements like attention to embodiment and to the more-than-human; here is the product of further thinking, a group of core understandings on which such a practice might be based.

- Like an ecosystem, therapy has no goal.
- Everything is connected; and it is through being fully *itself* that each being co-creates the whole.
- This co-creation happens spontaneously, with any sort of intervention from outside tending to be damaging.
- Looking more closely, in fact, there *is* no outside. The illusion of "outsideness" is something which ecology and therapy each challenge.

I shall look at these in turn, trying to give some examples of their practical implications.

Therapy has no goal

It is fundamental to ecological understanding that ecosystems are not "for" anything. They have no goal, and no intention; they are utterly unteleological. The whole extraordinary richness and complexity of life is the expression, the unfolding, of some very simple features inherent in life itself. Its nature is basically mathematical, in the sense that mathematics is an apparently uniquely good description of the universe: Complexity Theory shows how the repetition of little, straightforward algorithms—"instructions", we might say, but, in real ecosystems, instructions which have evolved rather than been given—leads to elaborate and unpredictable consequences: creation of everything out of almost nothing.

Some people seem to find this way of perceiving things scary, a description of universal meaninglessness. Personally, I find it awe-inspiring: rather than being made *by* anyone or anything, life bootstraps, *makes itself.* Wolf Singer (2005) describes the brain as an orchestra without a conductor. It seems that the whole of existence is an orchestra without a conductor, a continuous act of mutual co-creation. "Meaning" is a wholly different things from "purpose": life has no *purpose*, but it has an infinite amount of *meaning*, all the meaning you find in it!

What does this have to do with therapy? I suggest that one of therapy's important functions is—usually without talking about it explicitly—to disentangle *meaning* from *purpose*, and support people in exploring the possibility that they can live without "shoulds" and "oughts": the possibility that there are no "right" decisions, to be checked against some pre-established list, but only whatever decisions we find ourselves having made; nothing we are supposed to do, and no one we are supposed to be; and that our life means whatever we experience it to mean. One aspect of this dissolving of purpose is that therapy gives up any sense of its own purpose. This may seem paradoxical, and to some extent it is: what I have said could be seen as suggesting that therapy's purpose is to dissolve the notion of purpose! What I am talking about, though, is *function* not purpose, what therapy actually does rather than what it is "supposed" to do. The dissolving of purpose, *when not held as a goal*, tends to come about through the practice of therapy.

I wrote in an earlier article:

> Therapeutic practice, from a certain point of view, is an ongoing struggle by the therapist to live up to the aspirations of therapy—to become aware of and let go of her biases, judgements, wishes, demands for the client and reality to be a certain way. That's why and how being therapists, as well as hopefully being good for clients, is good for *us.* But the continuing paradox of therapy is that it can only be good for anybody insofar as it confronts and abandons its *intention* to be good for them. This is a corollary of the paradoxical theory of change (Beisser, 1970): not only does change

happen when the client stops trying to change—it happens when
the therapist stops trying to change them.

(Totton, 2007, pp. 24–25)

As clients, we project onto our therapist the demands which we are
accustomed to experiencing in our lives, and out of which, and out of
our resistance to which, we have constructed our identity. Althusser
(1971; see also Butler, 1993) calls this "interpellation", roughly trans-
latable as "hailing"—"Hey, you!"—in the way that a cop hails a sus-
pect. If we are addressed repeatedly in a particular way, we take on
that identity, together with its associated requirements. Maintaining
this interpellated self becomes the source of tremendous anxiety and
tension.

As therapists, then, we have a dilemma. Should we reinforce this
interpellation, "hailing" the client in ways they are accustomed to,
encouraging them to be the person they have been told they are/to be?
Or should we instead suggest that they are/can be someone else, someone new—who fits with *our own* picture of what people should be like?
Personally I don't find either of these options very appealing—although
in practice I can certainly slip into either of them. But when we do select
either option, it is because of a notion, however cloudy, that this will be
good for the client.

Paolo (a composite and fictionalized character) came to me because
he "felt depressed". When we explored what this meant, it became
apparent that what he mainly found difficult was taking action, of
almost any kind. This meant that he seemed apathetic; but in fact
he was anything but—inside him was a swarming, boiling crowd of
impulses, each of which immediately became blocked or cancelled out
by one or another injunction: Be Good, Be Nice, Look Before You Leap,
Don't Make Mistakes …

The obvious approach, which might indeed have worked quite well
in terms of changing his behaviour, would be to say something like:
"No wonder you're depressed! Anyone would be depressed if they had
that much to live up to! But you can choose to ignore those instructions,
and stand up for the 'Bad' part of you, the part that is human and
makes mistakes …" —and so on. The less obvious approach, which is
also certainly worth considering, would be to say: "Hmmm, yes, I see
the problem—mistakes are dreadful—best to *stay completely still* and

not take any risks"—to support the stuckness, in the hope of carrying it through to a place where it would naturally fall away.

I think, though, that each of these approaches—which of course both occurred to me—are in part a response to the dreadful uncomfortableness that stuckness creates in any reasonably empathic person, making us desperate to change the situation. Sitting with Paolo, I was very much aware of how his dilemma resonated inside *me*: of how much I am myself inhibited by similar internal messages, even if I (usually) do a better job of overcoming them.

The third course of action that I found, then, was to talk openly—awkwardly and haltingly—about the effect that his dilemma had on me; about how difficult it actually is to reconcile our own impulses with the needs of the larger groups of which we are part, and how confusing it becomes to try to work out what we do "really want". (In doing this I was struggling against my own injunction to be a skilful therapist.) Where Paolo tended to submit to the group will, I tend to flout it; but neither approach is truly satisfactory.

After several false starts, where I lapsed back into subtly telling him how he should be—that is, taking the role of his inner critics—we were able to reach a place where we could together simply hold and share the pain of the situation. And from this sharing, something new was born, not only in Paolo, but in me as well: a new realization, not just intellectual but embodied, that through accepting the genuine impossibility of wholly reconciling individual and group, together with the impossibility of separating them, the tension between the two can start to become creative, a field in which our energy might play.

Everything is connected

I have deliberately chosen the above vignette because it has no specific ecological or environmental content. I want to illustrate how ecological thinking can be applied in "ordinary" therapy; more specifically, to illustrate not only how we can work as therapists without a goal, but also how the relationship between group and individual needs reconceptualizing if therapy is going to become ecologically minded. Therapy very much tends to take the classic Western view that the individual is paramount, and that our job is to free individuals from the constraints and conditioning which limit their self-expression. This is both true and not true; it needs to pass through a dialectical process of thesis, antithesis and synthesis to reach another level.

Certainly therapy has traditionally suffered under the paradigm of "individual vs group". At some points in its history, it has tended to support the group and encourage the individual to submit to it, in the name of being "well-adjusted" or "well-adapted" (Totton, 2000, pp. 96–97, 106–107); at other points, it has tended to encourage the individual to rebel and find her supposed "real self" (Geller, 1982). Each of these positions is one-sided, and both are based on the assumption that individual and group are opposed.

Ecological ways of seeing, however—and they are not alone in this— encourage us to see that individual and group are complementary, even co-created (Totton, 2011, pp. 28–30; Macy, 1991b). The individual cannot exist or be understood without the group/s of which it is part; likewise, the group cannot exist or be understood without the individuals who make it up. We each bring our entire relational context into the therapy room with us—much as, in their psychoanalytic fieldwork in West Africa, Morgenthaler and Parin found that their "analysands" tended to literally bring their friends and relations to the sessions:

> Contrary to what might have been expected, the ... group exercised no sort of prohibitive function. Rather, it encouraged the young woman and even the analyst to make their relationship to each other more intense and more intimate. It was not long before they revealed the content of her wishes by making open demands, in words and gestures, for a sexual relationship.
>
> (Morgenthaler & Parin, 1964, p. 447)

In every therapy room, representatives of much larger groups are encountering each other. The client's family, their social networks, their political or spiritual organizations, their cultural and class groupings: all these are encountering not only the therapist's professional networks— this much we can be comfortable with—but also and more uncomfortably the therapist's family, social networks, political and spiritual organizations, cultural and class groupings. A problem or problems somewhere in the first network, we might say, has found its way to the second network, in the hope that this encounter will be helpful. But ultimately, everything is connected: client and therapist represent two points in one enormous network which has folded itself together to bring these two points into contact, in an attempt at self-healing—perhaps as one might put a burnt finger in one's mouth?

This is not how we usually see things; and it is reasonable to ask how, or whether, it is helpful to do so. It is helpful, I suggest, because it encourages us to rely on the wisdom of the collective—as it manifests *in us*. In effect, we have been chosen as the right therapist for the situation—and the choice is not primarily a matter of our skill or competence, but of *where we are situated* in relation to the larger network. In a sense the networks we belong to help constitute our unconscious, or at least our preconscious. Hence there is little to be gained by trying to conceal our own personality or allegiances: these are precisely what we have to offer to the situation.

If we again take Paolo as an example, among the many groups which were being brought together through our work were British and Italians; conformers and rebels; Catholics and pagans; anarchists and socialists; gay men and straight men; cafe culture and home-based culture. Also meeting each other were the ecologies of the Italian Alps and urban Milan, and of suburban London and rural Yorkshire. All of these encounters became significant at various points in our work. I think it is a struggle for therapists to move beyond the idea that such contrasts may be significant *for the client*, and realize that they are significant *for the therapist as well*. It is very tempting to protect our own subjectivity by treating it as a neutral medium within which the client's subjectivity is presented for examination; but this is far from the case. And by being willing to offer up our own position within the networks of culture and society to the therapeutic encounter, we set a tone of open undefensiveness which invites the client to do likewise.

What I am saying can be read in terms of the sort of relational approach which is now becoming widely known (Haugh & Paul, 2008; Mitchell & Aron, 1999); and certainly it includes those ways of working and thinking. What I want to contribute, though, is a further decentring of the individual. Not only is therapy about relationship; the relationship in question is not just between individuals, but also between *worlds*, and at certain moments we can sense directly how those worlds are *using* the two individuals to achieve something on a larger scale.

At the same time, though, we also need to hold the opposite emphasis: it is entirely through feeling and acting as individuals that we contribute to the development of the whole. In an ecosystem, each organism acts to further its own needs, and through this multiplicity of individual actions the conductor-less orchestra of the whole emerges in perfect synchrony. We perceive the same thing happening in group process: as most facilitators know, it is when each participant fully takes their own side—even, or perhaps even especially, when this is disturbing or irritating to the group—that the group as a whole is enabled to form and to grow. In taking their own side, each individual is representing an element of the group field (Mindell, 1992, Ch. 2). To trust the group is to trust ourselves; to trust ourselves is to trust the group. Individuality is *both* crucial *and* illusory. (This part of my argument is in dialogue with Andrew Samuels' (2011) recent work on individuality.)

Like all frames and boundaries, the therapeutic frame misrepresents reality, which is continuous rather than discrete. Like many frames and boundaries, though, the therapeutic frame can be immensely useful in bracketing and insulating those aspects of reality on which we wish to focus, for example the two individuals present in the room—so long as we don't take it too seriously, don't fetishise it and privilege it over the needs of the living moment. Paolo and I once visited a Catholic church together. On another occasion, we talked about going to a local cafe, but never actually went. These weren't casual or whimsical adventures, but important ways of introducing me to aspects of Paolo's world. They were only possible—and, I would argue, necessary—once we had formed a strong therapeutic relationship in the insulation of the therapy room.

What frame we apply to therapy depends on what aspect/s of reality we are seeking to explore. The hushed, holy isolation of the therapeutic pair which is currently the dominant model for our work derives from, and is appropriate to, a focus on early childhood experience, insulated (for many of us) within the mother-baby dyad: this focus is where the model largely developed. It can arguably be quite unhelpful, however, if we are exploring the client's membership of much larger sociocultural formations, or their relationship with the other-than-human and more-than-human. I would even suggest that the frame benefits from some adjustment when the work is focused on oedipal rather than pre-oedipal issues within the family.

It is worth recognizing that "frame" and "boundary" are both *spatial metaphors*. To use them commits us to a particular conceptualization of how to behave in therapy: it creates in our mind a picture of objective edges or thresholds which can be objectively crossed or not crossed, erased or preserved. How does it change our perception if we use a different spatial metaphor—perhaps a gravity field, strongest at the centre but diminishing imperceptibly and never quite ending? Or we could conceptualize it in some non-spatial way, as a protocol, say, or as a muscular tension, or as an altered state of consciousness; or perhaps most relevantly, as an attractor in a complex system (Piers, Muller & Brent, 2007). These all sound odd, but how much is that simply because they are unfamiliar?

Spontaneous co-creation

An emphasis on spontaneity is as much part of ecological awareness as an emphasis on connectedness. Both ideas follow from systems theory, which sees the world as a set of complex, self-organizing, adaptive systems, where nothing *causes* anything else in a linear sense, but everything mutually *responds* to everything else. This closely matches the Buddhist concept of *paticca samuppada*, "dependent co-arising" (Macy, 1991). Hence trying to isolate oneself from the world and exercise control over it is ultimately self-defeating—as we are indeed seeing with the current ecological crisis.

We also see this every day in the consulting room. A very high proportion of the difficulties that clients bring seem to me to be about illusions of controllability. They bring beliefs that they can and should be able to control their bodies, their feelings, their thoughts, their behaviour, their relationships … And the flip side of this, of course, is an implicit belief that others can control *them:* really it is the internalized other who is supposed to be controlling the various aspects of our process—and also, in a different sense, the internalized other whose recalcitrance and disobedience manifests in these processes.

It doesn't finally matter which aspect we identify with self, and which with other: the point is that we experience a split between different aspects of a single whole. We struggle to conduct the conductorless orchestra, which gives rise to countless miscoordinations as delays open up between various aspects of process. Because there is actually no overarching Self to act as conductor (Dennett, 1991; Nørretranders, 1999), it's as if a bassoon player, a violinist, a percussionist, and a couple of flautists were all trying to conduct simultaneously, while also performing their own parts. Chaos, but not in a good way. Left to its own devices, however, the orchestra coordinates *of its own accord*, just as ecosystems do, just as the universe does.

There is no outside

The idea of an overarching self is in effect the idea of an *outside*, a place to stand which is not itself part of the complex whole, but allows us to understand and control it. "Give me but one firm spot on which to stand, and I will move the earth", Archimedes said, according to Pappus (Partington, 1996, p. 24). But there is no such spot: nowhere outside our own frame of reference from which we can view things "objectively". Einstein showed us that this is so in a physical sense; but it seems a lot harder for us to grasp it emotionally and relationally.

I wrote in *Wild Therapy*:

> In the move from hunter gatherer society to agriculture, human beings tried to gain control over the world, over each other, and over the other-than-human and more-than-human. In doing this we split ourselves off from the world—it became, in fact, our "environment", rather than the whole of which we are an integral part. In Ursula LeGuin's resonant phrase, we learnt to live "outside the world" (LeGuin, 1988, 153). By trying to control the world we have made it *other*, and therefore dangerous and frightening. The more we seek control, the closer we seem to get to it, the further our goal recedes.
>
> (Totton, 2011, p. 2)

I can't improve on that formulation, but I want to add something about its relevance for the practice of therapy. Many people come to therapy for help in controlling their lives; and many practitioners try to give it to them. It is actually pretty near impossible to avoid being sometimes drawn into the pleasant illusion that this can be done; but it *is* an illusion, and one which creates great distress. Of course we can *manage* our lives better or worse (and therapists can come up with some useful tips); and we can insulate ourselves and our family, with money or with healthy lifestyles, for example. Living in a West European country gives us several layers of insulation to begin with. But we cannot prevent bad things from happening; and we certainly cannot prevent our bodies, our feelings, our relationships from changing of their own accord, in ways which might not be what the part of us that thinks it is "outside the world" would choose. To believe otherwise is comforting in the short term, but also a huge strain; and leaves us defenceless against disaster.

I frequently use quotations from Lao Tzu as an antidote to this way of thinking; and since I have just mentioned Ursula LeGuin, these two passages are from her translation (LeGuin, 1998, pp. 6–8).

> When you do not-doing
> Nothing's out of order.

(Tao te Ching, Ch. 3)

> Heaven and earth
> act as a bellows:

> Empty yet structured,
> it moves, inexhaustibly giving.

(Tao te Ching, Ch. 5)

"Doing not-doing", *wei wu wei*, is a phrase constantly repeated in the *Tao te Ching*. As LeGuin writes, "it's a thought that transforms thought radically, that changes minds" (LeGuin, 1998, p. 6): the thought that everything needful can happen without effort, of its own accord. "Doing not-doing" captures the paradox of individual and group: taking our own side in the knowledge that this is taking the group's side. The phrase is balanced, dialectical: "doing /not/ doing", yin and yang, "heaven and earth", ecosystemic process: it "acts as a bellows", powerfully pushing forward, yet without goals, "inexhaustibly giving", yet without generosity. It just is. And in my experience, the most powerfully transformative moments in therapy are about just-isness.

There was a moment with Paolo, near the end of our work together, when we had yet again gone around the cycle of stuckness, self-accusation, rage, and despair with which we were both by now so familiar. Pausing, not-doing, we caught each other's eye; and simultaneously giggled, chuckled, snorted. "And so on ...", Paolo murmured. "And so on," I agreed. From that point I don't think Paolo was ever again able to take his stuckness so seriously, or to locate it so firmly in the outside world.

Conclusion

In this chapter, I haven't written at all about what many people would assume to be the central feature of ecological therapy: taking clients out of doors and "into nature" (as if we could ever be out of it). While my clients and I do indeed sometimes work out of doors, this seems to me to be a corollary of much more crucial differences in therapeutic practice. It is perfectly possible to go out of doors but take the indoors with you!—In other words, to haul the traditional therapeutic frame up hill and down dale, through bush and briar, straining one's muscles and barking one's shins. Equally, it is possible to bring the out-of-doors indoors: to work in an ecological style while sitting in chairs in a consulting room. I frequently argue that doing body psychotherapy doesn't necessarily—though of course it can—involve touch, standing up or lying down, or even any explicit reference to bodies. In the same way, ecological therapy, what I call Wild Therapy (Totton, 2011), doesn't necessarily—though of course it can—involve going out of doors, or even discussing environmental themes. Also, it can mean going out of doors onto the high street as well as into the woods!

I feel convinced that the ideas discussed in this chapter, and those in *Wild Therapy* (Totton, 2011), have profound implications for therapy, just as they do for life. I don't feel that I have fully worked them out yet either in theory or in practice; and I certainly don't claim ownership of them, they have been around in written form for several thousand years and in oral form for a great deal longer than that. But it is some time since many of us really attended to them; and I think we need to do so, not only to develop our therapeutic practice, but to learn how to cherish the damaged world we live in and of which we are part.

CHAPTER TWENTY

Dangerous margins: recovering the stem cells of the psyche

Chris Robertson

> It's all a question of story. We are in trouble just now because we do not have a good story. We are in between stories. The old story, the account of how we fit into the world, is no longer effective. Yet we have not learned the new story.
>
> —Thomas Berry (1990)

Jason is a young man with a big heart that often gets him into untenable positions. He presents in therapy as a victim of his experience. It "happens" to him and it's unfair. Gentle explorations of what his investment might be in maintaining this position fall on stony ground. He is attached to the unfairness. The therapeutic relationship falls into a precarious impasse. He wants me to confirm his position—and I want to give him permission to deconstruct it.

I could attempt to begin a different sort of conversation—one that is about where we are stuck: a meta-narrative that attempts to surface the underlying dynamic between us. Or I could shift out of a conscious dialogue by introducing imagination, body experience or metaphor/story, and engage Jason in a fresh manner that allows his unconscious a stronger place in the therapy. This would open the space for the story to take off in many different directions—not random, but certainly bringing in a chaotic complexity that takes account of what is presently unseen.

It seems to me that ecopsychology may be in a similar impasse in attempting to engage the collective crisis facing humanity at this time. A conscious dialogue explaining the roots of our alienation and exhorting us to reconnect to our true interdependent state is unlikely to impact on our collective complex. By moving between the parallel process of therapeutic situation and the planetary crisis, between an imaginative story and an expositional one, I hope to show something of what an ecopsychological perspective can bring both to ecological concerns and to the consulting room.

Moving on from an earlier ecological activism Arne Naess suggested a deeper analysis was necessary—a *deep ecology* that emphasized our intrinsic relational interdependence with all species.

Since then, several significant contributions have been made to this analysis including:

- the denial of planetary problems is not a new phenomena, it follows a classic historical pattern. Cf. Jared Diamond in *Collapse: How Societies Choose to Fail or Survive* (Diamond, 2006).
- the abstraction and dissociation that takes place in the cultural shift from oral languages to the written word. Cf. David Abram in *The Spell of the Sensuous* (Abram, 1996) and Hugh Brody in *The Other Side of Eden* (Brody, 2002b).
- the alienation from our animal nature and illusory notions of control and mastery that come with the predictive capacities of our ego mind. Cf. Jerome Bernstein in *Living in the Borderland* (Bernstein, 2005).
- the collusion between religion and Newtonian science that denigrates nature and permits the cruel desecration of sacred sites, other species, and indigenous peoples. Cf. Joanna Macy in *World as Lover, World as Self* (Macy, 1991b).
- the narcissism of our present western culture that sees ourselves as the pinnacle of planetary evolution (anthropocentric superiority towards other species) and through this cultural complex sees our human needs as paramount. Cf. Arne Naess in *Thinking like a Mountain* (Seed, Macy, Fleming & Naess, 1993).
- the consumptive greed and insatiable hunger that powers our modern capitalist societies like an out of control eating disorder. Cf. Mary-Jayne Rust in "Consuming the earth" (Rust, 2008b).

These are all insightful contributions and go some way towards an understanding of why humanity continues to persist in its self-destructive behaviour. Yet they all point towards what is wrong with humankind. While agreeing that we do carry out violent destructive behaviour that is dangerous to other species, the planet and ourselves, this may need to be understood in a different context—less in classical diagnosis of what is wrong and more in terms of story.

When I shift the story just a little, to what *troubles* us rather than what is *wrong*, we get a different tone. If I am to talk about the pain I experience at the loss of species or the responsibility I feel towards indigenous cultures that have been decimated, this is a different communication—one that draws resonances from others through speaking from my experience.

To return to Jason: it would be tempting to proceed with an analysis of what is wrong. My training has enabled an ear for hearing this. Some of my language is already indicative of my clinical thinking. I have used the word "victim". A shift to speak more personally from my experience will set a different tone—a warmer, more empathic quality will be present. This carries its own dangers—that of a collusive relationship in which challenges are avoided.

But what if I assume that what is happening with Jason is "not wrong"? What if I start to listen to his troubles from that open place and attempt to understand how he comes to be where he is?

And now, coming back to our ecopsychological perspective, how would this approach look? To move to a place of compassionate perspective for humanity's destructive, narcissistic, greedy, and denigrating behaviour seems more difficult! It is rather like having a client who is admitting to abuse but not taking any responsibility. Something powerful gets stirred up—I could call it *righteous indignation*—and makes me want to confront him/her. This may be appropriate but it takes away the opportunity to be with the situation as it is: I am judging it again as "wrong".

A major part of the work of a systemic psychotherapist is to *positively connote* the complaint/symptom, in order to see how it works in the system, rather than focusing on the dysfunction. For instance within a family system, the therapist might positively connote a child's eating disorder as a means for the family to talk and stay together. This valuing the homeostasis of the system does not absolve responsibility or deny that dissociation from our own instincts or alienation from the planet has brought us into a crisis. It has. Our collective denial is a defence against the anxiety of being aware of this crisis, just as trauma victims dissociate and split off their experience.

What we are working with is an *unconscious process* that is not susceptible to rational analysis or well-meaning actions. Searles pointed out that we seemed in the grip of a common apathy that he recognized as symptomatic of unconscious ego defences against anxiety.

> The greatest danger lies in the fact that the world is in such a state as to evoke our very earliest anxieties and at the same time to offer the delusional "promise", the actually deadly promise, of assuaging these anxieties, effacing them, by fully externalizing and reifying our most primitive conflicts that produce those anxieties.
>
> (Searles, 1972, p. 373)

Actions may help, once the unconscious complex has been worked with, so that it no longer has the client, or our collective culture, in its grip. The systemic work of understanding how the symptom or apparent disorder has its function within the overall system, takes us into an empathic position, no longer being outside of the system judging it.

How to drop down and listen through to the dilemmas in this crisis? Sitting with clients, I notice how they want to draw me into their story; assimilate me to neutralise my otherness. If I can tune out of this known story, disengage my expectations and sink into sensing our mutual presence, my attention gets drawn to their unconscious complex. How might this work on a collective level? James Hillman gives us a pointer:

> The world, because of its breakdown, is entering a new moment of consciousness: by drawing attention to itself by means of its symptoms, it is becoming aware of itself as a psychic reality.
>
> (Hillman, 1998, p. 97)

The world is drawing attention to itself by means of its symptoms. While there is the economic pressure towards globalization, there is another complementary process away from individualistic egocentricity towards networked, interconnected communities that show deep concern for our wounded world. The world needs our engaged participation with it and its symptoms allow us a way to become aware of it as psychic reality.

This sort of ecosystemic thinking may help us in the much needed creation of a new story: a story that attempts to see through to what might be unfolding in the crisis; a story that recognizes the deep affinity between human flesh and the flesh of the world. Through our participatory engagement with the world we have co-evolved. David Abram writes,

> Our nervous systems, then, are wholly informed by the particular gravity of this sphere, by the way the sun's light filters down through the earth's atmosphere, and by the tug of earth's moon. In a thoroughly palpable sense, we are born of this planet, our attentive bodies coevolved in rich and intimate rapport with other bodily forms—animals, plants, mountains, rivers—that compose the shifting flesh of this breathing world.
>
> (Abram, 2010a, p. 97)

Psychotherapy with its emphasis on the client's self-reflection or even with the dynamic between therapist and client can absent itself from this intimate co-evolution. One of Hillman's dictums is "From mirror to window" (Hillman, 1989)—that if psychotherapists and clients spent less time looking in the mirror and more looking through the window, they might better attend to the world. He wants to break this mirror of self-reflection to free us from our self-absorption and release us back into the world. It is not *our* soul that individuates, it is the soul of the world.

Even this can become an anthropomorphic task. It is not just up to us to look out. It is not just for us to be aware of the world. *The world wants to look in.* The bird singing outside my window is asking to be heard. There is a potential reciprocal affinity through which the inside/outside distinctions no longer hold. The birdsong seems synchronistically attuned to the moment between the client and myself. The world is sensing us while we are sensing it. It is not a passive recipient of our attention but a deeply reciprocal partner. We are participants in the story that we are telling and is being told through us.

It is easy to recognize this reciprocity with animals. Neuroscience is increasingly showing the evidence of vicarious activity in mirror neurones. The more-than-human animals respond visibly to our attention. My dog is reading the subtle clues to my intentions. Sometimes he seems to know before I do what my intention is. When I engage my attention with a plant, the observable signs are less obvious. Plants are sensitive to their environment. Plant cells have features in common with nerve cells. They are not simply objects in our perceptual field but are joint participants within a shared field. Paul Shepard (1997) argues that our co-evolution with plants and animals has so deeply influenced our culture and thinking that they are inside of us as much as outside.

David Abram in a further challenge to our sense of being special, different from the rest of the planet suggests:

> It is even possible that this language we speak is the voice of the living earth itself, singing through the human form. For the vitality, the coherence, and the diversity of the various languages we speak may well correspond to the vitality, coherence, and diversity of earth's biosphere—not to any complexity of our species considered apart from that matrix.
>
> (Abram, 2010b, p. 102)

Working with a training group, I notice a feeling of something missing from the field between us. My loose intention was to move into some practical work but this feeling draws my attention. It is always difficult to attend to what is missing; it is a resonance with something unspoken or not attended to. I name this and one member who has not previously contributed begins to speak. She feels rather out of the group, on the margins. Other participants encourage her to join in and fail to grasp that their well-meaning invitation is part of the problem as it feels like an implicit rule that says people need to be clear about their participation. As we stay with the difficulties, moving from thoughts to a sensing of what is present, other members begin to own their discomfort with her ambivalence and this creates the space to recognize how she carries shadow ambivalences for this "open, accepting group". Perhaps the group was in the grip of the psychological construct of needing a sealed vessel to enable transformation—those not truly in the flask are marginalized.

Some persons seem prone to be shadow carriers or have a habit of occupying margins but if they are not to be scapegoats, the members of a system need to be permeable to what is expressing itself through them rather than what they think they are expressing. The tension between the marginal participant and the one wanting to be inclusive can be seen as tension between different aspects of the one group—expressing itself through its members.

This shift of perspective may be critical for psychotherapy. Instead of reading the field as one that comes from the individuals, an *interactive field*, we could see it as emerging through the individuals, a *synergetic field*. The synergy comes because the relationship between members seems pre-attuned. It emerges through them but is not created by them. The individual is not at the centre but is embedded in a reciprocal relationship with other members.

The shift in how we see the nature of transformation puts inner fulfilment into a secondary relationship. It is an affect of a wider transformation, not a cause. Jung said that we are in the psyche; the psyche is not in us. This reminds me of Jung's dream in which he sees a yogi who, much to Jung's surprise, had his face. Jung awoke thinking, "Aha, so he is the one who is meditating me. He has a dream, and I am it" (Jung, 1989, p. 323). And remarkably similarly, Tweedledee asks Alice where she would be if the Red King left off dreaming about her. She was, after all, "only a sort of thing in his dream!" (Carroll, 2007, p. 375).

A friend brings a dream that connects with the chapter even as I write.

> She is in the kitchen looking out into the garden and notices with surprise what looks like a baby orang-utan. Puzzled but charmed she goes out to investigate and is disconcerted to see that this is a human baby but one covered with an unusual amount of hair. Her whole attitude shifts from warm curiosity to anxious concern. How did this strange baby get into her garden? What should she do about it?
>
> Just then she notices a group at the back of the garden—adults and children who are also hairy and wild looking. Her husband arrives at this point and asks, "What's going on here?" Then on seeing a large amount of excrement on the side of the garden, he asks an adult, "Is this your children's?" The man rolls across the garden into the excrement and proceeds to smell and taste it. "Yes, definitely ours," he says.

On hearing this dream, I remembered a comment about the poverty of political discourse since the invention of the flush toilet. The shit was no longer faced: it all got flushed away. In contrast, part of the dreamer takes ownership … and more! The dream offers a possible hint to our sanitised culture in which our immune system is increasingly mistrusted to build its own defences.

There are many ways to engage this dream. We could do more about the nature of what we each have in our "garden". We could explore what we have lost in our sweet smelling culture of the ability to recognise kinship through smell. What stands out to me is the paradox of the baby—an image of potential combined with animal hair: a future primitive.

One thread of evolutionary theory suggests that evolution proceeds through the young of the species not specializing in the manner of the mature adult but staying flexibly adaptable to new evolutionary niches. This *neoteny* is very apparent in dogs that retain many infant characteristics, which give them the evolutionary advantage to read humans accurately.

Yet this baby human is covered in hair. Again the humour of the dream comes through. Are we being teased for being the only primate that is not born hairy? Or might the fine foetal hair, called "lanugo", which covers the six-month-old foetus in the womb and is usually shed before birth, be something that stays in the neoteny of the future … as if we might be reclaiming some of our primate nature in this evolutionary adventure?

Coming back from this speculation to my fictional client, Jason, I am thinking how his feeling of being at the effect of others (victim like) may have served him. In many ways it keeps him young. He feels like he is in a world of adults who have greater powers than he feels himself to have. I could suggest that he grows up and claims his adult status—a bit like exhorting western society to stop being so immature. Instead we start to explore his experience of "unfairness". This leads to a sense of his not feeling at home in his family and a wider sense of estrangement in life. He does however have a powerful connection with horses.

This feeling of estrangement from human culture but affinity with animals is not uncommon. Jerome Bernstein explores this pattern in *Living in the Borderland* (Bernstein, 2005). He describes the emergence of the "Borderland" as an experience of reality beyond the rational—a psychic space where the overly rational Western ego is in the process of reconnecting with its split-off roots in nature. His clients reported particular sensitivities to the sufferings of animals that he learnt to take at face value rather than as images of their internal world. He began to recognize this sensitivity as coming from a deep connection to the earth and possible evolutionary transformation. He thinks that new psychic forms are attempting to emerge and, while being resisted by the western ego in general, have impacted on this group of sensitized individuals.

And after all, *we may be at a juncture in evolutionary history for which there is no precedent.*

We have moved out of Nature's capacity to regulate us. Unlike other species, we have the powers to overcome environmental constraints, such as the limits of available food. The dangers are that this could lead us to extinction—but the corollary is that we may learn the lessons of self-regulation, rather than having nature correct our behaviour through environmental constraints.

Self-regulation is not that easy for us as individuals: it is far from a given for our species. From the epidemic of obesity in the west, to the 20 million tonnes of food thrown away in the UK alone, our lack of self-regulation is clear. A quick look at the recent banking crises, driven by short-term profit and precipitated by greed, shows the failures of banks' ability to self-regulate. And the horror of these events may be part of the painful process of facing into our collective denial.

Starting to self-regulate is a functional mutation that could take place at our present evolutionary threshold. While the evidence for it is small at present, this is not a basis for prediction. At junction points and thresholds, normal laws fail to operate. We enter a liminal space where the old means of regulation do not work but we have not yet developed new ones. These "borderlands" lie, like their territorial counterparts, at an in-between reality that is not governed either by what has come before or by what is attempting to manifest. They are intrinsically uncertain places to be in which small changes can be amplified.

They are described by the anthropologist Turner (1987) as *liminality,* and by Winnicott (1953) as *transitional space.* While being chaotic in nature, they are a source of creative potency. Winnicott considered such transitional spaces to be the location of cultural transformation. Psychotherapy has long explored events that constellate at boundaries or transitional spaces, starting with sacred dreams that took place in

Greek temples. The mysterious, chaotic nature of these thresholds has a dream quality and requires us to move into an imaginative mode, attending as if from peripheral vision or unexpected whispers from another reality.

Jason may be one of these disaffected but attuned individuals who suffer not so much from a personal trauma but a collective one. Attempting to understand his troubles solely from the viewpoint of his personal history is another form of reductionism. Although he had troubles in his childhood that may have sensitized him, his primary anxiety is not personal but rather that of our human collective attempting a radical evolutionary jump—one that seems to threaten our precious, if not precarious, sense of self. His staying young in his felt sense can be read as an adaptive psychological mutation. He needed to divorce himself from the matrix of adult human culture sufficiently not to specialize in the same way: not to fall into the destructive paradigm that controls our culture; ironically, to differentiate sufficiently not be party to the separation of the ego. And like many shamanic practitioners, he needs allies in this challenge: animals that are catalysts to recover his instincts and to reclaim a reciprocal affinity with the world; animals that mirror his own wounded animal and as kindred spirits offer healing and the development of compassionate concern.

As a relational psychotherapist, I am becoming increasing mindful of our companions on earth. I feel their attention on me as I practice. When I explore the client's relational background I include inquiry about his/her relationship with other species. Jason's deep resonance with the magic of the horse was what kept his soul alive in what seemed like a desecrated world to the sensitive child he was. Telling me stories about his relation to horses brought their magic into the room. These wondrous beings became our companions through his work. They seemed to hold a combination of grounded instinct and magical fantasy, of wild strength and feminine intuition that he sought to find in himself. They offered an alternative to the domestication to which he felt he had to submit.

In this deeper sense he had felt himself a victim to collective forces—powers over which he had no apparent say—and without the "horse-power", he might have succumbed to despair. Through participating in telling stories he began to retell his own story. We moved from stories about his past to imaginative stories co-created between us that reflected his present dilemma. In one such story, he removes the saddle of his favourite horse and attempts to ride bareback. The excitement of direct contact with the horse overcomes his fear of loss of control and he proceeds to gallop crazily away. Just when he is feeling intoxicated by this new power, the horse suddenly halts and he is thrown to the ground.

This story did not need much unpacking for him. It also offers us an interesting parallel to the potency and dangers of working in this borderland territory. They do offer powerful imaginal means of re-telling our story so that we are future-orientated rather than caught in past agendas. The dangers come when our egos become inflated from the transpersonal energies available at thresholds. To handle the power of wildness, we need not only practice with riding the waves of chaos but also humility. We need the holding of a relational field in which we recognize our inter-dependency whether this is a therapeutic rela-tionship, a working group, a community, or our resonance with the more-than-human world.

Part of our present difficulty comes because our dissociated ego feels our survival threatened at just these junctions where transfor-mation could occur. During a workshop, a participant reported the following:

> During an exercise on the course I had a scary, yet profound, expe-rience in which I found myself staring into a mirror, watching how my face rapidly rotted away until there was nothing left over my collar. I remember noticing that even if there was nothing there I still could see my shirt and the colour of my tie. This comforted me in a strange way, as it made me realise that there was still some life left in me.
>
> When we discussed my experience afterwards I realised that I had witnessed a spectacular shift within me. What was rotting away was my professional façade, or my professional face.
>
> (Wolde, 2008, n.p.)

Such experiences of ego loss within a holding environment are neces-sary precursors to coming through a collective transition. The present earthquake and tsunami in Japan show us the challenge for survivors to orientate themselves in a world that their minds cannot recognize. Given the anxiety generated by the uncertainty of transitional spaces, how can we hold and feel held enough to use the elemental energy creatively?

While I am focusing here on a collective crisis, psychoanalysis has explored how infants faced with severe separation anxiety may develop a *Second Skin* (Bick, 1968) to defend against the catastrophic experience of *unintegration*. It seems to me that we have collectively developed a second skin through our manic, driven culture in which there is no space to slow down and experience the anxiety that is kept at bay by constant activity and mental stimulation. This second skin is kept activated by a mixture of stress, information overload, and demanding workloads. Dreams are one of the few ways the angst can make itself known and we blot these out by waking suddenly and rushing to work. Yet the second skin is not seamless; there is a terrifying rupture opening in our collective skin through which both fears and longing can be sensed. Our world may fall apart or we may fall through into something strangely different.

Chaos Theory offers us the intriguing notion of *strange attractors* that operate within a chaotic system to constrain possible fluctuations. This metaphor shows how an apparently unordered (chaotic) system has recourse to patterns that are not readily recognisable but have a hidden order. This is helpful in understanding phase transitions, which are inherently unpredictable such as when water boils or freezes.

Transferring, with caution, this metaphor of attractors to ecosystems, it allows for the possibility of deep connections within the collective unconscious. The difficulties or dysfunction of a system are not just something that is wrong and need correcting. They are strong indicators of split off and unresolved issues within the system's wider culture that form constituent parts of its unique history. This unique history has its own evolving trajectory or entelechy which seldom reveals itself in linear or predictable fashions but creates an attractor field that influences the emerging direction. Thinking in terms of the rupture of our egosyntonic cultural skin as equivalent to the tear a snake initiates in shedding its skin, this renewal is to allow just those split off margins to emerge.

It is *as if* the ecological unconscious is dreaming us into a collective rite of passage. We are at this threshold needing to not only let go *of* our present anthropomorphic assumptions about our place on earth but also let go *to* a sensed but unknown transformation. This transformation is not something we can understand consciously or be in control of. It is an emergent probability that is attempting to evolve through us. While predicting what will come is not possible, we can be sure enough it will come from the margins.

Recent events in the Middle East, and in Egypt in particular, show how there can be profound transformations that are completely unexpected: unexpected because they come from the margins—in this case from the marginalized youth, who both shaped and were shaped by this collective ferment. The power of this ferment does not come from rational choice but from emotions. The other side of our fear of wild other-than-human is our passion and longing for them.

The dangerous potency which we banish to the margins of our tame, safe society and project onto the wild other-than-human, is the same energy that that we unconsciously act out in the destruction of our environment. This is the potency from which we dissociate in order to be "civilized" and which we will need to salvage if we are to negotiate our rite of passage—a passage through shadow lands that harbour the potential held in the penumbra of our consciousness. This potential in the shadow is like the *stem cells of the psyche* that could catalyse the regeneration of our collective story.

End reflections

Like all stories, this one has focused on some aspects of a bigger story and excluded others. While talking about shadow lands, I have created a few. These potent absences include our *collective narcissism*, our *need for reparation for our destructive behaviour*; for *physical embodiment*; for the *vitality of play* and *social justice*. While not denying responsibility for these exclusions, this particular story wanted to have the shape that it has drawing on the emergent coincidences, such as the friend's dream, that drew my attention. It seemed to particularly emphasize the elemental power that modern civilization has disowned, concreted over and now desperately need to recover before it draws us into an ecocidal catastrophe.

I hope to have shown that a story emphasizing conscious choice, whether therapeutic or ecological, is very limited in its ability to transform an unconscious complex. Using various therapeutic approaches as examples of working with unconscious processes, I have explored how we can shift the story by listening through to the rejected margins of the collective; to the whispered not-yet-felt/thought emerging.

This listening through can bring us to a different appreciation of what seems wrong and dangerous; to the regenerative potential of the wild psyche which is the synonymous with the earth's generative power.

While *stems cells of the psyche* is clearly a metaphor, I believe it is more than a metaphor of what simply gives future generations hope. Just as stems cells orchestrate regeneration in the physical organs, generative relationships transform how others perceive the world and act in it. It is suggested that our current crisis could also be an evolutionary threshold, a time when the earth is renewing itself—catalyzing self-regulation and reciprocal relationship with the other-than-human.

The Jason in you, or me, may still feel himself a marginal character but he has become engaged with his own story rather than being only an actor in it. The very nature of his complaints, his failings have become the ingredients of his sense of connection with the more-than human and a consequent sense of being held. This re-visioning of personal story to give a place to the "inferior" margins of the psyche parallels the collective challenge "to learn a new story".

In his powerful poem, *Last Night* Antonio Machado (1983) dreams of a beehive inside his heart where golden bees were making sweet honey from his old failures. It is indeed a sweet thought that it will not be my/your heroic achievements but our acknowledged failures through which the compassionate honey of the other-than-human will come.

REFERENCES

Aasen, A. (2007, August 15). Et sted blir til: Naturen som læringsmiljø. Project report for further education course in pedagogical development in kindergarten, Telemark University College.

Abram, D. (1996). *The Spell of the Sensuous: Perception and Language in a More-Than-Human World*. New York: Vintage Books.

Abram, D. (2010a). *Becoming Animal*. New York: Pantheon.

Abram, D. (2010b). Merleau-Ponty and the voice of the earth. *Environmental Ethics, 10*: 101–120.

Albrecht, G. (2005). Solastalgia, a new concept in human health and identity. *Philosophy Activism Nature, 3*: 41–44.

Albrecht, G., Sartore, G.-M., Connor, L., Higginbotham, N., Freeman, S., Kelly, B., Stain, H., Tonna, A. & Pollard, G. (2007). Solastalgia: The distress caused by environmental change. *Australasian Psychiatry, 15*(1): S95–S98.

Alcott, B. (2005). Jevons' paradox. *Ecological Economics, 54*: 9–21.

Alexander, C. (2005). *John Crow Speaks*. New York: Monkfish Book Publishing Company.

Althusser, L. (1971). Ideology and ideological state apparatuses. In: *Lenin and Philosophy and Other Essays*. London: New Left Books.

Anderson, J. (2009). Transient convergence and relational sensibility: Beyond the modern constitution of nature. *Emotion, Space and Society, 2*: 120–127.

Anisimov, O. (2007). Potential feedback of thawing permafrost to the global climate system through methane emission. *Environmental Research Letters, 2*. Retrieved October 1, 2011, stacks.iop.org/ERL/2/045016

Ansell, N. (2010, March 27). My life as a hermit. *Guardian Magazine*, pp. 26–30.

Attenborough, D. (1979). Gorilla encounters: *Life on earth* Episode 12. London: BBC. Retrieved October 1, 2011, from http://www.bbc.co.uk/programmes/p004j5sw

Avens, R. (1976). C.G. Jung's analysis of religious experience. *Journal of Dharma, 76*(1): 227–245.

Bache, C. (1981). On the emergence of perinatal symptoms in meditation. *Journal for the Scientific Study of Religion, 20*(4): 339–350.

Bache, C. (2000). *Dark Night, Early Dawn*. Albany, NY: SUNY Press.

Baiocchi, G., Minx, J. & Hubacek, K. (2010). The Impact of social factors and consumer behavior on carbon dioxide emissions in the United Kingdom. *Journal of Industrial Ecology, 14*(1): 50–72.

Barbalet, J. (2005). Weeping and transformations of self. *Journal for the Theory of Social Behaviour, 35*(2): 125–141.

Barlow, C. (1994). *Evolution Extended: Biological Debates on the Meaning of Life*. Cambridge, MA: MIT Press.

Batchelor, M. (1996). *Walking on Lotus Flowers; Buddhist Women Living, Loving and Meditating*. London: Thorsons.

Bateson, G. (1980). *Mind and Nature: A Necessary Unity*. London: Fontana.

Bateson, G. (2000). *Steps Towards an Ecology of Mind*. Chicago, IL: University of Chicago.

Bauman, Z. (2000). *Liquid Modernity*. Cambridge: Polity.

Becker, E. (1997). *The Denial of Death*. Berkeley, CA: Free Press.

Beisser, A. (1970). The paradoxical theory of change. In: J. Fagan & I. Shepherd (Eds.), *Gestalt Therapy Now: Theory, Techniques, and Applications* (pp. 77–80). Palo Alto, CA: Science and Behavior Books.

Bell-Scott, P. (1991). *Double Stitch: Black Women Write about Mothers and Daughters*. Boston, MA: Beacon Press.

Berger, L. (2009). *Averting Global Extinction: Our Irrational Society as Therapy Patient*. New York: Jason Aronson.

Berners-Lee, M. (2010). *How Bad are Bananas*. London: Profile.

Bernstein, J. (2005). *Living in the Borderland: The Evolution of Consciousness and the Challenge of Healing Trauma*. London: Routledge.

Berry, T. (1990). *The Dream of the earth*. San Francisco, CA: Sierra Club Books.

Berry, W. (1998/1973). The wild geese. In: *The Selected Poems of Wendell Berry*. Berkeley, CA: Counterpoint.

Bick, E. (1968). The experience of skin in early object relations. *International Journal of Psychoanalysis, 49*: 484–486.

Bigda-Peyton, F. (2004). When drives are dangerous: Drive theory and resource over-consumption. *Modern Psychoanalysis, 29*: 251–270.

Bion, W. R. (1961). *Experiences in Groups and Other Papers*. London: Tavistock.

Bion, W. R. (1984). *Second Thoughts: Selected Papers on Psychoanalysis*. London: Karnac.

Birkeland, I. (2005). *Making Self, Making Place*. Aldershot: Ashgate.

Birkeland, I. (2008). Cultural sustainability: Industrialism, placeless-ness and the reanimation of place. *Ethics, Place & Environment, 11*(3): 283–297.

Bixler, R. D., Floyd, M. F. & Hammitt, W. E. (2002). Environmental socialization: Quantitative tests of the childhood play hypothesis. *Environment and Behavior, 34*(6): 795–818.

Blatner, A. (2004). The developmental nature of consciousness transformation. *Revision, 26*(4): 2–8.

Blundhorn, I. (2001). Reflexivity and self-referentiality: On the normative foundations of ecological communication. In: C. Grant & D. McLaughlin (Eds.), *Language—Meaning—Social Construction: Interdisciplinary Studies* (pp. 181–201). Amsterdam: Rodopi.

Bodnar, S. (2008). Wasted and bombed: Clinical enactments of a changing relationship to the earth. *Psychoanalytic Dialogues, 18*: 484–512.

Bondi, L., Davidson, J. & Smith, M. (2005). Introduction: Geography's "emotional turn". In: J. Davidson, L. Bondi & M. Smith (Eds.), *Emotional Geographies* (pp. 1–16). Aldershot: Ashgate.

Bondi, L. & Fewell, J. (2003). "Unlocking the cage door": The spatiality of counselling. *Social and Cultural Geography, 4*(4): 527–547.

Bonta, M. (2005). Becoming-forest, becoming local: Transformations of a protected area in Honduras. *Geoforum, 36*: 95–112.

Bonta, M. & Protevi, J. (2004). *Deleuze and Geophilosophy: A Guide and Glossary*. Edinburgh: Edinburgh University Press.

Boston, T. (1996). Ecopsychology: An earth-psyche bond. *Trumpeter, 13*(2). Retrieved July 10, 2007, from http://trumpeter.athabascau.ca/index. php/trumpet/article/view/269/403

Bradshaw, G. A. (2009). *Elephants on the Edge: What Animals Teach us About Humanity*. New Haven, CT: Yale University Press.

Bradshaw, G. A. (2010). We, Matata: Bicultural living amongst apes. *Spring, 83*: 161–183.

Bradshaw, G. A. (2011). Can science progress to a revitalized past? In: D. Narvaez, J. Panksepp, A. Schore & T. Gleason (Eds.), *Human Nature, Early Experience and the Environment of Evolutionary Adaptedness*. New York: Oxford University Press.

Bradshaw, G. A., Capaldo, T., Lindner, L. & Grow, G. (2009). Developmental context effects on bicultural post-trauma self repair in chimpanzees. *Developmental Psychology, 45*: 1376–1388.

Bradshaw, G. A. & Sapolsky, R. M. (2006). Mirror, mirror. *American Scientist*, 94(6): 487–489.

Bragg, E. A. (1996). Towards ecological self: Deep ecology meets constructionist self-theory. *Journal of Environmental Psychology*, 16: 93–108.

Bragg, E. (1997). Ecopsychology and academia: Bridging the paradigms. *Ecopsychology Online*. Retrieved May 12, 2005, from http://ecopsychology.athabascau.ca/0197/

Brody, H. (2002a). *Maps and Dreams*. London: Faber & Faber.

Brody, H. (2002b). *The Other Side of Eden: Hunter-Gatherers, Farmers and the Shaping of the World*. London: Faber & Faber.

Bronfenbrenner, U. (1979). *The Ecology of Human Development*. Cambridge, MA: Harvard University Press.

Brown, N. W. (2011). *Psychoeducational Groups: Process and Practice*. London: Routledge.

Bruner, J. S. (1985). *Actual Minds, Possible Worlds*. Cambridge, MA: Harvard University Press.

Buber, M. (1952). *Good and Evil: Two Interpretations*. New York: Scribners.

Buechner, F. (1993). *Wishful Thinking: A Seeker's ABC*. San Francisco, CA: Harper.

Busch, F. (2007). "I noticed": The emergence of self-observation in relationship to pathological attractor sites. *International Journal of Psycho-Analysis*, 88: 423–441.

Bussey, M. (2006). Critical spirituality: Towards a revitalised humanity. *Journal of Future Studies*, 10(4): 39–44.

Butler, J. (1993). *Bodies that Matter: On the Discursive Limits of "Sex"*. London: Routledge.

Campbell, J. (2008/1949). *The Hero with a Thousand Faces* (3rd ed.). Novato, CA: New World Library.

Canda, E. R. (1988). Therapeutic transformation in ritual, therapy, and human development. *Journal of Religion and Health*, 27(3): 205–220.

Capra, F. (1989). *Uncommon Wisdom: Conversations with Remarkable People*. London: Fontana.

Carroll, L. (2007). *Through the Looking Glass*. London: Penguin.

Casey, E. (1993). *Getting Back into Place: Toward a Renewed Understanding of the Place-world*. Bloomington, IN: Indiana University Press.

Casey, E. (1996). *The Fate of Place: A Philosophical History*. Berkeley, CA: University of California Press.

Castree, N. (2005). *Nature*. London: Routledge.

Catling, S. (2005). Children's personal geographies and the English primary school Geography curriculum. *Children's Geographies*, 3(3): 325–344.

Celi, A. & Boiero, M. C. (2002). The heritage of stories: A tradition of wisdom. *American Studies International*, 40(2): 57–73.

Chartres, R. (2011). Royal Wedding Address. Retrieved April 29, 2011, from http://www.london.anglican.org/SermonShow_14544

Chawla, L. (1992). Childhood place attachments. In: I. Altman & S. M. Low (Eds.), *Human Behavior and the Environment: Advances in Theory and Research, Vol. 12: Place Attachment* (pp. 63–86). New York: Plenum.

Chawla, L. (1999). Life paths into effective environmental action. *Journal of Environmental Education, 31*(1): 15–27.

Clayton, S. (2003). Environmental identity: A conceptual and an operational definition. In: S. Clayton & S. Opotow (Eds.), *Identity and the Natural Environment* (pp. 45–65). Cambridge, MA: MIT Press.

Cobb, E. (1959). The ecology of childhood. *Daedalus, 88*(3): 537–548.

Cobb, E. (1977). *The Ecology of Imagination in Childhood.* New York: Columbia University Press.

Cohen, L. (2001). *God is Alive: Magic is Afoot.* Toronto: Stoddart.

Colebrook, C. (2005). The space of man: On the specificity of affect in Deleuze and Guattari. In: I. Buchanan & G. Lambert (Eds.), *Deleuze and Space* (pp. 189–206). Edinburgh: University Press.

Collins, M. (1998). Occupational therapy and spirituality: Reflecting on quality of experience in therapeutic interventions. *British Journal of Occupational Therapy, 61*(6): 280–284.

Collins, M. (2001). Who is occupied? Consciousness, self-awareness and the process of human adaptation. *Journal of Occupational Science, 8*(1): 25–32.

Collins, M. (2004). Dreaming and occupation. *British Journal of Occupational Therapy, 67*(2): 96–98.

Collins, M. (2006). Unfolding spirituality: Working with and beyond definitions. *International Journal of Therapy and Rehabilitation, 13*(6): 254–258.

Collins, M. (2007a). Spiritual emergency and occupational identity: A transpersonal perspective. *British Journal of Occupational Therapy, 70*(12): 504–512.

Collins, M. (2007b). Spirituality and the shadow: Reflection and the therapeutic use of self. *British Journal of Occupational Therapy, 70*(2): 88–90.

Collins, M. (2007c). Engaging self-actualisation through occupational intelligence. *Journal of Occupational Science, 14*(2): 92–99.

Collins, M. (2007d). Healing and the soul: Finding the future in the past. *Spirituality and Health International, 8*(1): 31–38.

Collins, M. (2008a). Spiritual emergency: Transpersonal, personal, and political dimensions. *Psychotherapy and Politics International, 6*(1): 3–16.

Collins, M. (2008b). Politics and the numinous: Evolution, spiritual emergency, and the re-emergence of transpersonal consciousness. *Psychotherapy and Politics International, 6*(3): 198–211.

Collins, M. (2008c). Transpersonal identity and human occupation. *British Journal of Occupational Therapy, 71*(12): 549–552.

Collins, M. (2010a). Engaging transcendent actualisation through occupational intelligence. *Journal of Occupational Science, 17*(3): 177–186.

Collins, M. (2010b). Spiritual intelligence: Evolving transpersonal potential towards ecological actualization for a sustainable future. *World Futures, 66*: 320–334.

Collins, M. (2010c). Global crisis and transformation: From spiritual emergency to spiritual intelligence. *Network Review, 103*: 17–20.

Collins, M., Hughes, W. & Samuels, A. (2010). The politics of transformation in the global crisis: Are spiritual emergencies reflecting an enantiodromia in modern consciousness? *Psychotherapy and Politics International, 8*(2): 162–176.

Collins, M. & Wells, H. (2006). The politics of consciousness: Illness or individuation? *Psychotherapy and Politics International, 4*(2): 131–141.

Costanza, R., Norton, B. G. & Haskell, B. D. (Eds.). (1992). *Ecosystem Health: New Goals for Environmental Management.* Washington, DC: Island Press.

Cresswell, T. (2004). *Place: A Short Introduction.* Oxford: Blackwell.

Crompton, T. (2008). *Weathercocks and Signposts: The Environment Movement at a Crossroads.* Godalming, UK: WWF-UK. Retrieved October 1, 2011, from www.wwf.org.uk/change

Crompton, T. (2010). *Common Cause: The Case for Working with our Cultural Values.* Godalming, UK: WWF-UK. Retrieved October 1, 2011, from www.wwf.org.uk/change

Crompton, T. & Kasser, T. (2009). *Meeting Environmental Challenges: The Role of Human Identity.* Godalming: WWF-UK. Retrieved October 1, 2011, from http://assets.wwf.org.uk/downloads/

Csikszentmihalyi, M. (1993). *The Evolving Self: A Psychology for the Third Millennium.* New York: Harper Collins.

Cushman, P. (1990). Why the Self is empty: Toward a historically situated psychology. *American Psychologist, 45*(5): 599–611.

Daly, H. E. (1977). *Steady-State Economics.* Washington, DC: Island Press.

Daniels, M. (2005). *Shadow, Self and Spirit.* Exeter: Imprint Academic.

Darwin, C. (2009/1916). *The Expression of the Emotions in Man and Animals.* London: Penguin.

Davies, J. (1998). The transpersonal dimensions of ecopsychology: Nature, non duality and spirit. *The Humanistic Psychologist, 26*(1–3): 60–100.

Davies, J. (2003). An overview of transpersonal psychology. *The Humanistic Psychologist, 31*(2–3): 6–21.

Davis-Berman, J. & Berman, D. S. (1994). *Wilderness Therapy: Foundations, Theory and Research.* Dubuque, IA: Kendall/Hunt.

De Rougemont, D. (1944). *La Part du Diable*. New York: Brentano.

Degenhardt, L. (2002). Why do people act in sustainable ways? Results of an empirical survey of lifestyle pioneers. In: P. Schmuck & P. W. Schultz (Eds.), *Psychology of Sustainable Development* (pp. 123–147). Dordrecht, Netherlands: Kluwer Academic.

DeLanda, M. (2005). *A Thousand Years of Nonlinear History*. New York: Swerve Editions.

DeLanda, M. (2006). *A New Philosophy of Society: Assemblage Theory and Social Complexity*. New York: Continuum.

Deleuze, G. & Guattari, F. (2003a/1980). *A Thousand Plateaus: Capitalism and Schizophrenia*. London: Continuum.

Deleuze, G. & Guattari, F. (2003b). *What is Philosophy?* New York: Verso.

Dennett, D. C. (1991). *Consciousness Explained*. London: Allen Lane The Penguin Press.

Derbyshire, D. (2009). Ten days left to buy traditional lightbulbs. *Daily Mail*. Retrieved March 31, 2011, from http://www.dailymail.co.uk/sciencetech/article-1208228/Ten-days-left-buy-frosted-lightbulbs-EU-ban-means-low-energy-ones-sale.html

Diamond, J. (2006). *Collapse: How Societies Choose to Fail or Survive*. London: Penguin.

do Rozario, L. (1997). Shifting paradigms: The transpersonal dimensions of ecology and occupation *Journal of Occupational Science*, 4(3): 112–118.

Dodds, J. (2011). *Psychoanalysis and Ecology at the Edge of Chaos: Complexity Theory, Deleuze | Guattari and Psychoanalysis for a Climate in Crisis*. London: Routledge.

Dopetype (2008). *Golden Compass* "Meet your own daemon" test. Retrieved June 1, 2011, from http://dopetype.wordpress.com/2008/11/22/the-golden-compass-deamon-test/

Du Nann Winter, D. & Koger, S. M. (2004). *The Psychology of Environmental Problems* (2nd ed.). Mahwah, NJ: Lawrence Erlbaum.

Dunne, B. J. & Jahn, R. G. (2003). Information and uncertainty in remote perception research. *Journal of Scientific Exploration, 17*(2): 207–241.

Durkheim, E. (1925/1961). *Moral Education: A Study in the Theory and Application of the Sociology of Education*. New York: The Free Press.

Eidelson, R. (1997). Complex adaptive systems in the behavioral and social sciences. *Journal Review of General Psychology, 1*(1): 42–71.

Elam, J. (2005). Mystical experience as a way of knowing. In: C. Clarke (Ed.), *Ways of Knowing: Science and Mysticism Today* (pp. 51–66). Exeter: Imprint Academic.

Eliade, M. (1961). *Images and Symbols*. New York: Sheed and Ward.

Ellis, S. (2010). *Wolf Within*. London: Harper.

Encarta World English Dictionary (1999). New York: St. Martin's Press.

Ewert, A., Place, G. & Sibthorp, J. A. (2005). Early-life outdoor experiences and an individuals' environmental attitudes. *Leisure Sciences, 27*(3): 225–239.

Exley, H. (Ed.). (1997). *In Beauty May I Walk ...: Words of Wisdom by Native Americans.* Watford: Exley Publications.

Fairbairn, W. R. D. (1992). *Psychoanalytic Studies of the Personality.* London: Routledge.

Fennell, M. (2009). *Overcoming Low Self-Esteem.* London: Robinson.

Feral, C. (1998). The connectedness model and optimal development: Is ecopsychology the answer to emotional well-being? *Humanistic Psychologist, 26*(1–3): 243–274.

Fink, B. (1995). *The Lacanian Subject: Between Language and Jouissance.* Princeton, NJ: Princeton University Press.

Fisher, A. (2002). *Radical Ecopsychology: Psychology in the Service of Life.* Albany, NY: SUNY Press.

Fjørtoft, I. (2001). The natural environment as a playground for children: The impact of outdoor play activities in pre-primary school children. *Early Childhood Education Journal, 29*(2): 111–117.

Fjørtoft, I. (2004). Landscape as playscape: The effect of natural environments on children's play and motor development. *Children, Youth and Environments, 14*(2): 21–44.

Fox, W. (1990). *Toward a Transpersonal Ecology: Developing New Foundations for Environmentalism.* Boston, MA: Shambhala.

Fox, W. (1990a). *Toward a Transpersonal Ecology: Developing New Foundations for Environmentalism.* Boston: Shambhala.

Fox, W. (1990b). Transpersonal ecology: "Psychologising" ecophilosophy. *Journal of Transpersonal Psychology, 22*(1): 59–96.

Frantz, C. M., Mayer, F. S., Norton, C. & Rock, M. (2005). There is no "I" in nature: The influence of self awareness on connectedness to nature. *Journal of Environmental Psychology, 25*(4): 427–436.

Freilander, A. & Landau, J. (1999). *Out of the Whirlwind: A Reader of Holocaust.* New York: Urj Press.

Freud, S. (1915). Thoughts for the times on war and death. *SE, XIV*, 273–300. London: Hogarth Press.

Freud, S. (1916). On transference. *SE, XIV*, 303–307. London: Hogarth Press.

Freud, S. (1927). The future of an illusion. *SE, XXI*, 1–56. London: Hogarth Press.

Freud, S. (1930). Civilization and its discontents. *SE, XXI*, 57–146. London: Hogarth Press.

Freud, S. (1936). *The Ego and the Mechanisms of Defense.* New York: Hogarth Press.

Freud, S. (1961). *The Future of an Illusion.* New York: W.W. Norton.

Geertz, C. (1973). *The Interpretation of Cultures*. New York: Basic Books.

Geertz, C. (1983). *Local Knowledge: Further Essay in Interpretative Anthropology*. New York: Basic Books.

Geller, L. (1982). The failure of self-actualization theory: A critique of Carl Rogers and Abraham Maslow. *Journal of Humanistic Psychology, 22*: 56–73.

Gendlin, E. (1978). *Focusing*. New York: Everest House.

Giddens, A. (1991). *Modernity and Self-Identity: Self and Society in the Late Modern Age*. Cambridge: Polity.

Glendenning, C. (1995). Technology, trauma and the wild. In: T. Roszak, M. E. Gomes & A. D. Kanner (Eds.), *Ecopsychology: Restoring the earth, Healing the Mind* (pp. 41–54). San Francisco: Sierra Club Books.

Glenn, J. C., Gordon, T. J. & Florescu, E. (2008). *State of the Future: Executive Summary*. World Federation of United Nations Associations. Retrieved August 1, 2008, from www.millennium-project.org/millennium/issues.html

Good, J. (2007). Shop 'til we drop? Television, materialism and attitudes about the natural environment. *Mass Communication and Society, 10*: 365–383.

Gore, A. (1992). *earth in the Balance: Ecology and the Human Spirit*. New York: Houghton Mifflin.

Grandin, T. & Johnson, C. (2005). *Animals in Translation*. London: Bloomsbury.

Green, V. (2004). *Emotional Development in Psychoanalysis, Attachment Theory and Neuroscience*. London: Brunner-Routledge.

Greenway, R. (2009). Teaching notes. Quoted in Ecotherapy News, Spring. Retrieved June 24, 2011, from http://thoughtoffering.blogs.com/ecotherapy/2009/06/the-ecotherapy-newsletter-spring-2009healing-our-relationship-with-nature-ecopsychology-in-action-psychotherapy-as.html

Greenway, R. (2010, March 27). Defining ecopsychology? *Gatherings: A Journal of Ecopsychology*. Retrieved October 1, 2011, from http://www.ecopsychology.org/gatherings/2009/03/defining-ecopsychology

Grieve, G. (2006). *Call of the Wild*. London: Hodder & Stoughton.

Grof, S. & Grof, C. M. (Eds.). (1989). *Spiritual Emergency: When Personal Transformation Becomes a Crisis*. Los Angeles, CA: Jeremy P. Tarcher.

Grof, S. & Grof, C. (1991). *The Stormy Search for the Self: Understanding and Living With Spiritual Emergency*. London: Mandala.

Grof, S. & Grof, C. (1993). Spiritual emergency: The understanding and treatment of transpersonal crises. In: R. Walsh & F. Vaughan (Eds.), *Paths beyond Ego: The Transpersonal Vision* (pp. 43–64). New York: Jeremy P. Tarcher/Putnam.

Grouzet, F. M. E., Kasser, T., Ahuvia, A., Fernandez-Dols, J. M., Kim, Y., Lau, S., Ryan, R. M., Saunders, S., Schmuck, P. & Sheldon, K. M. (2005). The structure of goal contents across fifteen cultures. *Journal of Personality and Social Psychology*, 89: 800–816.

Gruenewald, D. (2003a). The best of both worlds: A critical pedagogy of place. *Educational Researcher*, 32(4): 3–12.

Gruenewald, D. (2003b). Foundations of place: A multidisciplinary framework for place-conscious education. *American Educational Research Journal*, 40(3), 619–654.

Gruenewald, D. (2005). Accountability and collaboration: Institutional barriers and strategic pathways for place-based education. *Ethics, Place and Environment*, 8(3): 261–283.

Gruenewald, D. A. & Smith, G. (2007). *Place-Based Education in the Global Age: Local Diversity*. Philadelphia: Lawrence Erlbaum.

Guastello, S. (2004). Progress in applied nonlinear dynamics. *Nonlinear Dynamics, Psychology and Life Sciences*, 8(1): 1–15.

Guattari, F. (1995). *Chaosmosis: An Ethico-Aesthetic Paradigm*. Bloomington, IN: Indiana University Press.

Guattari, F. (2000). *The Three Ecologies*. London: Continuum.

Guiley, R. E. (2001). *Encyclopedia of Mystical and Paranormal Experience*. Edison, NJ: Castle Books.

Hamilton, C. (2004). *Growth Fetish*. London: Pluto.

Haraway, D. (2008) *When Species Meet*. Minneapolis, MN: University of Minnesota Press.

Harding, S. (2009). *Animate earth*. Totnes: Green Books.

Hardy, A. (1975). *The Biology of God: A Scientist's Study of Man the Religious Animal*. London: Jonathan Cape.

Hardy, A. (1984). *Darwin and the Spirit of Man*. London: Collins.

Harrison, D. & Svensson, K. (2007). *Vikingaliv*. Värnamo: Fälth & Hässler.

Hart, R. (1979). *Children's Experience of Place*. New York: Irvington.

Hartmann, T. (1998). *The Last Hours of Ancient Sunlight: Waking up to Personal and Global Transformation*. New York: Harmony Books.

Haskell, B. D., Norton, B. G. & Costanza, R. (1992). Introduction: What is ecosystem health and why should we worry about it? In: R. Costanza, B. G. Norton & B. D. Haskell (Eds.), *Ecosystem Health: New Goals for Environmental Management* (pp. 3–20). Washington, DC: Island Press.

Haugh, S. & Paul, S. (2008). *The Therapeutic Relationship: Perspectives and Themes*. Ross-on-Wye: PCCS Books.

Heidegger, M. (1977). *The Question Concerning Technology and Other Essays*. New York: Harper.

Heidegger, M. (1996). *Being and Time*. Albany, NY: SUNY Press.

Henriques, A. (2011). Personal communication.

Herzog, W. (2005). *Grizzly Man*. Film. Los Angeles, CA: Lionsgate Entertainment.

Herzogenrath, B. (Ed.). (2009). *Deleuze | Guattari and Ecology*. London: Palgrave Macmillan.

HH the Dalai Lama and Berzin, A. (1997). *The Gelug/Kagyu tradition of Mahamudra*. Ithaca, NY: Snow Lion.

Hillman, J. (1989). From mirror to window: Curing psychoanalysis of its narcissism. *Spring, 49*: 62–75.

Hillman, J. (1998). *The Thought of the Heart and the Soul of the World*. Dallas, TX: Spring.

Hillman, J. & Ventura, M. (1992). *We've Had a Hundred Years of Psychotherapy and the World's Getting Worse*. San Francisco, CA: HarperSanFrancisco.

Hirsh, J. B. & Dolderman, D. (2007). Personality predictors of consumerism and environmentalism: A preliminary study. *Personality and Individual Differences, 43*: 1583–1593.

Ho, D. Y. F. (1995). Internalized culture, culturocentrism, and transcendence. *Counseling Psychologist, 23*(1): 4–24.

Homburg, A., Solberg, A. & Wagner, W. (2007). Coping with global environmental problems: Development and first validation of scales. *Environment and Behaviour, 39*: 754–778.

Hopkins, R. (2008). *The Transition Handbook: From Oil Dependency to Local Resilience*. Totnes: Green Books.

Husserl, E., McCormick, P. & Elliston, F. (1981). *Husserl, Shorter Works*. Notre Dame, IN: University of Notre Dame Press.

Huxley, J. (1957). *New Bottles for New Wine*. London: Harper and Row.

Hyland, M. E., Wheeler, P., Kamble, S. & Masters, K. S. (2010). A sense of "special connection", self-transcendent values and a common factor for religious and non-religious spirituality. *Archive for the Psychology of Religion/Archiv für Religionspsychologie, 32*: 293–326.

Inayat Khan, V. (1999). *Thinking Like the Universe*. London: Thorsons.

Irwin, H. J. & Watt, C. A. (2007). *An Introduction to Parapsychology*. Jefferson, NC: McFarland.

Iwakabe, S. (1994). Psychotherapy and chaos theory: The metaphoric relationship between psychodynamic therapy and chaos theory. *Psychoanalytic Psychology, 11*(1): 1–19.

Jackson, T. (2009). *Prosperity without Growth*. London: earthscan.

Jacobi, J. (1980). *The Psychology of CG Jung* (7th ed.). London: Routledge & Kegan Paul.

Jacques, E. (1955). Social systems as a defence against persecutory and depressive anxiety. In: M. Klein, P. Heimann & R. E. Money-Kyrle (Eds.), *New Directions in Psychoanalysis: Significance of Infant Conflict in the Pattern of Adult Behaviour* (pp. 478–498). London: Karnac.

James, O. (2007). *Affluenza*. London: Vermilion.

James, W. (1911). *Memories and Studies*. New York: Longmans, Green, and Co.

Jarvis, M. (2005). *The Psychology of Effective Learning and Teaching*. Cheltenham: Nelson Thornes.

Jeffers, S. (1999). *The Little Book of Confidence*. London: Random House.

Jensen, D. (2000). *A Language Older than Words*. London: Souvenir Press.

Jordan, M. (2009a). Back to nature. *Therapy Today*, 20(3): 26–28.

Jordan, M. (2009b). Nature and self: An ambivalent attachment? *Ecopsychology*, 1(1): 26–41.

Jordan, M. & Marshall, H. (2010). Taking counselling and psychotherapy outside: Destruction or enrichment of the therapeutic frame? *European Journal of Psychotherapy and Counselling*, 12(4): 345–359.

Jung, C. G. (1940). *The Integration of the Personality*. London: Kegan Paul, Trench, Trubner.

Jung, C. G. (1946/1970). *The Fight with the Shadow*. Collected Works Vol. 10. Princeton, NJ: Princeton University Press.

Jung, C.G. (1959). *The Archetypes and the Collective Unconscious*. Collected Works Vol. 9. London: Routledge & Kegan Paul.

Jung, C.G. (1963). *Memories, Dreams, Reflections*. London: Collins and Routledge & Kegan Paul.

Jung, C. G. (1964). *Man and his Symbols*. London: Aldus Books.

Jung, C. G. (1969). Transformation symbolism in the Mass. 4. The psychology of the Mass. II: The psychological meaning of sacrifice. In: *Psychology and Religion: East and West. Collected Works*, Vol. 11. London: Routledge & Kegan Paul.

Jung, C. G. (Ed.). (1978). *Man and his Symbols*. London: Picador.

Jung, C. G. (1983). *Memories, Dreams, Reflections*. London: Flamingo.

Jung, C. G. (1989). *Psychological Reflections*. London: Ark.

Jung, C. G. (1993/1954). *The Practice of Psychotherapy*. London: Routledge.

Jung, C. G. (1993). *Memories, Dreams, Reflections*. London: Fontana.

Jung, C. G. (1994). The fight with the Shadow. In: R. Fields (Ed.), *The Awakened Warrior: Living with Courage, Compassion and Discipline*. New York: Jeremy P. Tarcher/Putnam Books.

Jung, C. G. (1998). *Jung on Mythology* (R. Segal, Ed.). London: Routledge.

Kahn, P. (1999). *The Human Relationship with Nature*. Cambridge, MA: MIT Press.

Kahn, P. H. (2006). Nature and moral development. In: M. Killen & J. G. Smetana (Eds.), *Handbook of Moral Development* (pp. 461–480). Mahwah, NJ: Lawrence Erlbaum.

Kals, E., Schumacher, D. & Montada, L. (1999). Emotional affinity toward nature as a motivational basis to protect nature. *Environment and Behavior*, 31: 178–202.

Kang, C. (2003). A psychospiritual integration frame of reference for occupational therapy part 1: Conceptual foundations. *Australian Occupational Therapy Journal, 50*: 92–103.

Kanner, A. D. & Gomes, M. E. (1995). The all-consuming self. In: T. Roszak, M. E. Gomez & A. D. Kanner (Eds.), *Ecopsychology: Restoring the earth, Healing the Mind*. San Francisco, CA: Sierra Club Books.

Kaplan, R. & Talbot, J. F. (1983). Psychological benefits of a wilderness experience. In: I. Altman & J. F. Wohlwil (Eds.), *Behavior and the Natural Environment* (pp. 163–203). New York: Plenum.

Kellert, S. R. (1996). *The Value of Life*. Washington, DC: Island Press.

Kerr, M. (2009). Personal journal.

Kerr, M. (2010). Personal journal.

Kerr, M. H. & Key, D. H. (2011). The Ouroboros: Towards an ontology of interconnectedness. *European Journal of Ecopsychology, 2*: 49–61.

Key, D. (2003). *The Ecology of Adventure*. Unpublished Masters thesis, Centre for Human Ecology, Edinburgh. Retrieved October 1, 2011, from http://www.ecoself.net/blog/wp-content/uploads/2010/07/TheEcologyofAdventure.pdf

Key, D. (2008). Personal journal.

Key, D. (2009). Personal journal.

Kidner, D.W. (2001). *Nature and Psyche: Radical Environmentalism and the Politics of Subjectivity*. Albany, NY: SUNY Press.

Klein, M. (1987). *The Selected Melanie Klein* (J. Mitchell, Ed.). New York: The Free Press.

Knapper, C. & Cropley, A. (1985). *Lifelong Learning and Higher Education*. London: Croom Holm.

Knebusch, J. (2008). Art and climate (change) perception: Outline of a phenomenology of climate. In: S. Kagan & V. Kirchberg (Eds.), *Sustainability: A New Frontier for the Arts and Cultures* (pp. 242–261). Waldkirchen: Verlag für Akademische Schriften.

Kolb, D. (1984). *Experiential Learning*. Hemel Hempstead: Prentice Hall.

Krupnik, I. & Jolly, D. (Eds.). (2002). *The earth is Faster Now: Indigenous Observations of Arctic Environmental Change*. Fairbanks, AK: Arctic Research Consortium of the United States.

Kubler-Ross, E. (1970). *On Death and Dying*. London: Tavistock.

Lakoff, G. (2006). *Thinking Points: Communicating our American Values and Vision*. New York: Farrar, Straus and Giroux.

Lakoff, G. & Johnson, M. (1980). *Metaphors We Live By*. Chicago, IL: University of Chicago Press.

Lasch, C. (1979). *The Culture of Narcissism*. New York: Norton.

Lasher, M. (2008). *Dog: Pure Awareness*. Kingsport, TN: Twilight Times Books.

Laszlo, E., Grof, S. & Russell P. (2003). *The Consciousness Revolution*. London: Elf Rock Productions.

Latour, B. (1993). *We Have Never Been Modern*. Hemel Hempstead: Harvester Wheatsheaf.

Layard, R. (2005). *Happiness: Lessons from a New Science*. London: Penguin.

Layton, L. (2008). What divides the subject? Psychoanalytic reflections on subjectivity, subjection and resistance. *Subjectivity, 22*: 60–72.

Lean, G. & Owen, J. (2008, July 13). "We've seen the future … and we may *not* be doomed". *Independent on Sunday*, pp. 8–9.

LeGuin, U. K. (1988). *Always Coming Home*. London: Grafton Books.

LeGuin, U. K. (Trans. & Ed.). (1998). *Lao Tzu: Tao Te Ching: A Book About the Way and the Power of the Way*. Boston: Shambhala.

Leopold, A. (1948). *A Sand County Almanac*. Oxford: Oxford University Press.

Levi, P. (1995). *Moments of Reprieve: A Memoir of Auschwitz*. London: Penguin.

Lewin, K. (1947). Frontiers in group dynamics. *Human Relations, 1*(1): 5–41.

Lewin, K. (1976). *Field Theory in Social Science: Selected Theoretical Papers*. Chicago, IL: University of Chicago Press.

Light, A. (2000). What is an ecological identity. *Environmental Politics, 9*(4): 59–81. London: Macmillan.

Louv, R. (2006). *Last Child in the Woods*. Chapel Hill, NC: Algonquin Books.

Lovelock, J. (1995). *The Ages of Gaia: A Biography of our Living earth* (2nd ed.). Oxford: Oxford University Press.

Lovelock, J. (2010). *The Vanishing Face of Gaia: A Final Warning*. London: Penguin.

Løvlie, L. (2007). The Pedagogy of Place. *Nordisk Pedagogik, 27*(1): 32–36.

Lucas, C. (2006). When spiritual emergence becomes an emergency. *Caduceus, 68*: 28–30.

MacDonald, L. (2010). Blog. http://archive.naturalchange.org.uk/blogs/louise-macdonald/

Machado, A. (1983). *Times Alone: Selected Poems* (R. Bly Trans.). Middletown, CN: Wesleyan University Press.

Macy, J. (1983). *Despair and Personal Empowerment in the Nuclear Age*. Philadelphia: New Society.

Macy, J. (1991a). *Mutual Causality in Buddhism and General Systems Theory: The Dharma of Natural Systems*. Albany, NY: SUNY Press.

Macy, J. (1991b). *World As Lover, World As Self*. Berkeley, CA: Parallax Press.

Macy, J. (1995). Working through environmental despair. In: T. Roszak, M. Gomes & A. Kanner (Eds.), *Ecopsychology: Restoring the earth, Healing the Mind* (pp. 240–259). San Francisco, CA: Sierra Club Books.

Macy, J. (2009). The story of the Elm Dance. Retrieved October 1, 2011, from http://www.joannamacy.net/theelmdance.html

Macy, J. & Brown, M. Y. (1998). *Coming Back to Life: Practices to Reconnect Our Lives, Our World*. Gabriola Island, BC: New Society.

Mahall, B. E. & Bormann, F. H. (2010, March 2). The earth has its own set of rules. *L.A. Times*. Retrieved October 1, 2011, from http://articles.latimes.com/2010/mar/02/opinion/la-oe-mahall2-2010 mar02

Mahler, M., Pine, F. & Bergman, A. (2000/1975). *The Psychological Birth of the Human Infant: Symbiosis and Individuation*. New York: Basic Books.

Maio, G. R., Pakizeh, A., Cheung, W. Y. & Rees, K. J. (2009). Changing, priming, and acting on values: Effects via motivational relations in a circular model. *Journal of Personality and Social Psychology, 97*(4): 699–715.

Maiteny, P. (2003). Psychological and cultural dynamics of sustainable human systems. In: *UNESCO Encyclopedia of Life-Support Systems*. Retrieved October 1, 2011, from www.eolss.net

Maiteny, P. (2004). Perceptions of nature by indigenous communities. In: J. Burley, J. Evans & J. A. Youngquist (Eds.), *Encyclopedia of Forest Sciences*. Oxford, UK: Elsevier.

Maiteny, P. (2009a). Completing the holistic perspective: Emotions and psyche in education for sustainability and the development of an ecosystemic conscience. Article 6.61.4.2, *The UNESCO Encyclopedia of Life Support Systems*. Retrieved October 1, 2011, from www.eolss.net

Maiteny, P. (2009b). Yearning for our niche: The role of meaningfulness in ecosystemic health. *Journal of Holistic Healthcare, 6*(3): 462–471.

Maiteny, P. (2009c). Finding meaning without consuming: The ability to experience meaning, purpose and satisfaction through non-material wealth. In: A. Stibbe (Ed.), *The Handbook of Sustainability Literacy: Skills for a Changing World* (pp. 178–184). Dartington: Green Books.

Manuel-Navarrete, D., Kay, J. J. & Dolderman, D. (2004). Ecological integrity discourses: Linking ecology with cultural transformation. *Research in Human Ecology, 11*(3): 215–229.

Marcuse, H. (1964/1991). *One-Dimensional Man* (2nd ed.). London: Routledge.

Marks-Tarlow, T. (2004). The self as a dynamical system. *Nonlinear Dynamics, Psychology, and Life Sciences, 3*(4): 311–345.

Maslow, A. (1999). *Toward a Psychology of Being* (3rd ed.). New York: Wiley.

May, R. (1976). *The Courage to Create*. London: Collins.

Mayer, F. S. & Frantz, C. M. (2004). The connectedness with nature scale: A measure of individuals' feeling in community with nature. *Journal of Environmental Psychology, 24*: 503–515.

McCormack, D. P. (2009). Becoming. *International Encyclopedia of Human Geography, 6*: 277–281.

McLean, P. (2011). *The Impact of a Values-based Change Method on the Environmental Performance of an Organisation*. Unpublished MSc thesis for Graduate School of the Environment, Centre for Alternative Technology and University of East London.

McLellan, G. (2009). Blog. Retrieved February 3, 2010, from http://www.naturalchange.org.uk/blogs/gavin-mclellan

Mcnaghten, P. & Urry, J. (1998). *Contested Natures*. London: Sage.

Meltzer, D. (1967). *Psychoanalytical Process*. Perthshire: Clunie Press.

Meltzer, D. (1992). *The Claustrum: An Investigation of Claustrophobic Phenomena*. Perthshire: Clunie Press.

Merchant, C. (1983). *The Death of Nature: Women, Ecology and the Scientific Revolution*. San Francisco, CA: Harper.

Merleau-Ponty, M. (1962). *Phenomenology of Perception*. London: Routledge & Kegan Paul.

Miller, D. (2010). *Stuff*. Cambridge: Polity.

Miller, J. (2004). *The Transcendent Function: Jung's Model of Psychological Growth through Dialogue with the Unconscious*. Albany, NY: SUNY Press.

Miller, M. (1999). Chaos, complexity, psychoanalysis. *Psychoanalytic Psychology*, 16: 355–379.

Miller, R. (2005). *The Revolution in Horsemanship*. Guilford, CT: The Lyons Press.

MIND. (2007). *Ecotherapy: The Green Agenda for Mental Health*. London: MIND.

Mindell, A. (1988). *City Shadows: Psychological Interventions in Psychiatry*. London: Arkana.

Mindell, A. (1992). *The Leader as Martial Artist*. Portland, OR: Lao Tse Press.

Mindell, A. (2000). *Quantum Mind: The Edge Between Physics and Psychology*. Portland, OR: Lao Tse Press.

Mindell, A. (2002). *The Deep Democracy of Open Forums: Practical Steps to Conflict Prevention and Resolution for the Family, Workplace, and World*. Charlottesville VA: Hampton Roads.

Mindell, A. (2008). Bringing deep democracy to life: An awareness paradigm for deepening political dialogue, personal relationships, and community interactions. *Psychotherapy and Politics International*, 6(3): 212–225.

Mishan, J. (1996). Psychoanalysis and environmentalism: First thoughts. *Psychoanalytic Psychotherapy*, 10(1): 59–70.

Mitchell, E. (2011). Edgar Mitchell and the big picture effect. Interview by Jules Evans. Retrieved October 1, 2011, from http://www.politicsofwellbeing.com/2011/01/edgar-mitchell-on-space-travel-and-big.html

Mitchell, S. A. (1988). *Relational Concepts in Psychoanalysis: An Integration*. Cambridge, MA: Harvard University Press.

Mitchell, S. A. & Aron, L. (1999). *Relational Psychoanalysis: The Emergence of a Tradition*. Hillsdale, NJ: Analytic Press.

Mollon, P. (1993). *The Fragile Self: The Structure of Narcissistic Disturbance*. London: Whurr.

Monbiot, G. (2009, March 21). George Monbiot v Aga: "It's still a woefully inefficient use of fuel". *The Guardian*. Retrieved March 31, 2011, from   http://www.guardian.co.uk/environment/georgemonbiot/audio/2009/mar/21/monbiot-aga-carbon-emissions-debate

Moon, J. (2000). *Reflection in Learning and Professional Development*. London: Kegan Page.

Morgan, M. (1995). *Mutant Message Down Under*. Wellingborough: Thorsons.

Morgenthaler, F. & Parin, P. (1964). Typical forms of transference among West Africans. *International Journal of Psycho-Analysis, 45*: 446–449.

Morton, T. (2007). *Ecology Without Nature: Rethinking Environmental Aesthetics*. Cambridge, MA: Harvard University Press.

Morton, T. (2010a, October 15). Presentation as part of the Panel Discussion "Promiscuous Ontologies". RMLA Convention, Albuquerque, New Mexico.

Morton, T. (2010b). *The Ecological Thought*. Cambridge MA: Harvard University Press.

Muir, J. (1911). *My First Summer in the Sierra Boston*. New York: Houghton Mifflin.

Nabhan, G. P. & Trimble, S. (1994). *The Geography of Childhood: Why Children Need Wild Places*. Boston, MA: Beacon Press.

Næss, A. (1973). The shallow and the deep, long-range ecology movement. *Inquiry, 16*: 95–100.

Naess, A. (1985). Identification as a source of deep ecological attitudes. In: M. Tobias (Ed.), *Deep Ecology* (pp. 256–270). San Diego, CA: Avant Books.

Naess, A. (1986). The deep ecological movement: Some philosophical aspects. *Philosophical Inquiry, 8*: 10–31.

Naess, A. (1988). Self realization: An ecological approach to being in the world. In: J. Seed, J. Macy, P. Fleming & A. Naess (Eds.), *Thinking Like a Mountain* (pp. 19–30). Gabriola Island, BC: New Society.

Næss, A. (1989). Ecosophy and gestalt ontology. *The Trumpeter, 6*(4): 134–137.

Narvaez, D. & Gleason, T. (2011). Developmental optimization. In: D. Narvaez, J. Panksepp, A. Schore & T. Gleason (Eds.), *Human Nature, Early Experience and the Environment of Evolutionary Adaptedness*. New York: Oxford University Press.

Neisser, U. (1995). Criteria for an ecological self. In: P. Rochat (Ed.), *The Self in Infancy: Theory and Research* (pp. 17–34). Amsterdam: North-Holland/ Elsevier Science.

Nicholls, L. (2007). A psychodynamic discourse in Occupational Therapy. In: J. Creek (Ed.), *Contemporary Issues in Occupational Therapy: Reasoning and Reflection* (pp. 55–86). Chichester: Wiley.

Nicholson, S. (2003). *The Love of Nature and the End of the World: The Unspoken Dimensions of Environmental Concern.* Cambridge, MA: MIT Press.

Noë, A. (2008). The life is the way the animal is in the world: A talk with Alva Noë. *Edge: The Third Culture.* Retrieved October 1, 2011, from http://www.edge.org/3rd_culture/noe08/noe08_index.html

Noë, A. (2009). *Out of our Heads: Why You are not Your Brain and Other Lessons from the Biology of Consciousness.* New York: Hill and Wang.

Norcross, J. C. & Goldfried, M. R. (1992). *A Handbook of Psychotherapy Integration.* New York: Basic Books.

Norgaard, K. M. (2009). *Cognitive and Behavioural Challenges in Responding to Climate Change.* World Bank Policy Research Working Paper 4940. Retrieved October 1, 2011, from http://ideas.repec.org/p/wbk/wbrwps/4940.html

Nørretranders, T. (1999). *The User Illusion: Cutting Consciousness Down to Size.* London: Penguin.

Olwig, K. (1989). The childhood deconstruction of nature. *Children's Environments Quarterly, 6*(1): 19–25.

Olwig, K. (1991). Childhood, artistic creation, and the educated sense of place. *Children's Environments Quarterly, 8*(2): 4–18.

Orr, D. (1992). *Ecological Literacy, Education and the Transition to a Postmodern World.* Albany, NY: SUNY Press.

Ouspensky, P. D. (1950). *The Psychology of Man's Possible Evolution.* New York: Hedgehog Press.

Palmer, J. A., Suggate, J., Bajd, B., Hart, P., Ho, R. K. P., Ofwono-Orecho, J. K. W., Peries, M., Robottom, I., Tsaliki, E. & Van Staden, C. (1998). An overview of significant influences and formative experiences on the development of adults' environmental awareness in nine countries. *Environmental Education Research, 4*(4): 445–464.

Palombo, S. (1999). *The Emergent Ego: Complexity and Coevolution in the Psychoanalytic Process.* Madison, CT: International Universities Press.

Paulson, T. (2005). Inseminating elephant takes 2 Germans, an ultrasound and a very long wait. *Seattle Post-Intelligencer Reporter.* Retrieved June 21, 2011, from http://www.seattlepi.com/default/article/Inseminating-elephant-takes-2-Germans-an-1167610.php

Peters, R. (1987). The Eagle and serpent: The minding of matter. *Journal of Analytical Psychology, 32*: 359–381.

PhinnyWood.com. (2011). Zoo tries again to artificially inseminate elephant Chai. Retrieved June 2011, from http://www.phinneywood. com/2011/06/09/zoo-tries-again-to-artificially-inseminate-elephant-chai/

Piers, C., Muller, J. P. & Brent, J. (Eds.). (2007). *Self-Organizing Complexity in Psychological Systems.* Lanham, MD: Jason Aronson.

Pramling Samuelson, I. & Kaga, Y. (2008). *The Contribution of Early Childhood to a Sustainable Society.* Paris: Unesco.

Preece, R. (2006). *The Wisdom of Imperfection: The Challenge of Individuation in Buddhist Life.* Ithaca, NY: Snow Lion.

Preece, R. (2009). *The Courage to Feel: Buddhist Practices for Opening to Others.* Ithaca, NY: Snow Lion.

Prendergast, J. J. (2003). Being together. In: J. J. Prendergast, P. Fenner & S. Krystal (Eds.), *The Sacred Mirror.* St Paul, MN: Paragon House.

Prentice, H. (2003). Cosmic walk: Awakening the ecological self. *Psychotherapy and Politics International*, 1(1): 32–46.

Pullman, P. (2003). *The Golden Compass.* New York: Laurel Leaf.

Raine, K. (1975). *The Land Unknown.* London: Hamish Hamilton.

Randall, R. (2005). A new climate for psychotherapy? *Psychotherapy and Politics International*, 3(3): 165–179.

Randall, R. (2009a). Loss and climate change: the cost of parallel narratives. *Ecopsychology*, 1(3): 118–129. Retrieved March 31, 2011, from http://www.liebertonline.com/doi/pdfplus/10.1089/eco.2009.0034

Randall, R. (2009b). *Carbon Conversations: Six Meetings about Climate Change and Carbon Reduction.* Cambridge: Cambridge Carbon Footprint.

Rappaport, R. A. (1984/1948). *Pigs for the Ancestors: Ritual in the Ecology of a New Guinea People.* New Haven, CT: Yale University Press.

Rappaport, R. A. (1999). *Ritual and Religion in the Making of Humanity.* Cambridge: Cambridge University Press.

Ravindra, R. (1990). *The Yoga of the Christ.* Shaftesbury, UK: Element.

Reason, P. (2002). Justice, sustainability, and participation. *Concepts and Transformation*, 7(1): 7–29.

Reist, D. M. (2004). *Materialism vs. an Ecological Identity: Towards an Integrative Framework for a Psychology of Sustainable Living.* Unpublished doctoral dissertation.

Rescher, N. (2009). *Ideas in Process: A Study on the Development of Philosophical Concepts.* Lancaster: Gazelle.

Reser, J. P. (1995). Whither environmental psychology? The transpersonal ecopsychology crossroads. *Journal of Environmental Psychology*, 15: 235–257.

Rickinson, M. (2001). Learners and learning in environmental education: A critical review of the evidence. *Environmental Education Research, 7*(3): 207–320.

Rickinson, M., Dillon, J., Teamey, K., Morris, M., Choi, M. Y., Sanders, D. & Benefield, P. (2004). *A Review of Research on Outdoor Learning.* London: National Foundation for Educational Research and King's College London.

Robinson, R. M. (2007). *Ordinary Women, Extraordinary Wisdom: The Feminine Face of Awakening.* Alresford: O Books.

Rogers, C. (1951). *Client-Centred Therapy.* London: Constable.

Rogers, C. R. (1980). *A Way of Being.* New York: Houghton Mifflin.

Rogers, L. (2010). *Bearwalker of the Northwoods.* London: BBC. Retrieved October 1, 2011, from http://www.bbc.co.uk/programmes/p004vwxn

Roll, W. G. (1997). My search for the soul. In: C. Tart (Ed.), *Body Mind and Spirit: Exploring the Parapsychology of Spirituality.* Charlottesville, VA: Hampton Roads.

Romanyshyn, R. (2007). *The Wounded Researcher.* New Orleans, LA: Spring Journal Books.

Roosevelt, T. (1916). *A Book-Lover's Holidays in the Open.* New York: Charles Scribner's & Sons.

Roszak, T. (1992). *The Voice of the earth: An Exploration of Ecopsychology.* London: Simon and Schuster.

Roszak, T., Gomes, M. E. & Kanner, A. D. (Eds.). (1995). *Ecopsychology: Restoring the earth, Healing the Mind.* San Francisco, CA: Sierra Club Books.

Russell, C. (2006). Charlie responds to the story of Timothy Treadwell. In: *Letters from Charlie.* Retrieved October 1, 2011, from http://cloudline.org/

Russell, P. (2009). *Waking up in Time: Our Future Evolution and the Meaning of Now.* London: Cygnus.

Rust, M.-J. (2004). Creating psychotherapy for a sustainable future. *Psychotherapy and Politics International, 2*(2): 157–170.

Rust, M.-J. (2005). Ecolimia nervosa. *Therapy Today, 16*(10): 11–15.

Rust, M.-J. (2008a). Climate on the couch: Talk at the Guild of Psychotherapists, London, November 17, 2007. *Psychotherapy and Politics International, 6*(3): 157–170.

Rust, M.-J. (2008b). Nature hunger. *Counselling Psychology Review, 23*(2): 70–78.

Rust, M. J. (2008c). Consuming the earth: Unconscious processes in relation to our environmental crisis. Keynote lecture at CAPPP Conference, Bristol. Retrieved October 1, 2011, from http://www.mjrust.net/downloads/Consuming%20the%20earth.pdf

Sabini, M. (Ed.). (2002). *The earth Has a Soul: The Nature Writings of C. G. Jung*. Berkeley, CA: North Atlantic Books.

Sacks, A. (2008). The therapeutic use of pets in private practice. *British Journal of Psychotherapy, 24*(4): 501–521.

Safran, A. (1998). *La Saggezza della Kabbalah*. Florence: Giuntina.

Samuels, A. (1993a). *The Political Psyche*. London: Routledge.

Samuels, A. (1993b). "I am place": Depth psychology and environmentalism. *British Journal of Psychotherapy, 10*(2): 211–219.

Samuels, A. (1998). "And if not now, when?": Spirituality, psychotherapy, politics. *Psychodynamic Practice, 4*(3): 349–363.

Samuels, A. (2001). *Politics on the Couch: Citizenship and the Internal Life*. London: Karnac.

Samuels, A. (2011). Where have all the individuals gone? The shadow of solidarity. Workshop at the conference *"We're All in This Together?'— Power, Inequality and Diversity"*, London, May 7–8.

Santostefano, S. (2008). The sense of self inside and environments outside: How the two grow together and become one in healthy psychological development. *Psychoanalytic Dialogues, 19*: 513–535.

Sawaya, R. (2010). Positive feedback mechanisms and climate change: The runaway effects that could accelerate global warming. *Suite 101*. Retrieved October 1, 2011, from http://www.suite101.com/content/positive-feedback-mechanisms-and-climate-change-a189162

Schore, A. (1999). *Affect Regulation and the Origin of the Self: The Neurobiology of Emotional Development*. Hillsdale, NJ: Lawrence Erlbaum.

Schroll, M. (2007). Wrestling with Arne Naess: A chronicle of ecopsychology's origins. *Trumpeter, 23*(1): 28–57.

Schultz, P. W. (2000). Empathizing with nature: The effects of perspective taking on concern for environmental issues. *Journal of Social Studies, 56*: 391–406.

Schultz, P. W. (2001). The structure of environmental concern: Concern for self, other people, and the biosphere. *Journal of Environmental Psychology, 21*: 327–339.

Schultz, P. W. (2002). Inclusion with nature: The psychology of human-nature relations. In: P. Schmuck & P. W. Schultz (Eds.), *Psychology of Sustainable Development* (pp. 61–78). Boston, MA: Kluwer Academic.

Schultz, P. W. & Zelezny, L. (1999). Values as predictors of environmental attitudes: Evidence for consistency across cultures. *Journal of Environmental Psychology, 19*: 255–265.

Schwartz, S. H. (1992). Universals in the content and structure of values: Theoretical advances and empirical tests in 20 countries. In: M. Zanna (Ed.), *Advances in Experimental Social Psychology, Vol. 25* (pp. 1–65). Orlando, FL: Academic Press.

Schwartz, S. H. (2006). Basic human values: Theory, measurement, and applications. *Revue française de sociologie, 47*(4): 249–288.

Scourfield, J., Dicks, B., Drakeford, M. & Davies, A. (2006). *Children, Place, and Identity*. London: Routledge.

Scull, J. (2009). Ecopsychology: Where does it fit in psychology 2009? *Trumpeter, 24*(3): 68–85.

Searles, H. (1960). *The Nonhuman Environment in Normal Development and in Schizophrenia*. Madison, CT: International Universities Press.

Searles, H. (1972). Unconscious processes in relation to the environmental crisis. *Psychoanalytic Review, 59*: 361–374.

Seed, J., Macy, J., Fleming, P. & Naess, A. (1988). *Thinking Like a Mountain: Towards a Council of All Beings*. Philadelphia: New Society.

Seed, J., Macy, J., Fleming, P. & Naess, A. (1993). *Thinking Like a Mountain: Toward a Council of All Beings*. Gabriola Island, BC: New Society.

Senders, V. L. (1994). Interhelp, whence and whither? Design for a play in three acts. *Interhelp News, 1*(Fall): 4–9. Retrieved October 1, 2011, from http://www.interhelpnetwork.org/pdf/history.pdf

Sessions, G. (Ed.). (1995). *Deep Ecology for the 21 st Century*. Boston, MA: Shambhala.

Sewall, L. (1999). *Sight and Sensibility: The Ecopsychology of Perception*. New York: Tarcher/Putnam.

Shanahan, J. (1993). Television and the cultivation of environmental concern. In: A. Hansen (Ed.), *The Mass Media and Environmental Issues* (pp. 181–197). Leicester: University of Leicester Press.

Shanahan, J., Morgan, M. & Stenbjerre, M. (1997). Green or brown? Television and the cultiavtion of environmental concern. *Journal of Broadcasting & Electronic Media, 41*: 305–324.

Shaules, J. (2007). *Deep Culture: The Hidden Challenges of Global Living*. Clevedon: Multi Lingual Matters.

Shea, J. (2004). *Spiritual Wisdom of the Gospels Year A*. Collegeville, MN: Liturgical Press.

Sheldon, K. M., Nichols, C. P. & Kasser, T. (2011). Americans recommend smaller ecological footprints when reminded of intrinsic American values of self-expression, family, and generosity. *Ecopsychology*, in press.

Sheldrake, R. (2006). Morphic fields in world futures. *Journal of General Evolution, 62*(1–2): 31–41.

Shepard, P. (1997). *The Others: How Animals Made us Human*. Washington, DC: Island Press.

Shrum, L. J., Burroughs, J. E. & Rindfleisch, A. (2005). Television's cultivation of material values. *Journal of Consumer Research, 32*: 473–479.

Siebert, C. (2009, July 8). Watching whales watching us. *New York Times Magazine*. Retrieved October 1, 2011, from http://www.nytimes.com/2009/07/12/magazine/12whales-t.html?_r=2&emc=eta1

Singer, W. (2005). The brain—an orchestra without a conductor. *Max Planck Research, 3*: 15–18.

Siri, V. (1998). Dreaming with the first shaman (Noaidi). *Revision, 21*(1): 34–39.

Slaughter, R. A. (1999). Towards a responsible dissent and the rise of transformational futures. *Futures, 31*: 147–154.

Smith, M., Davidson, J., Cameron, L. & Bondi, L. (2009). *Emotion, Place and Culture*. Aldershot: Ashgate.

Snyder, G. (1990). *The Practice of the Wild*. San Francisco, CA: North Point Press.

Somerville, M. (2007). Place literacy. *Australian Journal of Literacy and Language, 30*(2): 149–164.

Somerville, M. (2010). A place pedagogy for "global contemporaneity". *Journal of Educational Philosophy and Theory, 42*(3), 326–344.

Speth, J. G. (2008). *The Bridge at the Edge of the World: Capitalism, the Environment, and Crossing from Crisis to Sustainability*. New Haven, CT: Yale University Press.

Speth, J. G. (2009). Doing business in a postgrowth society. *Harvard Business Review* (September): 18–19.

Spitzform, M. (2000). The ecological self: Metaphor and developmental experience. *Journal of Applied Psychoanalytic Studies, 2*(3): 265–285.

Stacey, R. (2006). Complexity at the edge of the basic-assumption group. In L. Gould, R. Stapley & M. Stein (Eds.), *The Systems Psychodynamics of Organizations: Integrating Group Relations, Psychoanalytic, and Open Systems Perspectives* (pp. 91–114). London: Karnac.

Stenner, P. (2008). A.N. Whitehead and subjectivity. *Subjectivity, 22*: 90–109.

Stewart, I. & Joines, V. (1987). *TA Today*. Nottingham: Lifespace Publishing.

Sumner, G. & Haines, S. (2010). *Cranial Intelligence: A Practical Guide to Biodynamic Craniosacral Therapy*. London: Singing Dragon.

Suzuki, D. T. (1969). *An Introduction to Zen Buddhism*. London: Rider.

Tanner, T. (1980). Significant life experiences. *Journal of Environmental Education, 11*(4): 20–24.

Tarnas, R. (1996). The Western world view: Past, present and future. In: R. E. Di Carlo (Ed.), *Towards a New World View: Conversations at the Leading Edge*. Edinburgh: Floris Books.

Tarnas, R. (2000). Is the modern psyche undergoing a rite of passage? In: T. Singer (Ed.), *The Vision Thing: Myth, Politics and Psyche in the World*. London: Routledge.

Tarnas, R. (2006). *Cosmos and Psyche: Intimations of a New World View.* New York: Viking.

Taylor, S. (2005). *The Fall.* New York: Winchester.

Teilhard de Chardin, P. (1960). *Le Milieu Divin: An Essay on the Interior Life.* London: Collins.

Teilhard de Chardin, P. (1969). *Human Energy.* London: Collins.

Thøgersen, J. & Crompton, T. (2009). Simple and painless? The limitations of spillover in environmental campaigning. *Journal of Consumer Policy, 32*: 141–163.

Tolle, E. (2005). *A New earth: Awakening to Your Life's Purpose.* London: Penguin.

Totton, N. (2000). *Psychotherapy and Politics.* London: Sage.

Totton, N. (2007). Therapy has no goal. *Therapy Today, 18*(9): 24–26.

Totton, N. (2011). *Wild Therapy: Undomesticating Inner and Outer Worlds.* Ross-on-Wye: PCCS Books.

Trungpa, C. (1973). *Cutting Through Spiritual Materialism.* Boulder, CO: Shambala.

Turner, V. (1987). Betwixt & between: Liminal periods in rites of passage. In: L. C. Mahdi (Ed.), *Betwixt & Between: Patterns of Masculine and Feminine Initiation* (pp. 3–19). Chicago, IL: Open Court.

Victor, P. (2008). *Managing Without Growth.* Cheltenham UK: Edward Elgar.

Volk, T. (1998). *Gaia's Body: Towards a Physiology of earth.* New York: Springer-Verlag.

Vygotsky, L. (1978). *Mind in Society: Development of Higher Psychological Processes.* Cambridge, MA: Harvard University Press.

Vygotsky, L. (1986). *Thought and Language.* Cambridge, MA: MIT Press.

Wackernagel, M., Schulz, N. B., Deumling, D., Linares, A. C., Jenkins, M., Kapos, V., Monfreda, C., Loh, J., Myers, N., Norgaard, R. & Randers, J. (2002). Tracking the ecological overshoot of the human economy. *Proceedings of the National Academy of Sciences, 99*: 9266–9271.

Walsh, R. & Shapiro, D. H. (1983). In search of a healthy person. In: R. Walsh & D. H. Shapiro (Eds.), *Beyond Health and Normality: Explorations of Exceptional Psychological Well-Being* (pp. 3–12). New York: Van Nostrand Reinhold.

Walsh, R. & Vaughan, F. (1983). Towards an integrative psychology of well-being. In: R. Walsh & D. H. Shapiro (Eds.), *Beyond Health and Normality: Explorations of Exceptional Psychological Well-Being* (pp. 388–431). New York: Van Nostrand Reinhold.

Warren, K. J. (2000). *Ecofeminist Philosophy: A Western Perspective on What it is and Why it Matters.* Lanham, MD: Rowman & Littlefield.

Washburn, M. (1995). *The Ego and the Dynamic Ground*. Albany, NY: SUNY Press.

Watson, K. (1994). Spiritual emergency: Concepts and implications for psychotherapy. *Journal of Humanistic Psychology, 34*(2): 22–45.

Watts, A. (1957). *The Way of Zen*. New York: Pantheon.

Watts, A. & Huang, A. C. (1975). *Tao: The Watercourse Way*. New York: Pantheon.

Wegscheider-Cruse, S. (1991). *Learning to Love Yourself: Finding Your Self-worth*. London: Health Communications.

Weintrobe, S. (2010, October). On healing split internal landscapes. "Engaging with Climate Change: Psychoanalytic Perspectives" Conference.

Wells, N. & Lekies, K. (2006). Nature and the life course: Pathways from childhood nature experiences to adult environmentalism. *Children, Youth, and Environments, 16*: 1–24.

Whatmore, S. (1999). Nature culture. In: P. Cloke, M. Crang & M. Goodwin (Eds.), *Introducing Human Geographies* (pp. 4–11). London: Arnold.

Whitaker, D. S. (1985). *Using Groups to Help People*. London: Routledge and Kegan Paul.

Whitehead, A. N. (1978). *Process and Reality, Corrected Edition* (D. R. Griffin & D. W. Sherburne Eds.) New York: Free Press.

Whitehead, A. N. (2004/1920). *The Concept of Nature*. New York: Prometheus.

Wilden, A. (1987). *The Rules Are No Game: The Strategy of Communication*. London: Routledge and Kegan Paul.

Wildlife Trust. (2004). EcoHealth: New journal bridging human, wildlife, ecosystem health and disease emergence. Press release. Retrieved October 1, 2011, from http://www.ewire.com/display.cfm/Wire_ID/2144

Williams, B. J. (2007). Pueblo parapsychology: Psi and the longbody from the Southwest Indian perspective. *Australian Journal of Parapsychology, 7*(2): 134–163.

Wilson, E. O. (1978). *On Human Nature*. Cambridge, MA: Harvard University Press.

Wilson, E. (1984). *Biophilia*. Cambridge, MA: Harvard University Press.

Wilson, E. O. (2003). *The Future of Life*. London: Abacus.

Winnicott, D. (1953). Transitional objects and transitional phenomena. *International Journal of Psychoanalysis, 34*: 89–97.

Winnicott, D. (1971). *Playing and Reality*. London: Routledge.

Winnicott, D. (1987). *Through Pediatrics to Psychoanalysis: Collected Papers*. London: Karnac.

Wolde, M. (2008). Personal communication from workshop.

Woodland Park Zoo. (2011, March 14). Zoo's commitment to elephant conservation continues with artificial insemination. Retrieved June 17, 2011, from http://www.zoo.org/page.aspx?pid=1597

Wright, P. A. (1998). Gender issues in Ken Wilber's transpersonal theory. In: D. Rothberg & S. Kelly (Eds.), *Ken Wilber in Dialogue: Conversations with Leading Transpersonal Thinkers* (pp. 207–236). Wheaton, IL: Quest Books.

WWF. (2009). *Natural Change: Psychology and Sustainability*. Retrieved October 1, 2011, from http://www.naturalchange.org.uk/natural-change-report/

Wyld, H. C. (1961). *Universal English Dictionary*. London: Waverley.

Yalom, I. D. (1970). *The Theory and Practice of Group Psychotherapy*. New York: Basic Books.

Yalom, I. (1989). *Love's Executioner*. London: Penguin.

Yontef, G. (1988). *Awareness Dialogue and Process*. Gouldsboro, ME: Gestalt Journal Press.

Yunt, J. D. (2001). Jung's contribution to an ecological psychology. *Journal of Humanistic Psychology, 41*(2): 96–121.

Zavestoski, S. (2003). Constructing and maintaining ecological identities: The strategies of deep ecology. In: S. Clayton & S. Opotow (Eds.), *Identity and the Natural Environment*. Cambridge, MA: MIT Press.

Zelezny, L. (1999). Educational interventions that improve environmental behaviors: A meta-analysis. *Journal of Environmental Education, 31*(1): 5–14.

Žižek, S. (1989). *The Sublime Object of Ideology*. London: Verso.

Žižek, S. (1991). *Looking Awry: An Introduction to Jacques Lacan Through Popular Culture*. Cambridge, MA: MIT Press.

Žižek, S. (2007). Censorship today: Violence, or ecology as a new opium for the masses. Retrieved October 1, 2011, from http://www.lacan.com/zizecology1.html

INDEX